IDANNA PUCCI
The Trials of Maria Barbella

Idanna Pucci grew up in Florence, Italy, and is an award-winning documentary filmmaker. In 1973, she moved to Bali, where she dedicated herself to the study of Balinese mythology. Her *Bhima Swarga: The Balinese Divine Comedy* is used in Bali to teach local culture. She now divides her time among Florence, Bali, and New York.

The Trials of

MARIA BARBELLA

The Trials of

MARIA BARBELLA

The True Story of a 19th Century
Crime of Passion

IDANNA PUCCI

Translated by Stefania Fumo

Vintage Books
A Division of Random House, Inc. / New York

FIRST VINTAGE BOOKS EDITION, MARCH 1997

Library of Congress Cataloging-in-Publication Data
Pucci, Idanna, 1945–
[Fuoco dell'anima. English]
The trials of Maria Barbella : the true story of 19th-century
crime of passion / by Idanna Pucci ; translated by Stefania Fumo.
p. cm.
Originally published : New York : Four Wall Eight Windows, 1996.
ISBN 0-679-77604-4
1. Crimes of passion—New York (State)—New York—History—19th
century—Case studies. 2. Murder—New York (State)—New York—
History—19th century—Case studies. 3. Trials (Murder)—New York
(State)—New York—History—19th century—Case studies. 4. Capital
punishment—New York (State)—New York—History—19th century—Case
studies. 5. Barbella, Maria. 6. Brazza, Countess di, b. 1862.
I. Title.
[HV6053.P8313   1997]
364.1'523'097471—dc20   96-28269
CIP

Vintage ISBN: 0-679-77604-4

Book design by Debbie Glasserman

Random House Web address: http://www.randomhouse.com/

Printed in the United States of America
10 9 8 7 6 5 4 3 2 1

This book is dedicated to:

My godchildren: Fiona McGarry, Adrian Hubert,
Emmina Bini, and Kyra Ward,
who are still too young to understand
that all stories are not fairytales
and that many stories do not end.

And to my mentor and friend,
the late Professor Barbara Stoler Miller,
who continues to inspire and encourage me.

De lo que fui no tengo sino estas marcas crueles
porqué aquellos dolores confirman mi existencia.

Of all that I was, I bear only these cruel scars,
because those griefs confirm my very existence.

—Pablo Neruda

PROLOGUE

$\mathcal{T}$he pursuit of the past can sometimes seem an adversarial task in which our opponents precede us by several lifetimes, capitalizing on their advantage, misplacing and destroying clues. Such an adversary is the drunken Austrian soldier sleeping away the night of December 17th, 1917, on the enormous Venetian carpet of my ancestral home in northern Italy. His garrison has occupied the estate.

Dominated by the ruins of a tenth-century castle, the grounds of Brazzà are laden with snow. Nearby is the chapel, where years later I would be baptized and where, in turn, I baptized my doll. Except for the creaking of branches under the white weight, all is silent. The only wakeful presence is the ember of my adversary's cigarette burning the eighteenth-century carpet. Soon a terrible fire explodes in the white landscape. It does not spread to the park, but the villa is consumed and with it all of Cora Slocomb di Brazzà's possessions.

The fire destroys the diaries Cora kept as a child in New Orleans and those she wrote later as a woman of two worlds. Memorabilia is lost: her portrait as the Queen of Carnival in 1881, her wedding pictures, her correspondence.

———

I was named Idanna after my maternal grandmother, the only child of Cora Slocomb and Detalmo di Brazzà, and until recently I knew little more about Cora than that she was my great-grandmother. I was born in Brazzà, Italy, near Udine, in the great white villa that was rebuilt after the fire, but I was removed from that enchanted domain, and from my mother, at an early age. As an old Gypsy had predicted, circumstances forced my mother to sail to another continent and abandon everything she loved.

Each September, caravans of Gypsies, migrating south to the Camargue from Hungary, would camp for a few nights outside our gates. Hand in hand, my mother and I would hurry out to visit them. I sat beside her while her palms were being read, under the shade of an acacia tree, intent on every word. These occasions provided my first intimations of the wider world, a place made in the image of its transient narrators, mysteriously governed by "adventure" and "destiny." Filled with wonder, I, too, stretched out my three-year-old palms to be examined by the old woman. She pronounced her judgment: I, too, would be uprooted.

The notion of "destiny" helped me to accept my mother's mysterious departure for Africa. In Florence, where I grew up in my father's home near the Duomo, the severance from my maternal branch was complete. The oblivion of my great-grandmother Cora was final: her possessions had burned and her name was not mentioned in our household.

It was years later, reunited with my mother in Switzerland, before I idly inquired about my American great-grandmother; I encountered secrecy at first. "Cora" was mentioned in a whisper, as if a great mystery were trapped in the mere utterance of her name. But one day, my mother and I were roaming through her apartment, which was like a family shrine, holding a few relics of life in Brazzà. "That belonged to my grandmother Cora," mother said, indicating a porcelain flower vase. "She painted it herself. It's the only one left." The design was of large blossoms: deep red garden-grown roses on a white background.

"This was in Brazzà next to my mother's bed," she said, touching an eighteenth-century Venetian two-drawer chest: Venetian like the fateful carpet, and like the gilded mirror. I vividly remembered the mirror; in the middle of its tarnished surface, like an image in a lagoon, I had seen my own face for the first time.

"Where is the mirror?"

"I had to sell it," my mother answered quickly. I imagined it in a Palm Beach residence. If certain pieces of furniture, even just an old cup, could tell their story. . . .

I opened the bottom drawer of the chest. Inside was a booklet, about seventy pages long, printed on handmade paper. The texture of the cover was rough and brownish like that of recycled cardboard. I don't know why, but I held it in my hands as if it were a magic relic. What struck me first was not so much the title, *Storia di Maria Barbella,* but rather the strange pseudonym of the author: "DEDIBS." An acronym? The cover was adorned with art deco flowers and leaves. Next to the word "Storia" was a tiny drawing of a three-leafed clover.

"DEDIBS. . . ." I pronounced the word quietly in Italian, thinking it sounded like the English word "dead," something dead. . . . At the bottom of the cover was written: "Rome, 1920." The preface was a single page:

The reader of this book will surely think that the author's talent lies mainly in his imagination. But these lines comprise a precise account of an event which took place in the United States of America in the years 1895–1896.

The name of the story's second heroine, the benefactress of Maria, is withheld, for this Lady is well known in Italy. Her fame derives from her commitment to the cause of the poor peasant women and laborers. She founded, sponsored and managed several organizations to improve their condition and the development of their artistic talents and craft, in the name of justice and human dignity.

During the 1905 earthquake of Monteleone, which was not as tragic as that of Messina, with only 800 victims, this Lady alone went to the people's rescue. She travelled abroad and managed to raise more than 60,000 liras, adding 17,000 of her own. In the devastated regions, she established several cooperative schools like those she had founded in Friuli.

Her humanitarian work won her a standing ovation in Parliament. While reading this story, written without embellishments, those who are acquainted with the international circles of philanthropy will probably succeed in guessing the Lady's name. . . .

I drew a deep breath. Anonymous, both author and heroine. What could be more intriguing in a true story?

"Mother, do you know what 'DEDIBS' stands for?"

She glanced at the cover and replied: "Oh, that's my grandfather. DE for Detalmo, DI for di, B for Brazzà, and S for Savorgnan: Detalmo di Brazzà Savorgnan. It's something he wrote and printed privately two years before he died."

> "Is the 'Lady' his wife?"
>
> "Yes . . . I don't know why he conceals it. . . ."
>
> "It must have been her wish," I suggested.
>
> "Well, it's possible. He loved her very much. . . ."

I spent a sleepless night, a "notte bianca" as the Italians say, immersed in my great-grandfather's ode to my elusive great-grandmother, Cora, and her protégée, Maria. It was dawn when I closed the book. I went to the window and stared at the still surface of the lake in the distance and at the fiery reflection of the sun rising from behind the Alps. I was under the spell of Maria, a young Italian woman who weighed one hundred and five pounds and stood under five feet. She had occupied a cell in Sing Sing. The glass of the only window had been painted over: prisoners on death row were forbidden to look out.

The spell of the story became an obsession. I needed to learn more. I resorted to old newspapers and the memories of whomever I could locate. I delved into subjects I had hitherto ignored, such as the history of capital punishment. My search ultimately led me from continent to continent, from New York to New Orleans, and across Italy. But the information I needed belonged to the age of carriages, gas lamps, and great steamships unloading human cargoes on the docks of the New World. More than once, I was anticipated by my old adversary: fire.

Too often I would find a promising source in ashes. When Maria Barbella arrived in New York, in 1892, Ellis Island had just become the quarantine and registration point for immigrants. But that very year, a fire on the island destroyed all evidence of her passage. I had to go to the village of Ferrandina, Italy, to learn the exact date of Maria's departure.

The popular Italian-language newspaper *Il Progresso Italo-Americano* was one of several papers in America that covered Maria's ordeal extensively. Archives for the year 1896 survived. But a fire in the paper's New York headquarters had consumed all issues from the year 1895. No library in the United States or in Italy possesses a trace of *Il Progresso* from 1895. Sometimes it seemed to me that the Austrian soldier of 1917 had released a genie.

My mother hinted that Detalmo had left some memoirs. My uncle, now the sole proprietor of Brazzà, told me about a trunk there which might contain them. So I revisited my childhood home. Neglect had altered Cora's park, and an earthquake had reduced the medieval castle to ruins.

The trunk in question was crammed with loose pages concerning my great-grandparents, mixed with the memorabilia of three wars. Fishing out pages at random, I began to reassemble their lives: their New York wedding; their visits to Louisiana; Detalmo's scientific essays; Cora's sketches; her unfinished novel (strangely titled "Lovemaking on Wheels"), her play, "A Literary Farce," published in Boston in 1896. I also found the complete transcript of Maria Barbella's appeal, printed by Wynkoop, Hallenbech, Crawford Printers, New York, 1895. All these became valuable sources.

My next pilgrimage was to 1205 Esplanade, at the corner of St. Claude Street in New Orleans, the Renaissance-style mansion where Cora was born. It had been one of the most extravagant homes in nineteenth-century New Orleans. Cora's father had bought it from a merchant by the name of Henry Morton Stanley, adoptive father of the famous explorer of Africa. Cora had slept in one of the second-floor bedrooms and had descended the great staircase with the mahogany bannister. The library of first editions had nurtured her literary taste. The house must have retained traces of her.

I walked north from the old U.S. Mint, away from the Mississippi River and the French Quarter, but I did not find a number 1205 on Esplanade. After the death of her husband, Cora's mother sold the grand house to the Archdiocese of New Orleans which eventually demolished it, over the objections of landmark societies. While protesters had failed to stop the demolition, they were able to obstruct all subsequent development. I found a littered, weed-covered lot, surrounded by a rusty wire fence.

Despite the ravages of fires and time, I was gradually able to reconstruct the story of Maria Barbella and the "Lady," my great-grandmother. My account is drawn from many sources: archives, memoirs, transcripts, and newspapers. The wandering palmreaders of my childhood knew better than psychologists what could move the human heart, and chance was their domain. Had I not been confronted with those transient educators so early in life, I would probably not have been so inspired by the coincidences of fire, and by the booklet of DEDIBS. Audible throughout this story is the spirit of the proud husband, Cora's first biographer and the instigator of my search. I am grateful for all the discretion of his narrative. Had he been more explicit, less modest, and less secretive, I might never have looked further.

Vedrassi li alberi delle gran selve di Taurus e di Sinai, Apennino e Talas scorrere per l'aria da oriente a occidente, da aquilone a meridie, e portarne per l'aria gran moltitudine d'omini. O quanti vòti, o quanti morti, o quanta separazion d'amici e di parenti! O quanti fien qualli che non rivederanno più le lor provincie né le lor patrie, e che morran sensa sepoltura, colle loro ossa sparse in diversi siti del mondo!

The trees of the vast forests of Taurus and of Sinai, of the Appenines and of Atlas, shall be seen speeding by means of the air from east to west, and from north to south, and transporting by means of the air a great quantity of men. Oh, how many vows! How many deaths! What partings between friends and relatives shall there be! How many who shall nevermore behold their own lands or their native country, and shall die unsepulchred and their bones be scattered in diverse parts of the world.

Prophecies: Of Sailing in Ships,
Leonardo da Vinci

The Trials of
MARIA BARBELLA

CHAPTER ONE

This is how I saw the events leading up to the death of Domenico Cataldo:

It happened a long time ago, in the heart of Manhattan. She was a seamstress. She was poor, but she dressed with care. In 1895, women wore long wide skirts, several underskirts, corsets, tailored blouses, and stockings even in summer. When a man wanted a woman, he had to make his way through layers and layers of material—unless, obviously, she desired him enough to take her clothes off.

But Maria said she did not remember a thing about her first night with a man. When she woke up in a room on Chrystie Street, her clothes were not torn and Domenico Cataldo was lying next to her. He promised to marry her, swearing his eternal love. That was how it all started.

On April 25, 1895, the heat in New York reached a twenty-four-year high. At three-thirty in the afternoon the temperature jumped suddenly from 52 to 90 degrees. If the rise in temperature had not been so extreme, perhaps Maria would have acted differently at nine-forty-five the following morning.

On Thursday the 25th, as usual, she had gone to work. She spent ten hours a day at Louis Graner & Co., a cloak manufacturer at 541 Broadway. If she took work home and sewed until midnight, she managed to earn eight dollars a week. She was paid by the piece. But in the preceding month, in the time since she had left her family and gone to live with Domenico Cataldo, she could no longer work after hours. Her situation was desperate and, as often happens in matters of the heart, she could not bring herself to admit the truth. The traditional code of honor of Southern Italy was deeply rooted in Maria. Domenico had seduced her with a promise of marriage, and now she was consumed with fear that he would break his word.

It had been an unbearably hot day. Maria had been handling heavy wool cloth for long hours over the sewing machine, and the stale air and the incessant hum of the machines intensified her already anguished state of mind.

When she walked back to Domenico Cataldo's rooms it was past 9:30 in the evening. She glanced into the Tavolacci Bar, at 428 East Thirteenth Street, but Domenico wasn't there. So she continued, bypassing two more buildings to reach their five-story tenement. She climbed the stairs. It was dark. Her legs felt heavy as lead, and despite the fact that she was only twenty-two years old, it took her a long time to reach the second-floor doorway to the two-room apartment.

She entered, lit the gas lamp in the kitchen, and then collapsed onto the mattress on the floor in the other room: Domenico hadn't even bought her the bed he'd promised. Her head ached; she felt feverish. Hot, humid air came through the small window. She had no idea where Domenico was. She had been seeing less and less of him, and she never knew when he would return. Tired and fearful, she felt too weak to eat, or even to take her clothes off. Thinking about death, she fell into a deep sleep.

Maria woke suddenly, in the middle of that Thursday night. Domenico was on top of her. She could not see his face, but she could smell beer on his breath. Like that, in the dark, he could have been anyone. Brutally, he penetrated her. Maria remained motionless and silent. Moments later he was asleep, sprawled out next to her, disheveled and drenched in sweat.

Maria woke late on Friday morning, numb and still feverish. The tiny apartment felt like an oven and Domenico, dressed and already wearing a hat, was racing about the room: he seemed to be looking frantically for something. Nervously he opened a drawer, rummaged through it, and slammed it shut. Maria watched him speechlessly, her big dark eyes wide open and her heart beating madly. He ransacked the chest, throwing everything out, shouting that he wanted his bankbook, that he was leaving America, that he was going back to Italy. She stood up in a flash and took his arm. Swearing, he pushed her away. She fell onto the floor and, in a voice which did not sound like her own, screamed that she was going to call the police. At that moment the door opened and Maria's mother came in. Filomena Barbella was breathless, although she had climbed those stairs many times before to plead with Domenico to keep his promise. She was hoping once more that he would make up his mind to marry her daughter. But when he saw the exhausted woman, Domenico pushed her violently aside and ran out, slamming the door behind him. Then he ran down the stairs and into the bar, two doors down. It was nine-thirty.

The bar had a small counter up front with a table next to it, and two more tables in the back. The owners, Vincenzo and Caterina Mancuso, were there, and one customer—a man Domenico obviously knew, because, after ordering a beer, he sat next to him at the table near the entrance. The man took out a deck of cards, mixed them deftly, and dealt them out. Mrs. Mancuso was busy cleaning while her husband watched the Neapolitan *briscola* game from behind the counter.

Ten minutes later, Maria came in. Very calmly, she laid a hand on Domenico's shoulder and waited. He did not even raise his eyes. "Will you come back and talk it over with my mama?" she whispered in Italian, not realizing that her mother had followed her.

"Talk what over?" Domenico answered, shrugging his shoulders to dislodge her hand.

"Our marriage. Come. Let's go and get married right away." . . . "I don't need a new dress or anything. I'll come as I am."

"*Only pigs marry!*" shouted Domenico, laying a card down. Maria put her left hand on his shoulder. Domenico made another movement as if to rid himself of her. But just at that moment, as if propelled by a spring, he jumped up. A razor flashed in the air. Convulsively clutching his throat with his hands, Domenico ran out of the bar. Maria fell to the ground, her face and clothes stained with blood. Someone screamed; everybody but Maria came out of the bar and saw Domenico cross the street, his hands gripping his neck, his body bent forward. Staggering, he continued to run toward Avenue A until he hit a fence; despite the now-gushing blood, he got up again and began to run through the crowd of horrified bystanders, who parted to let him through. Finally, when he reached the avenue, he fell backward onto the sidewalk and lay in the gutter, twitching faintly.

A moment later he was dead.

When Maria appeared at the doorway of the bar, she looked as if she were in a trance. Wholly indifferent to the shouts and the confusion, she walked toward Mr. Porzio's grocery; calmly, she washed her hands in the bucket of water on the sidewalk near the shop window and then disappeared into the building where she lived.

At home, she took off the blood-stained cotton dress, washed her hands again—this time with soap—and her face. She drank a glass of water. Then she opened the closet and took out her good dress: a serge jacket with puffed sleeves, which she put on over a blue blouse edged in white, and a skirt of the same dark blue material as the jacket. She changed into a pair of new black leather boots and tightened the laces. She also put on her most beautiful hat, which was black, with a wide brim, two big black feathers, and a blue velvet ribbon. She made the makeshift bed and tidied the rooms. Finally, she brought a chair to the window and sat down.

Meanwhile, police agents James Hay and John O'Reilly, having heard screams and

Artist's sketch of Maria Barbella testifying. The World, April 27, 1895.

seen a great crowd pour into the street from the nearby tenements, rushed to the scene and found Domenico Cataldo's
body. Great pools of blood stained East Thirteenth Street; the
red trail showed that Cataldo had staggered about four hundred feet before collapsing on the corner of Avenue A.

Somebody shouted out the murderer's name, pointing to
the tenement at number 424. The officers went to the building
and up to the second floor, where the door was open. For a split
second they thought there had been a mistake. That tiny
woman, sitting near the window with wide-open eyes and a
childlike expression, could not have been the murderess. But
then she spoke:

"Me take his blood so he no take mine. Say me pig marry."
This is what Maria said in her rudimentary English to the two
men who handcuffed her.

Hay and O'Reilly first took her to the police station at East
Twenty-Second Street, and from there a Captain Smith transferred her to the East Fifth Street command post, where
Domenico Cataldo's body had been taken. On the body they
had found a twelve-inch-long knife, twenty-seven cents, a
cheap watch, and a Bleecker Street Savings Bank book showing
a total deposit of 923 dollars.

While she waited at the police station, Maria sat quietly, her
tiny hands folded in her lap. She was pale and calm; she did not
know that just fifty feet away from her lay Domenico's body,
still warm.

They interrogated her. Maria answered calmly and always in
a low voice; she spoke in Italian, now and then using an English
word, but with difficulty. Only two people were able to understand her: detective John M. O'Rourke and Bernardino
Ciambelli, editor of the Italian daily *Il Progresso Italo-Americano*,

who had rushed to the station to meet her. The woman seemed absolutely unaware of the fact that she had committed a crime and spoke of Domenico as if he were still alive.

The news had traveled like lightning in the Italian neighborhood of Mulberry Street. Mott Street was in mourning. People came and went from number 136, where Maria's family lived. Her mother could not stop crying. They had been in the United States just three years and, with the exception of the two youngest children, Carmela and Giovanni, no one in the family spoke English. The father held his head in his hands.

Crowds surrounded the police station all afternoon. In the streets, people animatedly discussed the killing far into the night. Many did not find it at all strange that Maria had killed Domenico Cataldo. That man had abused her, had torn her from her family, and had violated her. "Only pigs marry!" he had shouted at her. None of those present could ignore the enormity of that insult. Maria had been taken by Domenico and he had refused to maintain the promise of marriage. What else could she have done to avenge her honor? For them, Maria's act was not a crime but self-defense. The woman had not had any choice.

That evening, Maria had been transferred to the jail at the Essex Market police station. There she was held in a common cell, without bail, and charged with murder.

The heat was still oppressive. On the spot where Domenico Cataldo had died, the glittering pool of blood slowly changed color, first to green and then to black, blending into the darkness of the night. At dawn the street sweepers washed it away. Among them, perhaps, was Louis Cataldo, Domenico's brother, who worked as a street cleaner.

CHAPTER TWO

$\mathscr{O}$n a June morning, one month after Maria Barbella's arrest, Cora Slocomb, Countess di Brazzà, was having breakfast with her husband, Detalmo, on the terrace of their country house in the Friuli region of Italy. As she leafed through *The New York Times,* which, as usual, had arrived weeks after publication, Cora's glance was drawn to a short paragraph. The tiny headline had almost escaped her: KILLED BECAUSE HE REFUSED TO MARRY HER. *A young woman, Maria Barbella, cuts Domenico Cataldo's throat.*

Cora threw the newspaper to the ground, paced up and down the terrace, then stopped, leaned on the parapet and stared out at the countryside. It was harvest time, and the peasants could be seen working in the fields. Several rows of mulberry trees stretched as far as the eye could see, interspersed with vineyards and orchards. The avenue leading to the house was white as chalk because of the summer dust. The ruins of the medieval castle, shrouded in wisteria, did not seem entirely abandoned.

Detalmo looked up from his newspaper and watched his wife, wondering what she was thinking. Cora turned, picked up the *Times* and held page five out to him, pointing to the paragraph in question. He read it and, unimpressed, handed it back to her. She looked straight into his eyes and said: "Another poor Italian immigrant at the mercy of the American courts."

Astonished that Cora had immediately taken the murderess's side, Detalmo was also curious about his wife's reaction. Was it perhaps because the killer was a woman, young and Italian? Cora had a very special intuition. He knew she was too fair to take the woman's side automatically. She thought that men and women represented opposite elements: equally important, but with distinctive strengths, complementary but different. Detalmo, unlike many of his colleagues, was in favor of women's demands for the vote and higher salaries. He thought that women should have the right to speak and to be heard, and that they did indeed have much to complain about.

"I wonder where that poor girl is, in that stifling heat," Cora said suddenly. She was thinking of the letter she had just received from her aunt Sally Townsend, who lived in Oyster Bay, Long Island, on a property surrounded by oak trees and bordering on the Roosevelts' estate. Her aunt had written how, that year, summer had arrived unusually early: 90 degrees, and it was only June!

"A woman does not kill lightly, it's not in her nature. It must certainly have been self-defense," Cora remarked.

Detalmo did not answer. He felt that his wife was already determined to find out more about the young woman. Cora was obstinate and sincere, and she fought every injustice to the very end. Detalmo loved her for that very reason. He preferred a woman who could speak her mind to one who was passive and eager to please. Meeting his expectations, Cora immediately prepared to send a telegram to her Aunt Sally. Although her hair was already arranged in the soft chignon which suited her so well, she was still in her silk robe, so she ran into the house to dress. Then she called Nonino, the coachman, and asked him to take her to Udine, five miles away. She wanted to be certain that the telegram, urgent as it was, would be clear and unmistakable.

> DEAR AUNT SALLY, PLEASE READ ARTICLE PAGE FIVE, SEC-
> OND COLUMN, NEW YORK TIMES, APRIL 27 STOP LOOK INTO
> MARIA BARBELLA'S SITUATION STOP TELEGRAPH RESPONSE
> STOP GREETINGS TO ALL, CORA.

Detalmo watched the open carriage pass the gate. Seated next to his wife was Idanna, their seven-year-old daughter, in her straw boater, her long fair hair blowing in the wind. At that moment, he knew that the young Italian immigrant was not going to disappear from their lives.

Front view of the mansion at Brazzà.

—

When Maria Barbella's case attracted Cora's attention, she and Detalmo had already been married for eight years. They had always kept separate rooms in the tacit belief that their passion would last only in the full respect of each other's privacy. They considered themselves lucky to own a house which allowed them such a luxury, and they were more in love now than on the day of their wedding, which took place in New York on October 18, 1887.

In December of that year they had arrived in Brazzà together for the first time. The carriage approached the gates of the estate by way of the long avenue lined with snow-laden acacias. Cora's glance ran over the entire facade of the white villa, then stopped at the front door, where a red rose bush was in full bloom.

"My dear, tell me . . . what place is this, where roses bloom in the snow?" she asked, turning to Detalmo.

"It is Brazzà, our home," he answered, taking her by the hand and leading her into the house.

Soon the Stars and Stripes flew above the entrance of the estate, next to the tricolor of the Italian kingdom. The old families of the area expressed a certain discomfort at such patriotic ardor. Was the young countess perhaps an eccentric nouveau-riche American? But Cora was sure that the neighbor's attitude would disappear sooner or later, and that her dynamism, as well as her American bathroom and American typewriter, would eventually be appreciated by the local inhabitants of the drowsy hills of her adopted country.

Born and raised in New Orleans in the most difficult period of the Civil War, Cora was the daughter of Confederate Captain

Cuthbert H. Slocomb and of his wife, Abigail Day, an energetic and willful Quaker. As a young man, Cora's father had financed the Washington Artillery, commanding its Fifth Battalion with heroic distinction. After the Civil War, Cuthbert became one of the pillars of the local community. Thanks to his hardware business, he had accumulated a significant fortune. He was also president of the Bank of Louisiana and of the Louisiana Equitable Insurance Co., first vice president of the Louisiana Mechanics Agricultural Association, and a volunteer fire fighter in New Orleans. However, when he died at the age of forty-two, these were not the things for which he was remembered.

His obituary, citing his good works, filled an entire page of the January 31, 1873, edition of the *Evening Picayune:*

> . . . In all the misfortunes to which our people have been subjected, the kind hand, open purse and cheering voice of Capt. Cuthbert H. Slocomb have always been seen, felt and heard.
>
> When the rear of the city was overflowed, he manned a boat and daily delivered provisions to hundreds of poor and suffering and in this holy work sowed the seed of the disease from which he died.
>
> As an enterprising, liberal citizen he had no superior. He was always ready to give time and money to whatever tended to beautify the city or improve the condition of its people, and now as a last offering we can almost say that he has given his life to help the poor and needy. . . .

Cora was just eleven years old when her father died, but he had managed to instill in her those values that would later inspire her to fight for social justice and Maria Barbella's cause.

Wealthy, intelligent, and gifted, Cora received a first-rate education. By age eighteen, she spoke fluent French and Ger-

man, and, having traveled to Europe several times, truly felt
herself to be a world citizen. At twenty-one, she was admitted
to the prestigious Munich Academy to study painting under
Frank Duvenek, an Ohio-born artist who was well-respected at
the time.

Three years later, in the spring of 1887, Cora went to Rome,
where she fell in love with Detalmo di Brazzà, a man eighteen
years her senior. Soon after, she fell ill with typhoid fever.
Unable to help her, Detalmo left Rome and returned to Brazzà.
Their love was still a well-kept secret. They had seen each other
only a few times, and never alone. When Detalmo finally
received the news that Cora was out of danger and wanted to
meet him in Sorrento, where she was convalescing, he went to
her immediately.

They met in Cora's private sitting room. She wore a dressing
gown and was seated on a chaise longue. When he saw her,
Detalmo was startled: due to her illness, her head had been
completely shaved. Having anticipated his reaction, she
smiled, pointing to the wig which was propped up nearby. "I've
had it made with my own hair," she said quietly, "but I decided
not to wear it today, so that you could see me as I really am."
Detalmo recognized the magnificent golden chestnut hair. He
could not speak and looked into her eyes, which were larger,
bluer, and livelier than he remembered. He proposed marriage,
and Cora accepted without hesitation.

Three days later, Cora received a proposal of marriage from
the German prince Wilhelm von Wied, who later became the
king of Albania. She had met him in Munich. The situation
amused her: Detalmo's timing had been perfect. She wrote a
letter to her aunt Sallie Day, who lived in New Orleans and was
just two years her senior. Sallie had married her maternal uncle
Robert Day, and Cora was very attached to her.

Sorrento, July 20, 1887

My Dear Sallie:

As you know I am still weak from my long illness, but still I do not wish you to hear from anyone else of my engagement to a Roman named Detalmo di Brazzà. He belongs to one of the oldest families in Italy and his name is in the Golden Book of Rome (if you remember your history you will know what that means) but his golden heart and mind are what have won my affection. The only misfortune is that he is a very busy man and runs the large estate of his family, so that we will not be often in America.

He is very handsome and dark as a Titian, reserved and stylish, amusing in conversation, and has a very tender heart and a character more like papa's than any man I have met. He considers himself too old for me, being 43, but as we love each other very much, I told him that it made no difference and I was glad of a strong arm to lean upon.

All my fortune is to be settled upon me, as he has means of his own. We are to winter in Rome in a family palace built by Giulio Romano, the favorite pupil of Raphael. This palace was originally built for the Cenci family (Leonardo painted a famous portrait of the beautiful Beatrice Cenci). In the summer we have the country place called Brazzà, [after] an old medieval castle in the chestnut-clad hills that lie between Venice and Trieste, where one of the largest seats of the family is situated.

We are to marry quietly in New York in early October. I thank God that He spared my life for such happiness as the love of a man like Detalmo. I feel like the man in the scriptures who, when he found the pearl of great price, sold everything. I have sought long but I have found what I wanted. The nation is nothing when you find the man you revere. I almost venerate Detalmo. How he fell in love with me, at first sight, during a "banal" conversation at an overheated soirée in Rome I cannot tell, for he must have thought me as frivolous as all the rest. I realized at once that he was not like the other men. I struggled hard against my feelings. But when they told me I might die, I realized the only thing that cost me anything to leave behind on earth was "he" and so I knew that if God spared me it was also for him.

He came to Sorrento to see me as soon as he heard I was well enough to see anyone, and fancy me, who wished always to keep my liberty, I placed my future into his hands with a sigh of relief as we became engaged on the shores of the Mediterranean.

My ring is a smooth polished blue flamed sapphire, almost black and, as one looks into it, it has just the color of the water as we leaned over the edge of the boat the day after he proposed to me.

This must travel around among you, as I am not strong enough to write each one fully. And, of course, it will begin with Marie Louise and end back to you, after all have read it.

You will think me sentimental, but typhoid infection is dangerous. We shall travel for a month after our wedding in America and come down to New Orleans before we sail back to Rome.

The business that interests him most is his flour mill in Brazzà. You see some Italians are energetic!

His father was a sculptor and there is a statue of his on the Pincio, one of the hills of Rome, besides lots more in the palaces and country places. I shall have many brothers-in-law, but only three of them are married, one brother to a Russian, another to a Belgian; one sister is married to a prominent nobleman in the province of Perugia. Detalmo is the fifth of sixteen children. I am to meet my mother-in-law the day after tomorrow. I was told about her intelligence long before I met Detalmo, so it must be true. She is seventy-one years old and I send you a copy of the letter she wrote to me when Detalmo proposed to me. Of course it is in French, and I translate it so it will be easier for you. Detalmo knows little English, but I shall teach him before the wedding, as

he is very quick to learn. I wish I could write longer, but I am still
weak so that my pen refuses to travel.

Yours Affectionately
Cora

P.S. Detalmo is just at the age his father was when he married. He
is a count and has three other names, but we need not bother about
them. One brother, Pietro, is the rival of Stanley in Africa but has
not yet had the time to write his book, being only 37 years old. It
seems as if my letter will never end—so good-bye, Cora.

Her mother-in-law had written to her:

Salsomaggiore, July 10, 1887

My dear daughter,

   From what Detalmo has told me about you, you will permit me
to call you by that sweet name. My son asks for my consent to your
union. He tells me you are necessary for his happiness and all that he
says about your heart and mind makes me see that I must also rejoice
at acquiring the right to your affection. I should like to express my
feelings to you better, but my son will tell you that my heart is
warmer than my pen. God bless you my dear child and give to you
and Detalmo the happiness which I enjoyed with his beloved father.

Your mother,
Giacinta di Brazzà

Cora's letter—the only one that survived the fire which later
destroyed all of Cora's personal belongings . . . and much, much
more—reached all four of her maternal aunts. It was sent first to
Marie Louise Day Sanders in England. Then it crossed the
Atlantic and reached Sally Day Townsend, on Long Island. From
there it traveled to aunt Amelia Day Starkey in New London,
Connecticut. And finally it crossed America by train toward
New Orleans and young aunt Sallie Day, wife of uncle Bob.

CHAPTER THREE

*I*n the summer of 1887, when Cora Slocomb announced her engagement to Detalmo in Sorrento, Maria Barbella was living not far away. She was about to turn sixteen in her native village of Ferrandina, in the Basilicata region.

Founded in 1496, Ferrandina, with its houses clustered on top of a hill, resembled a fortress. The dazzling Mediterranean sun had bleached its ochre walls, which, from a distance, appeared white. Steep stone pathways interlaced with myriad dead-end alleys to form a labyrinth. At dawn, the entire village would wake to the echo of animal hooves.

The men would go to gather wood in the valley on mules. Sometimes they stopped to rest under the centuries-old olive trees. In between villages, in the surrounding valleys, the ruins of ancient temples and prehistoric dwellings could still be seen. The women always sat by their front doors. They mended clothes, chatted, prepared meals. . . . Whatever they could do without stirring from their straw chairs they did on the spot, in the enormous living room that was the street. Often a woman would be crying over the death of a newborn: infant mortality was high. Maria's mother had lost five children, four of them after Maria's birth. The women all dressed alike: a long black skirt, a black

FERRANDINA
Gruppo di Popolane

Women of Ferrandina.

fitted corset, and a white blouse. Hens and goats roamed freely in and out of the houses. The street was their farmyard.

Two families owned all the surrounding lands. They lived in ghostly palaces in the center of Ferrandina, overlooking the church of Maria Santissima della Croce. The rest of the population, the peasants, worked their land and battled the harsh elements: gale force winds in the winter and paralyzing heat in the summer. Many of those who did not die ended up emigrating to America.

They would depart on foot, in groups of twenty or more. Entire families, including their unmarried adult children, would leave their loved ones to try their luck in the New World. They brought with them the Virgin Mary, Saint Rocco, patron of Ferrandina, and God. If they were lucky, they managed to catch the mail coach, which took them along the dirt road to Matera, down sloping fields and over the Basento

Street of Ferrandina.

River. At Matera, they were usually forced to continue to Naples on foot, reaching the docks and the waiting ships at least a week later. The journey to Naples took almost as long as the journey to America.

Maria did not realize it, but her father, Michele, had been thinking of emigrating to America for some time. Her older brother, Giuseppe, was already there. Michele Barbella was known in the village because, besides working the land, he was able to make ends meet thanks to his skill as a tailor, a job he loved. The two wealthy families would call on him whenever the expensive clothes, custom-made for them in the capital, needed alterations. Their measurements, especially those of the ladies, were constantly changing: either they lost weight and their clothes had to be taken in, or else the stitches had to be let out once more. Maria, too, had learned to sew.

Accompanying her mother to and from the public fountain at the edge of the village, where women took turns washing their linen, Maria never imagined there was any reason to cross the ocean. However, one day, soon after her birthday on October 24, 1892, she helped her mother pack a few belongings, including her father's tape measure and scissors, and gather up the flock of her younger brothers and sisters: Antonia, Carlo, Giovanni, and Carmela. At dawn, one by one, they walked out of the two-story house at number 8, Via De'Mille, and her father shut the small weathered wooden door behind them just in time for them all to climb onto the mail coach that was heading down to the valley. When they passed in front of the cemetery, below the village, her mother made the sign of the cross.

A few weeks later, after an arduous ocean crossing, Maria Barbella became one of the 247,000 Italians who landed in the United States in 1892. Once in New York, she felt as if she had never left home. It was as if Ferrandina had been transplanted along the Mulberry Bend alleys of Little Italy.

At that time, some 70,000 Italians lived in Little Italy. Their life was not very different from the one they had relinquished. The poverty was the same, if not worse. Whatever part of Italy they had come from, their faces were lined with the hardships they had left behind and continued to endure.

The narrow streets and alleys were little more than tunnels through four- or five-story brick buildings, dismal overcrowded tenements. Despite the colorful religious images hanging on the walls, the bright patchwork quilts on the beds, and the occasional bunch of lilacs in the spring, these "homes" seemed more like stables than dwellings fit for human beings.

On Saturdays, the open-air Mulberry Street market was always in full swing, however disappointing the goods. With much loud shouting and dogged bargaining, the immigrants bought and sold hard, moldy bread leftovers from rows of great sacks; they haggled over spoiled meat, wilted vegetables, fruit that was almost rotten, eggs that had broken in transit and were sold by the spoonful for omelets, and fish that had long been strangers to water. The whole neighborhood was permeated by the odor of decay. Goods which on Fifth Avenue would have been considered garbage were human sustenance here. From time to time the sanitation inspectors came and dumped these substandard offerings into the East River, but business as usual would soon resume.

Often, the men would sit in the barbershops having their beards and mustaches trimmed or go to the bar for a beer and a game of cards. Under the lowered brims of their black hats, smoking their pipes, they hatched schemes for the future; the more enterprising among them would return to Italy and impress their fellow villagers with their earnings and tales.

During the icy winters, women scurried about, their heads covered by black shawls, speaking to each other in dialect, invoking their patron saints. In the summer the people of the neighborhood spent most of their time on the sidewalks in front of their tenements. The organ grinder walked slowly through the streets with his little monkey that bowed, pirouetted, and held out a hat for money. Singers and dancers, carnival troupes, and small opera companies performed outdoors on feast days. In mid-August, the day of Saint Gennaro's miracle was the occasion for an important festival. If the saint's blood, kept in an ancient crystal phial in the Naples cathedral, liquefied, news of the miracle would arrive by telegraph and all the church bells of Little Italy would ring in unison while the inhabitants fell to their knees and crossed themselves.

Silk banners and perfume of anisette, in honor of Garibaldi's unification of Italy in 1860, accompanied the September 20th procession. The band invariably played Verdi, and when the music soared the crowd would be moved, thinking of their homeland so far away.

Life in the neighborhood was bound to the *padrone* system. Entrepreneur, loan shark, banker, the *padrone* watched over the existence of the poor immigrants. His agents in Italy painted an idyllic picture of America, drew up labor contracts with the peasants, tearing them from their land and bringing them across the ocean for the *padrone*'s profit. This was slavery, the Italian way.

Giuseppe Barbella, Maria's older brother, was one such peasant. In the United States, he had worked under the *padrone* system. Having established himself, he brought the rest of his family to America, as many other young people did under the same circumstances.

The unions had little influence over these immigrants, who seemed indifferent to the privileges of naturalization. Certain that if they became American citizens they would be drafted into the military, they kept to themselves. They lived under the illusion that this separatism was acceptable, because America was a free country.

In their autonomous world, so far from home, they nurtured beliefs and superstitions as ancient as the villages they had left behind. They had their own rules of justice, and they avoided the American courts. The traditional code of honor was an unquestioned reality, a kind of second nature; if violated, honor could only be regained by revenge. "An eye for an eye, a tooth for a tooth," was the centuries-old law everyone accepted with the utmost fatalism.

One night in November 1893, Maria Barbella spoke with Domenico Cataldo for the first time. Some eleven months had passed since her arrival in New York. She was returning home to Elizabeth Street, where her family then lived. She stopped at Domenico Cataldo's shoeshine booth on the southeast corner of Canal and Elm Streets. She passed by him every day because his booth was on the way to the sweatshop where she worked. Usually she lowered her eyes and kept going. That night, however, she returned his smile. He asked her to please stop for a moment. She looked at him with her great hazel-colored eyes. Her pink cheeks and full figure attracted him. And she was short, just right for him.

Domenico, with his black hair and well-tended mustache, had a good physique, notwithstanding the beginnings of a paunch. He had full cheeks, a slightly aquiline nose, and a narrow forehead. Although he thought himself handsome, he really was not, and his skin was pockmarked from smallpox. Yet Maria found him attractive.

Maria did not have much to say. Her family was from Basilicata; she was a seamstress; she had gone to work immediately

Maria Barbella, from an engraving at the time of the first trial.

after her arrival and since then she had done nothing but sew. Cataldo told her that he, too, came from Basilicata, from Chiaromonte, which was true; that he had a thousand dollars in the bank, which was a little more than the truth; that he was twenty-eight years old, which was a little less than the truth; and that he was tired of his bachelor's life, which was entirely false. He ended by saying that if he found the right girl, he would marry her and invest his savings in a barbershop.

That was how the love story began. For Maria, Domenico was simply an honest man who came from the same region she did. She was well acquainted with hardship, but as far as love and human nature were concerned she was naïve. Furthermore, she was certain that she was ugly and insignificant, because no young man had ever courted her; her sister Antonia, who was two years younger, was already married and had two children. Domenico made her feel special.

During that cold week in November, Maria stopped several times at Domenico's booth and finally let him escort her almost all the way home. She began to leave her house earlier in the morning and to come back later and later at night. Her mother became suspicious and asked her a few questions. Maria, who had not told her parents about Domenico out of fear they would not approve, now confessed the truth. She had met a good young man from Chiaromonte who wanted to marry her. Soon he would come to meet them.

But Domenico never did go to Maria's home. Every day he walked her to the door, but always had a ready excuse not to climb the stairs. "Not today, I'm late, tomorrow . . . tomorrow . . ." he said, every time. Maria was in love and she believed him. Meanwhile, the days went by. Finally Michele Barbella lost his patience and ordered his daughter never to see Domenico again.

Maria had to obey. She did what a woman usually does in order to forget a man. She avoided him and even changed jobs, moving to a sweatshop on Broadway. For more than a year, Maria and Domenico never met, not even by chance. While Maria had resigned herself to the idea of having lost her sole opportunity to get married, Cataldo proved to be less compliant. He certainly was not prone to mad infatuations, but he knew that Maria loved him. He was sure of himself and did not want to forego the possibility of having her.

Determined to seduce Maria, he managed to find out where she worked and waited for her one day outside the building on Broadway. As soon as she saw him, she passed him by and kept walking. He ran after her and grasped her arm, begging her to stop. He besieged her with a flood of words: he said that he had missed her terribly, that he could not go on without her and that he wanted to marry her. Maria listened, staring at him with her great wide eyes. At one point, though, she managed to interrupt him: "Good-bye, it's late . . . please let me go . . ." she said timidly, and ran off.

But Domenico was not ready to admit defeat. Night after night, with unrelenting determination, he waited for Maria at the factory exit. Ten days later, he began once more escorting her home. Maria was afraid they would be seen and would leave him a block away from her house. He would reassure her by saying that he would soon introduce himself to her parents. Once more, he made her feel special, even beautiful.

And so the love story resumed. It was the middle of March 1895.

CHAPTER FOUR

$\mathcal{C}$ora and Detalmo di Brazzà were a striking couple. Cora was the epitome of a late-Victorian beauty. Her skin was smooth, her shoulders round; she was endowed with the mandatory hourglass figure which most women of the time achieved only with constricting girdles, and at the cost of their health. Her eyes were aquamarine, large and arresting, and when she moved, she did so with grace and dignity, making herself seem taller than she actually was.

Detalmo was tall and classically elegant, with a full beard and dark eyes. He was Cora's perfect counterpart. Like her, he was a nonconformist. An eccentric streak ran in his family: two of his brothers, who left to explore the French Congo, died there. The city of Brazzaville owes its name, in fact, to Pietro di Brazzà. Detalmo looked after the family properties, but his true passion was for civil engineering. He was a scientist-inventor with the culture and polymathic energy of a nineteenth-century gentleman. Science, like his choice of a wife, was an escape from provincialism.

In Cora he had found a kindred soul. Their marriage was based on the enthusiasm for life which animated them both. Omnivorous readers—from books on Africa to prayer books—

they nevertheless had their individual preferences. Detalmo was especially fond of scientific tracts with complex illustrations of new inventions such as hydraulic pumps or rotaries; Cora loved novels, the margins of which she filled with notes. For this reason she often bought two copies of the same book: one for herself and one for her husband.

It was probably because of the distance from her native country that Cora maintained a voluminous correspondence and subscribed to *The New York Times,* the New Orleans *Daily Picayune,* the *North American Review,* which kept her abreast of the latest publications, and, for Detalmo's benefit, *Scientific American.*

The village mailman was kept busy, and Nonino, the coachman, was often rushed off to Udine so that the letters could leave before the post office closed. Cora also wrote to people she did not know personally, and perhaps would never meet, such as John Ruskin and Elizabeth Cady Stanton, whom she admired for her struggle for women's suffrage. She felt as if some of these epistolary friends were as close to her as those who lived nearby.

The clicks of the typewriter echoing throughout the house were as familiar a sound to Detalmo as the buzz of cicadas in June. During ocean crossings; on the Orient Express between Venice and Paris; in the first-class compartment on the Direttissimo, the train connecting Udine to Rome, Cora tirelessly wrote and wrote: letters, plays, novels. . . . Brazzà was her capital, certainly not her retreat.

Cora and Detalmo's ideas were unusual for their time. Both were convinced that wealth brings happiness only because it provides the opportunity to do some good for others. Improving the condition of the poor was a cause which they shared with equal determination. They understood that times were changing and that the social realities of the "Old World" were driving more and more poor Europeans to emigrate. They also knew that the New World bristled with dangers for the emigrants. And what would become of Italy if all the young people left? Detalmo was not one of those country gentlemen who prospered on the peasants' backs: He considered his lands to be fertile enough to support everyone, and did his best to provide the peasants with the means to live in a dignified way. Was it not better to put what one had to good use, rather than to struggle for a better life in a country whose language, laws, and customs were entirely unknown?

Cora and Detalmo's views on the new century, which was imminent, differed slightly. The great technological discoveries were about to bring vast changes to everyone's lives, and the worry over what would happen should machines take over was great. Would manual skills become useless? And if the traditional values were to disappear, what would the elders teach the new generations? Would their role in society still have meaning? These questions Cora answered with a defense of her correspondent John Ruskin's nostalgic ideas, while Detalmo hoped for a gradual transition into modernity. On one point, however, they did agree: Progress could be defined as such only if the values of the past were not entirely erased, but fused with those of the future. An idea which was utopian perhaps, but which animated their spirits and was actualized in their daily lives. The Brazzà gates were always open, and no management changes were carried out without input and advice from the peasants. Detalmo and Cora hoped, naïvely perhaps, that their efforts would stem depopulation in the area due to emigration. In other words, they hoped to defeat History.

During her early years in Louisiana, Cora had learned to make lace, following designs handed down through her mother's

Quaker family. Soon after settling at Brazzà, Cora introduced this art into the Friuli region, integrating it with the local decorative motifs and making it a means to improve the peasant women's conditions. She created a lacemaking cooperative, which was not only the first of its kind in Italy, but also became one of the most active centers of lace production in the country. The cooperative provided the women with a means of sustenance without keeping them from their domestic or farm work, employing them during the long winter months when it was impossible to labor in the wheat and corn fields. By 1891 the industry was in full swing. On a wave of enthusiasm, and thanks also to Cora's business acumen, orders arrived from the United States, France, England, Hungary, and even Chile. The American market was the largest, but it was protected. Marketer, pedagogue, and now trade reformer, Cora struggled for the abolition of American tariffs on foreign lace and was able to have them reduced from sixty to fifteen percent, convincing the U.S. Commerce Department that the reduction of import tariffs would diminish the influx of immigrants.

Cora would often hold entertaining seminars for the lacemakers on how to conquer the American market. "You must make exotic and original designs," she would tell them. "Americans worship the new. They fear being caught with old styles."

The Brazzà lacemakers soon acquired fame as the "queen's lacemakers," thanks to the regular orders which came from Queen Margherita of Italy, who had a great regard for Cora. At the 1893 International Exposition in Chicago, Brazzà lace was chosen as a prime example of Italian craftsmanship. Standing next to the samples she was so proud of, Cora spoke on the life of Italian peasant women. Speaking in front of a large audience was not new to her, and she liked to improvise. Her speech, which was subsequently published that year in Chicago in *The Congress of Women,* was mostly extemporaneous.

The race which inhabits Friuli and speaks its language is robust, handsome, intelligent and patient. The women do not work as regularly as the men in the fields. . . .

. . . The women in the high-perched villages are the first to spy the thunder caps scudding along toward the quarter of the heavens which arches their homes, and they hurry to the churchtower and ring the bells to call the laborers from the fields and the old to their prayers. They ring with a will, for they believe that by establishing an aerial commotion through the swinging, reverberating bells the devastator can be warded off.

Since peasant and proprietor suffer alike from the terrific hail and storms, the gentlefolk of Friuli are seeking in every way to render their tenants familiar with all the means for rapidly substituting fresh crops for those destroyed. They also seek to supply them with other means of earning a livelihood in inclement weather so that they may maintain their families and meet their financial obligations with the proceeds of their manual industry. . . .

. . . Oh my compatriots, you and I grew up with tales of Mafia and bloodshed poisoning our hearts against the Sicilians; but the Mafia brotherhood was born as the inevitable defense against centuries of repression under foreign rulers. You and I read of the Sicilian vespers, the rebellion reeking with blood against the Angevins in 1282. . . .

The lacemakers of Brazzà know scores of such stories. Learning thus daily of the great influence for good which even the lowliest can exert, let us also learn from them never to neglect the smallest opportunities, for they are the stepping-stones to bridge the deep chasm of egotistical selfishness which lies between our frail humanity and the great example of St. Francis of Assisi. . . .

Among our lacemakers, there are the handicapped—those who are so crippled that they are unable to leave their homes.

Yet each day, the young girls, some no older than six, travel on foot to these homes to instruct these gnarled hands in the intricacies of the twists and delicate turns involved, so that they too feel part of the creation of these masterpieces which have come to be known as the lace of Brazzà. . . .

Cora had summed up her personal philosophy in the so-called "Seven Rules of Harmony," listed in the lacemaking school's cooperative regulations. A flier with the seven rules was distributed to the buyers and hung at the entrance to each of the three buildings on the grounds of the estate that Cora had designated for the lacemakers.

1. May the sacred spirit of peace be a living power in your life so that you may contribute time, thought and money to its cause.
2. Never listen without protest to unjust accusations against the members of your family or your community.
3. Try to understand the spirit of national laws and obey them; but try also to take interest in the modification of those laws which, in your view, oppress any given class of society.
4. May your thoughts and active efforts serve to develop a national and patriotic spirit, and do not criticize without prior knowledge the administration of the family and the nation.
5. Treat the birds and animals, and all living creatures in the world of flora and fauna with kindness and justice. Do not destroy, unless it is for your survival or for the protection of the weak. Make it your duty and purpose to plant, nourish, and propagate all that might lead to the moral and physical improvement of your family, home, and nation.
6. Teach your children and employees the spirit of justice and peace, trying to develop around you sentiments of harmony.
7. Let not a day pass without a word or a single action that may help transmit the cause of peace, whether at home or outside.

Cora was so sensitive to the problems of peace and nonviolence that as a member of the American National Council on Women she was the president of the Committee on Peace and Arbitration. Also, despite her American nationality, in 1895 she was elected president of the Italian Association of Women's Industry.

Cora chose the three-leafed clover as her symbol because, she said, if one already possesses a four-leafed clover, the hope of finding the lucky one was nil. That symbol became such a source of inspiration to her that the wonderful park of Brazzà, which included Himalayan deodaras, cedars, tropical palms, weeping willows, and countless other varieties of trees and plants, was redesigned in the shape of a three-leafed clover.

The best time to visit the magnificent park was on the day of celebration of the lacemaking schools, when prizes were given out for the year's best samples. In June 1895, the celebrations began as usual with a Mass in the private chapel. A Unitarian, Cora nevertheless felt at ease in all sanctuaries and sat in the first pew along with the younger lacemakers, who wore their traditional costume. Her white lace blouse was an example of their work.

Guests were everywhere, inside the villa, in the rose garden, and in the park. Nonino, the coachman, did not want to disturb his mistress during Mass to give her the alarming telegram which had arrived from America and so he searched for Detalmo and gave it to him. It came from Oyster Bay, Long Island:

MARIA BARBELLA IN NEW YORK CITY JAIL STOP TRIAL SET FOR MID-JULY STOP OUTLOOK NOT GOOD.

Detalmo showed his wife the telegram only after all their guests had left. It was late in the evening and they sat on the terrace to

Cora Slocomb, Countess di Brazzà.

enjoy the soft breeze coming from the Adriatic. Cora read the message and then looked inquiringly at her husband. Maria Barbella was a potential scapegoat for the brutal American discrimination against Italians. . . . And Detalmo knew that, although Cora was American by birth and Italian by marriage, she believed in a kind of justice without nationality, one which would serve the poor and the rich in the same way. So he was not surprised when Cora said that she might have to take the steamer to New York, in order to meet Maria and hear her story. The girl almost certainly did not speak any English, and probably no one had wondered whether Domenico Cataldo had abused her, forcing her to defend her honor. The foreboding of a struggle between life and death possessed Cora.

"If America does not have enough prisons to jail all the criminals, there is plenty of land in which to build new ones," she remarked. "The steel magnates and robber barons could invest in such ventures. But obviously capital punishment is the easiest way out."

Detalmo was listening. Maybe social justice exercised over his wife the same attraction that Africa had on his brothers: It was a challenge requiring sacrifice, which did not exhaust itself in the altruistic impulse but rather was a part of the search for the self, almost a sacred vocation.

Cora was insistent she could travel to New York alone. But on July 6, when the North Star Line steamship *Nomadic* left Liverpool for New York, there were two passengers registered under the name of Brazzà on board. Cora had brought her easel and paints, as well as her typewriter. She was writing a novel about the experience of an anthropologist living with the Piman Baja Indians of the Sierra Madre. Detalmo had brought his new invention: a postal registration machine he wanted to present to the scientific community in New York.

CHAPTER FIVE

*T*he New York prison, perhaps the purest example of Neo-Egyptian architecture of the nineteenth century, was a majestic building. With a massive portico, upheld by enormous columns, it occupied the entire block between Franklin and Centre Streets. The polished floors of the corridors would not have soiled a lace handkerchief. But this stately, seemingly immaculate building concealed the most terrible conditions: The basements were permanently covered with stagnant water, and when the tide rose the drains overflowed, so that a nauseating stench of fouled earth insinuated itself everywhere. The cells, situated above an open drainage pool, stank of the sewer. Malaria was rampant.

Completed in 1840, this architectural masterpiece had been built on pilings sunk into the marshy ground of the Old Collection Pond. The pilings were deep, but not sufficient to allay fears of a collapse under the weight of that monumental granite mass. And, in fact, the site had sunk so much by 1895 that the foundation of the building barely surpassed the level of Broadway, which was nearby.

The cells, little more than caves carved out of the thick granite walls, were arranged in four layers crossed by a long and narrow courtyard. Two coal-burning stoves heated the building, but the two bottom floors were constantly freezing. The cells were nine by five feet and received light and air solely through narrow slits set very high up in the walls. Each cell was closed by a heavily fortified barred door about five feet high. There were 298 cells, but at that time the average prison population was approximately five hundred people. Inmates were often doubled up in their cells, taking turns to sleep on the one cot.

The name of John Fallon, the head warden, was always uttered in a whisper. The prison was a place of detention and not a penitentiary, so all its occupants were to be regarded as innocent until their trials; and yet, under Fallon's wardenship, the innocent and the guilty alike suffered brutalities worse than those inflicted in the state penitentiaries. The atrocious conditions in which the inmates found themselves gave rise to the name by which the prison was known: the Tombs.

During 1895, fifty thousand prisoners crossed the threshold of the Tombs. Maria Barbella was one of them. The exact date of her arrival is uncertain. It is highly probable, however, that it was the beginning of May when the municipal van, known as the "Black Maria," brought her from the Essex Market prison to the Tombs.

The women's section had forty-nine cells, which held about sixty inmates. For some reason, Maria was alone. Her tiny body made the cell, whose only amenities were a ceramic bowl, a towel, and a piece of soap, seem almost large. From home, Maria had brought her toothbrush.

The women, unlike the men, were locked up only at night. At six-thirty in the morning the clinking of the matron's keys could be heard as, one by one, every cell was opened. After having washed, dressed, and tidied their cells, the women emerged into the hallway where they spent the day sitting on chairs. Maria must have felt a bizarre similarity to the women of Ferrandina who did their chores seated at the entrance to their houses. But the Tombs's hallway was not Via de' Mille: Here there was a roof instead of the sky, and menacing bars ran along the entire perimeter of the internal courtyard.

It was in that hallway that a tall, distinguished lady, dressed in black, extended her slender kid-gloved hand to Maria and introduced herself. Her name was Rebecca Salomé Foster, but to the detainees she was known simply as Mrs. Foster. Since she had arrived at the Tombs, Maria had not spoken a word and had eaten very little. Looking very pale, she timidly shook the stranger's hand.

A native of Mobile, Alabama, Mrs. Foster was the widow of General John A. Foster, who had died in 1890. She lived in the city, in the elegant Park Avenue Hotel, and she summered in Riverdale. And yet, for the past fourteen years, she had not missed a single one of her daily meetings with the inmates at the Tombs; she listened, she comforted, she gathered their outbursts and their confidences. But her support was not just moral: a great portion of her significant fortune was allotted to the prisoners and their families. Her dedication to this cause had earned her the sobriquet of the "Tombs Angel," which satisfied her desire for anonymity.

Mrs. Foster seemed wholly at ease in the prison: she had no difficulty in getting her bearings and moved briskly up and down the stairs, in and out of the cells; even the wardens treated her with respect. Her fame had also reached the Justice Department: Judges, lawyers, and reporters knew her well and there was no courtroom in New York to which she was not admitted.

Mrs. Foster was immediately struck by Maria's composure and thought her physical appearance pleasant. Maria, for her part, felt that she could trust the tall lady dressed in black. The girl knew nothing about the workings of justice, and Mrs. Foster did not tell her that the worst was yet to come, that those first signs of insomnia and lack of appetite would soon coalesce into panic. Mrs. Foster knew that the road ahead would be much longer than Maria could ever imagine.

Each day, the girl spoke of her past without reticence. Her big hazel eyes brightened when she softly uttered Domenico Cataldo's name and told the story of how they met. But she was absolutely silent about more recent events.

"Long me here?" she would ask in broken English.

"I don't know," Mrs. Foster invariably answered. "Soon you will be put on trial . . ."

"Trial?" Maria did not even know the word.

"They will ask you some questions. They will ask a lot of people questions. They want to find out if you're guilty of premeditated murder."

Maria would not answer. She remained motionless, her eyes fixed on her hands intertwined in her lap. Mrs. Foster wondered whether the girl had understood the meaning of "premeditated murder," but would not have the heart to ask.

Maria spent two and a half months in the Tombs, and every day a member of her family came to visit her. Giovanni, her younger brother, told her the latest news from Mott Street and brought her some sewing so that the time would pass a little more quickly. He also gave her a rosary which Maria put in her pocket.

One afternoon, her mother came. She was very agitated, and her tired, drawn face made her seem far older than her forty-nine years. The entrance guards called the matron, who let her inside. In the trembling light of gas lamps, Mrs. Barbella was taken to a small, dismal room to be searched, according to the rules. The woman was sobbing, and with reason.

That morning an eviction notice had been served to the Barbella family. They owed a month's rent. It was either pay or be thrown into the street. The family lived in three stifling rooms on the top floor of a five-story building, for which they paid ten dollars a month. Since the day of Maria's arrest, her father, the tailor, had stopped working; he did nothing but come and go from the Tombs, anguished over his daughter's fate. He did not know where to turn for help.

Mrs. Foster was present when Mrs. Barbella told Maria the terrible news of their pending eviction. She tried to reassure her, but Filomena clung to her daughter, seeking comfort in the embrace. Maria remained silent, but, for the first time, Mrs. Foster noticed her eyes glaze over with tears.

The next day an envelope from an anonymous benefactor reached the Barbella home: It contained the amount necessary to pay the rent for May.

Father Ferretti of the Baxter Street Church of the Transfiguration also went to the Tombs. Maria did not want to see him: she was afraid of him because the priest personified absolute authority. But he addressed her by name and spoke to her the way the Ferrandina parish priest would have done. He was the typical Italian village curate: plump, bald, and rosy-cheeked. The expression on his face was that of a man who had listened to many sins and had forgiven and forgotten them all. Seated in a corner of the cell, he spent more than half an hour with Maria who, kneeling, whispered her confession to him. Then he made a sign of the cross on her forehead and gave her the Eucharist. For some days after that Maria slept better and regained her appetite.

Then, one evening, her legal counsel appeared.

In particularly difficult cases, the court usually entrusted the defense of indigent defendants to a prominent lawyer. But it was to a little-known attorney by the name of Amos Evans that the notable Judge John W. Goff decided to appoint the case of the Italian immigrant.

Evans's associate was Henry Sedgwick, a lawyer whose first case was Maria's. Sedgwick was tall and pale: The blue eyes were cold as ice behind thick lenses, and the dark thin hair, parted in the middle, seemed glued to his head. By contrast, Evans was a man of about fifty, portly, with a long, curled mustache and an irrepressible tendency to pontificate.

The two lawyers reached the Tombs at six o'clock in the evening, a rather unusual hour for a first-time consultation with a client. Mrs. Foster had just left when the matron told Maria that two gentlemen wanted to speak to her. The girl was scared to death and beset the woman with a torrent of Italian, refusing to follow her into the visiting room. The matron tried to convince her that the two lawyers were there to help her. Maybe the trial was imminent, and everything would work out for the best. . . . Nothing could convince Maria. The girl refused to budge. The matron then had to lift her and pull her by the hand through the crowded hallway. Maria walked as if she were in a trance, unaware of the curious glances of the other inmates.

When she entered the visiting room, Evans and Sedgwick greeted her formally and motioned for her to sit down. The girl obeyed, keeping her hands tightly wound in her lap, staring first at one and then the other of the two men. Both placed their briefcases on the table, opened them, pulled some documents out, closed them, and placed the cases on the ground. Their gestures were so synchronized that only the obvious difference in their appearance gave an indication that they were not the same person.

A thousand questions churned in Maria's mind. Those two strangers, her friends? How was that possible? Why on earth should they help her? Who had told them about her? They did not even speak Italian. Astonishment made her speechless. Suddenly a door opened and another man came into the room. He was of medium height, had a mustache, thick sideburns, and small round glasses. He took off his hat, and, in English with the two men and in Italian with Maria, he excused himself for being late.

Benedetto Morossi, an Italian, had been working as a court interpreter for a few years. He had worked with Amos Evans on his latest case. Vincenzo Nenno, also Italian, had killed his wife: during the trial the defense had wanted to plead insanity, but Evans had been opposed. Now, locked on death row at Sing Sing, Vincenzo was clearly showing signs of his mental illness. This event had deeply affected Morossi, who could not entirely hide his coolness toward Evans, speaking to him and his associate in a detached, formal manner. When he addressed Maria his voice assumed a friendlier tone.

The meeting lasted less than an hour. The two lawyers asked Maria many questions and took notes, without once looking her in the eye. Morossi translated, trying to be as clear as possible and at the same time attempting to explain to Maria the procedures of the trial, which was to take place very soon. But Maria was disoriented: it seemed that her native tongue, too, had become unintelligible to her. She could only repeat the obsessive refrain of how Cataldo had broken his promise of love and had betrayed her, of how he had been about to return to Italy. *"Say me pig marry!"* Yes, it was Domenico's razor; he had just bought it. She could not remember anything else.

Suddenly, Evans and Sedgwick looked at each other; they signaled, took their briefcases, opened them, replaced all the documents, closed them with a jerk, stood up in unison, shook Maria's hand with a bow of their heads, and disappeared. Morossi told Maria that the trial date had been set for July 11; he told her not to worry. Then he left hurriedly in the attorneys' wake. Maria remained there, seated in the dimly-lit room, shaken by the news of her impending trial. She did not even notice that the guard was waiting for her.

That first meeting with attorneys Evans and Sedgwick was to be the last. Maria saw her lawyers again only on Thursday, July 11, in court.

CHAPTER SIX

*T*he elevated passage connecting the Tombs to the Criminal Courts bore an appropriate name: the Bridge of Sighs. On the day of the trial, a stifling July morning, Maria crossed the Bridge of Sighs on Mrs. Foster's arm.

She had spent the week making herself a new dress. Mrs. Foster had given her a bolt of blue cotton, and her mother had brought all the sewing items, including a pair of scissors which the warden, after some hesitation, had granted her permission to use. Under the eyes of the matron, who watched her through the open door of the cell, Maria had spread the material on the floor and cut out gigot sleeves, a collar with a pleated flounce, a pleated skirt, and a close-fitting bodice which emphasized the shapeliness that had so attracted Domenico Cataldo. The dress, once basted, was sewn by her father, who worked day and night so that it could be ready by the day of the trial.

Maria entered the courtroom wearing the new dress and a dark gray felt hat trimmed with organza flowers and feathers.

The day was leaden, thick with clouds and humidity. Neither air nor light came in through the five open courtroom windows. Not even the two enormous ceiling fans stirring the hot air provided relief.

The courtroom buzzed with activity: Men in black business suits came in and out, spoke in serious tones and continually moved documents from one bench to another. When she entered the room, Maria recognized one of her attorneys, Amos Evans, who bowed deeply to Mrs. Foster.

"I did my best to choose two jurors from the South. Usually they show more clemency toward those who commit extreme acts to vindicate a loss of honor."

"Are there any Italian jurors?" asked Mrs. Foster.

"I'm afraid not."

"And why not?" she said, astonished.

Evans could not answer.

One by one, twelve men took their places in the jury section. Mrs. Foster stared at them attentively, wondering which of them might be from the South.

The courtroom was packed with people, mostly Italian immigrants: many came merely out of curiosity, but there were also those in search of strong emotions. A woman with a lined face and a distraught air sprang out of the crowd and clutched Maria: it was her mother. Crying, she clasped her daughter in an embrace that revealed her immense pain. It was not easy to separate them. Maria's father was asked to accompany his wife out of the courtroom. Henry Sedgwick, Evans's colleague, came in hurriedly, looking for his seat. Then came the prosecution lawyers, McIntyre and Lauterbach, who took their places to the right of the judge. McIntyre's thick mustache hid his mouth almost entirely, while Lauterbach had a pointed, prominent chin and a nervous tic that made his upper lip tremble slightly. Aside from these differences, the two men were of similar build, kept their hair tidily slicked back, and wore identical blue bow ties, which stood out against their starched white collars.

"The People versus Maria Barbella!" announced the clerk. "Hear! Hear! All rise, the Superior Court for the County of New York is now in session, the Honorable John W. Goff, judge, presiding. God save the United States of America and this Honorable Court."

Everyone stood up. The tall, thin Judge Goff made his entry, moved the solid oak high-backed chair, and sat down.

"Sit down, please," he muttered, placing a folder on the desk and scanning the courtroom with his gray eyes.

Maria grasped Mrs. Foster's hand.

John W. Goff. Apprehensively, Mrs. Foster remembered a story she had read in *Life Magazine.* Maybe it was just gossip, but the rumors had not been laid to rest despite the denials. Apparently, when he was ten years old, Goff had encountered a little girl who had been crushed by a horse in the road. As the horse galloped away, the girl, lying on the ground, cried out for help. The future judge threw himself on her and began to beat her. Fortunately, someone rushed to her aid, pushing her attacker away. Afterwards, the little boy had thus explained his behavior: "God wanted to punish this girl, and I helped him."

Reserved and distinguished, the Anglo-Irish Judge Goff seemed to have descended straight from Dublin into that high office of the American court. His Oxford-cloth shirt was immaculate and his silk tie was held by a silver clasp. He had a benevolent aspect, but to Mrs. Foster's eyes he seemed cold. His penetrating gaze worried her.

At ten o'clock, Assistant District Attorney McIntyre's opening statement plunged the courtroom into a deathly silence:

"The prosecution has every reason to think that Miss Barbella premeditated the murder of her lover, Domenico Cataldo. On the basis of the irrefutable evidence in our possession, we have concluded that, before the murder, Maria Barbella was perfectly conscious of the gravity of the crime. It is our intent to produce evidence which will fully confirm the charge of murder in the first degree brought against Miss Barbella."

Maria understood only the word "murder." The expression "first degree" had no meaning for her.

Deputy Assistant District Attorney Lauterbach stood up and spoke: "Agent Hay, first to arrive on the scene of the crime, was informed of the upheaval on East Thirteenth Street. He followed the track of blood which went from the bar at number 428 East Thirteenth Street to number 211 Second Avenue where he found Domenico Cataldo's body." His voice was not as solemn as McIntyre's, and his nervous tic made his nose wrinkle.

"Agent John O'Rourke of the East Fifth Street police station took Maria Barbella's confession: she admitted having entered the bar while Domenico Cataldo was playing cards. Then, after having grasped the man by the hair and pulled his head back, she had cut his throat. Then she had run away. Domenico ran after her, but almost immediately he had fallen to the ground dead. The woman confessed that she had been relieved when she saw him fall because she was afraid of him."

While Lauterbach spoke, Mrs. Foster sat thoughtfully, evaluating the discrepancies which Evans seemed to disregard.

Police Officer James H. Hay was called to the witness stand. "I confirm what has been related by attorney Lauterbach," he stated. "I found Domenico Cataldo with his throat cut. I immediately sought medical help and called an ambulance."

Officer O'Reilly's deposition coincided with Hay's. "I went immediately to Miss Barbella's apartment where, hidden behind a stool, I found a bloody cotton dress," he added.

No reaction on Evans's part.

Then it was East Fifth Street police station agent John O'Rourke's turn. This thickset Irishman had learned Italian while stationed at Mulberry Bend. "Maria Barbella's confession was made in Italian in the presence of Captain Wiegand and an Italian reporter," he stated.

Finally the defense intervened.

"I ask the court that Agent O'Rourke repeat in Italian the defendant's exact words," Sedgwick requested. The judge motioned his agreement. O'Rourke repeated Maria's confession, pausing after each sentence to translate it into English for the jury's benefit.

"Miss Barbella told me she went to live with Domenico Cataldo at number 424 East Thirteenth Street when he promised to marry her. He showed her his savings book which had a deposit of four hundred dollars. However, the man did not keep his promise and continually put it off: so she cut his throat."

"Objection!" Evans shouted. "The officer cannot translate himself. We have an interpreter here." And he pointed to Benedetto Morossi, the Italian assistant Maria had met at the Tombs.

"Objection dismissed," answered Goff. "The witness has the court's permission to translate his own words."

A hum came from the crowd.

"The murderess had often argued with the victim before the crime was committed," O'Rourke continued. "The mother would sometimes intervene in these arguments. He continued to refuse to marry her. She had lost her reputation."

"Just a moment! Is the stenographer writing everything down?" Sedgwick shouted. Beard, the stenographer, looked at the lawyer and nodded: he had studied Italian in preparation for the trial. Sedgwick appeared surprised and adjusted his glasses, seemingly embarrassed.

Then O'Rourke opened a large brown envelope he had brought to the stand. He pulled a razor out of it and approached the judge. "Your Honor, here is the razor used by Miss Barbella," he said handing it to the judge. "Do you see the nick?"

Several people stood on tiptoe trying to catch a glimpse of the blade glimmering in the judge's hand. Goff examined it and then returned it to the agent.

"The nick must have been caused when the murderess threw the razor to the ground." With these words O'Rourke concluded his testimony.

Evans did not say a word.

The court then called Deputy Coroner John Huber to the stand.

"On Domenico Cataldo's throat I found a wound caused by a knife about six inches long. The wound began on the left, approximately halfway between the chin and the lower mandible, and ended at the bone immediately beneath the right ear. All the neck tissues through to the spinal column had been lacerated, exposing the vertebrae themselves. The man lost all his blood within a few instants," declared the doctor all in one breath.

"Death occurred due to the loss of blood then?" asked the judge.

"The cause of death was the cutting of the arteries that reach the heart."

The next witness was Bernardino Ciambelli, the editor of *Il Progresso Italo-Americano,* who had been present at Maria's first interrogation. "I remember a rather unusual statement Miss Barbella made during the course of her first confession to the police. It seems that one day, after Domenico had given her something to drink, she lost consciousness. Then the man must have . . . taken advantage of her."

The courtroom exploded. Mrs. Foster looked straight in Amos Evans's direction, without being able to capture his attention.

"Silence!" Goff shouted, grasping the gavel with his bony fingers and rapping vigorously. The noise died down.

"I saw Maria at the door of the bar," stated Michael Snyder, a thirteen-year-old witness. "Her hand was all covered in blood and her dress, too, was stained with blood."

Leopoldo Porzio, a Barbella family friend and the grocer next to the Tavolacci Bar on East Thirteenth Street, smiled at Maria while going to take his place in the witness stand. "Me finish wuosh window . . . Maria wuosh hands . . . me no foget, many people, many confusion . . . ," he managed to say before his nervousness prevented him from continuing. He was the last witness to be called by the prosecution before the court adjourned for an hour.

All the jurors left. Judge Goff had a lunch date with an old friend of his, the diplomat Joseph H. Choate, in the nearby Astor House. McIntyre and Lauterbach left together. The crowd moved toward the exit. Mrs. Foster and Maria were the last to stand up. The girl was upset: two and a half months had passed since she had last seen her friend Leopoldo. Only close relatives were admitted to the Tombs.

During the pause, Evans and Sedgwick hurriedly improvised a line of defense for their client: Domenico Cataldo made a practice of seducing women with false promises of marriage. Maria had been one of his victims.

The hour passed quickly. The ceiling fans continued to hum, but the oppressive heat was increasing: Mrs. Foster unbuttoned her gloves, pulled a silk fan out of her handbag and began to wave it. Maria, seated beside her, was able to share the draft. The fan swayed consolingly in the hand of her friend, blurring its pattern of pink roses.

When the trial resumed, Mrs. Foster tried to explain to Maria that her defense was about to begin. Henry Sedgwick, in a clear, loud voice, gave the opening statement:

"Your Honor, Maria Barbella's crime was provoked by Domenico Cataldo's depraved lasciviousness. It is a well-known fact that Italian women hold chastity in the highest consideration, almost more than their very lives. It is extremely rare to meet in the streets of New York an Italian woman whose moral behavior is not absolutely irreproachable. Domenico Cataldo tricked the young Maria Barbella. He was a gambler, a libertine of the worst kind. . . ." He spoke with a persuasive indignation, but he was interrupted by Goff's peremptory tone:

"We ask that attorney Sedgwick confine himself to the facts of the case."

"On the morning of the murder, Filomena Barbella followed her daughter into the bar. As she had already done many times previously, she begged Domenico Cataldo to maintain his promise of marriage. He refused, saying that Maria did not have an appropriate dress. The girl answered that she did not care and that she was ready to marry him immediately, in the dress that she was wearing. But he continued to play cards. Suddenly he stated that for a sum of two hundred dollars he might be persuaded to marry her. At those words, Mrs. Barbella protested: 'But Domenico, you know how poor we are. We don't have that kind of money!' At which he laughed cruelly and pronounced his famous last words: 'Only pigs marry!' That was when, driven by her desperation, in a moment of blind rage, Maria Barbella inflicted the fatal blow, killing the man she loved."

These statements caused a furor among the public; taking advantage of the moment's tension, Evans stood up and began to speak emphatically:

"Your Honor, the prosecution has not demonstrated the premeditation and deliberation on the part of the accused for the crime of which she is indicted. I therefore ask this honorable court to remove the charge of first-degree murder from the indictment and to try Maria Barbella for second-degree murder."

Silence fell in the courtroom. Mrs. Foster's heart almost stopped. Maria stared at the pleats of her skirt.

"Request denied!" The judge's voice rang out. Evans seemed to deflate on his chair. Sedgwick and Mrs. Foster exchanged a worried look. Maria did not have the faintest idea what had just happened.

It was at that point that the defense called Maria. Mrs. Foster motioned to her to stand up.

"My dear, it's your turn now. You must do nothing but tell the truth and everything will go well," she murmured to her. Guided by the Tombs Angel, the girl moved hesitantly towards the witness stand.

"I met Domenico at the corner between Canal and Elm Street." Maria spoke in Italian in a trembling voice. "I walked by him every day on my way to work and he always looked at me." Here she paused to let Morossi, whose English was barely understandable, translate.

"One evening he spoke to me and I answered him." Again she had to pause for the translation.

"He told me he wanted to meet my parents and ask their consent to marry me. I answered him that, yes, he could come to our house. . . ."

Morossi translated.

"He often came to pick me up at work and walked me home, but he always refused to come upstairs." Maria's voice was soft. "This went on for many weeks, until I understood that he did not intend to introduce himself to my parents. So I began to go to work by another route."

Morossi translated.

"One day he came to work and begged me to go by the same street as I used to. 'I want to see you every day,' he said. But I didn't pay any attention to him. Then he came again to wait for me at work, and that time he promised that he would come to our house because he wanted to marry me."

Maria again had to stop and wait for Morossi.

"I believed him. . . . One day he invited me to meet a woman from his village. At first I refused, but he insisted, so I followed him to a house on Baxter Street. . . ." This time Morossi's voice overlapped slightly with Maria's.

"But it was a man who opened the door, not a woman. I did not go in. I ran home. Then I left my job and stayed home to work with my father, as I used to do in Ferrandina. One day, from the window, I saw Domenico. At that time, our rooms faced the street. I left the house secretly, hoping he would return upstairs with me. Instead he told me he wanted to marry me without my parents' consent. It was none of their business, but ours only, he said. It seemed absurd to me and I left him there, on the street. Finally my father ordered me never to see him again."

Maria appeared calm and not at all confused by all the interruptions for the translation. Mrs. Foster, on the other hand, was more and more irritated by Morossi's bad English and his tedious tone of voice.

"I did not see him for many months."

"How many?" asked Evans. "Oh . . . I don't remember. . . ." Maria was uncertain.

"Continue," the lawyer urged her on.

"One day he came again to pick me up at my job on Broadway. Again he asked me to marry him. A long time had gone by and he had not forgotten me. One afternoon I went for a walk with him . . ."

"Which afternoon? Do you remember the date?" Evans intervened.

"It was on a Thursday. . . ."

"What day of the month?"

"March 28," Maria answered, without hesitation this time. "We walked around until evening, and then we stopped in a bar on Chrystie Street, where he offered me a drink. . . ."

Evans stepped forward. "What kind of drink?"

"A soda . . ." Maria answered, "then it got all dark and he was pushing me up some stairs and laughing. . . ."

She could not continue and hid her face in her hands. Two of the jurors were visibly moved. The crowd became so restless that Goff suddenly announced a twenty minute recess.

"Don't stop now. . . ." Mrs. Foster whispered in her ear during the break. "You're doing well. Don't be afraid. . . ."

Maria made an effort to regain her self-control. Goff reentered and she was able to continue her story.

"I remember a lamp, a woman. She took us into a room . . . I heard the sound of a key turning and locking a door. . . . It was dark and I couldn't breathe, then I don't know. . . ."

Morossi translated.

"I lost some blood. I know because when I woke up he showed me a handkerchief. 'It's true, you're a good girl,' he told me. 'You will be my wife.' Then he . . . held me down again. We stayed in that room for a long time."

"For how long?" asked Evans.

"I don't know. . . . He went out and came back with another soda, but I didn't want to drink anymore."

After Morossi had translated, the attorney waited for Maria to continue, but the girl remained silent.

"And then, what happened?" he urged her.

Maria turned on the lawyer an absent gaze: it was as if she had fallen into a trance. Her silence and the heat were trying

Goff's patience. "Is that all?" the judge asked coldly. The question woke her up.

"I screamed," she continued. "Then someone knocked on the door. A woman wanted to know what was happening."

Morossi's monotonous voice interrupted her again.

" 'Leave us alone,' Domenico shouted at her. Then he took me by the shoulders and said: 'Let's go.' I did not want to. 'I'm not leaving here unless it's to get married,' I answered him. 'I can't go home like this.' There, that's just what I told him."

The story had reached its climax, but the jury was not paying attention because of Morossi's labored translation.

" 'Before I marry you, I want to find a house for the two of us,' he told me. Then the woman came back and she asked us to go away. While we were leaving, I heard him whisper: 'We'll be back on Sunday.' Then I screamed: 'No! No! I'm calling the police.' I was terrified. 'No, don't do it, don't do it,' shouted the woman, holding me back."

Mrs. Foster handed Maria a glass of water. She drank while Morossi translated.

"We left. He took me home. I begged him to come upstairs, but he refused. When I arrived upstairs my mother asked me why I was late and what was wrong. I told her I felt ill."

"Why did you hide these events from your parents?" Goff asked her.

Morossi repeated the question.

"Because I was ashamed . . . Domenico might still have come to my parents' . . ."

Morossi's voice was a flat drone. The jury was visibly impatient and the judge interrupted him with a blow of the gavel.

"The court is adjourned until tomorrow."

Everyone stood up to leave. Maria was disoriented: she had not finished her story.

"Tomorrow," Mrs. Foster reassured her, taking her by the arm and leading her back into the Tombs over the Bridge of Sighs.

That night, on the way home, the Tombs Angel bought the evening edition of several dailies. The *Brooklyn Daily Eagle* contained a brief piece titled: MARIA BARBERI ON TRIAL. *Tried for the murder of her unfaithful lover.* "Barberi" instead of "Barbella": A peculiar error, mused Mrs. Foster, familiar with the allusive power of a literary device. The word "Barberi" evoked the razor and had connotations of savagery. The report intermingled accuracy and fantasy.

> . . . Policeman Hay of the East 22nd Street Station testified that he saw Domenico Cataldo with his throat cut, lying on the sidewalk in front of the grocery at 211 Second Avenue. Policeman O'Reilly sent for an ambulance. Hay followed the trail of blood which led up to a saloon at 428 East 13th Street, where he found the door locked. In front of a store next door, he found the young woman who had committed the crime. Policeman O'Rourke of the First Avenue police station took her confession. . . . Maria Barberi said that Cataldo had $400 in the bank and she added to this $400 of her own. He had asked to marry her and she agreed on the condition he would give her all his money. . . .

There were many discrepancies. In the courtroom, Agent Hay had not stated that the door to the bar was locked nor that O'Reilly had been the one who called the ambulance. Domenico had been found on the corner of Avenue A and not of Second Avenue. Agent O'Rourke was not stationed at the First Avenue precinct but rather at East Fifth Street. As for

Maria's economic motives in agreeing to marry Domenico, these were outright inventions.

The *New York Herald* was even more sensational. The article was titled: MARIA BARBERI TAKES THE WITNESS STAND. The headline type continued: *Her face and figure present an interesting case for the expert criminologist.* WHY DID SHE KILL CATALDO? *The prosecution charges premeditated murder. Her lawyer pleads the exasperation of insulted womanhood.* "PIGS MARRY" HE HAD TOLD HER. There were drawings portraying Mrs. Foster and Maria sitting in court, also a decidedly unflattering illustration of Mrs. Barbella. Describing Maria's appearance, the newspaper said:

> . . . If Professor Cesare Lombroso were in this city he would point to Maria as a confirmation of many of his conclusions concerning female offenders. Her countenance shows the predominance of the animal nature. Her jaws are heavy, the forehead is low and the ears stand out prominently. The right side of the face is larger than the left. Indeed, the asymmetry is so marked that the face looks as if it had been violently twisted toward the right . . .

Mrs. Foster was outraged. Maria was a pleasant-looking woman. She was not a great beauty, but her eyes and voice were quite charming. The *Sun* published a fairly accurate report:

> . . . The case is one of the most extraordinary ever held in the criminal courts of this country, and while it lacks the dramatic features which characterized the trial of Chiara Cignarale and other women tried for murder in the first degree, it is nevertheless interesting for the fact that the defense rests solely upon the sympathetic temperament of the jury as against the law. . . .

Assistant District Attorney McIntyre said it was one of the
hardest cases he has ever tried.

The *World,* soon to be Maria's enemy, at the outset was one of
her supporters. Its headline was: MARIA'S CONFESSION
DEFORMED. *Maria's sobbing tale of murder shouted in bad
English by an interpreter.*

"What a pity she doesn't speak English!" The remark was made
by a well known lawyer who happened in at the trial. . . . It was
a tale of confession, not of defense, and nobody who listened as
it was whispered by the girl to the phlegmatic interpreter, and
by him voiced in stentorian, execrable English to the jury, could
fail to perceive how different it would have sounded had the girl
been able to tell it to them herself. The jury looked bored.

All the newspapers concluded that the trial would probably
end on the following day, but Mrs. Foster suspected it would
continue a bit longer.

On Friday, July 12, many new faces were present in the courtroom. Maria's parents sat in the first row: her mother, who
seemed dazed, did not match the exotic description which had
appeared in that morning's edition of the *Herald:*

Her head is bare and hoops of gold glitter in her ears. This,
together with the thick black hair, dark complexion and great
black shawl wound around her shoulders, gives her the appearance of an Indian.

Maria resumed her story at the point where she had left off, in
a soft voice and with the same pauses for Morossi. Three feet
away she could barely be heard.

"The day after Chrystie Street, Domenico told me not to worry; he had found us a place to live and we would be married soon. 'Marry me today,' I urged him. 'Come and speak to my parents.' 'We don't need them,' he said over and over. 'We'll go to city hall, just you and me . . . Now go to work and in three days we'll get married, three days, I promise you.' "

Maria couldn't take her eyes off her parents.

"I saw him again on that Sunday. He told me the apartment was almost ready. 'Marry me first,' I proposed again, 'and then I'll come with you.' He answered: 'All right, don't worry.' That Monday he told me the apartment was ready. 'Come with me, let's go get married. But first I want to show you the apartment.' So I went. The two rooms were empty. Not a chair, nothing. He ordered me to wait while he went to fetch the furniture. I didn't want to. 'No! First marriage, then the furniture. I am more important than furniture.' He promised me that he was only going away for a few minutes and he added that I shouldn't worry, that afterwards we were going to city hall. I insisted. Then he got angry and threw me onto the ground. After that first time, he had not touched me again. He held me down and did it again with me . . . Then he left me there, alone."

A faraway rumble of thunder was heard. Morossi translated, Maria continued: "He came back with a man who helped him bring up a table, two chairs, a closet, a chest, and a mattress. From that moment on we lived together. I could not go back home to my family. Every day, I begged him to marry me. He always put it off. On April 20 he told me that he was never going to marry me. 'I'll find you a young man willing to marry you,' he told me. 'I'll tell him you're a widow. I'll buy you a black dress. You'll marry him because I want you to. Then, I'll come to visit you while he's at work.' That's what he told me."

Now, despite Morossi, the jury seemed interested. Maria sat perfectly still: fragile but determined. Her lawyers did not dare interrupt her.

"Two days later, he asked me to meet three young women he knew. Every now and then one of them was to come to the house with a man and I was to let them in and then leave them alone, and they would pay me fifty cents. 'I can't do that,' I cried, 'I beg you, marry me . . . that way I can go back home and continue to earn my living with my work, I don't want anything else!' "

Her voice faded. Morossi came closer to Maria, to hear what she was saying. It had begun to rain very hard and the windows had to be shut. Maria then began the story of what happened on the morning of April 26.

"I ran to the bar and I saw him . . . he was playing cards . . . he was going to leave by the first ship . . . I ran back toward home, but then I changed my mind and went back to the bar. I thought. . . ." She stopped.

"What did you think?" Evans asked her.

"I don't remember. . . ."

At this point Sedgwick approached her. "Do you remember whether Domenico Cataldo told you anything?"

"No. . . ."

Evans intervened: "Just one moment; ask her what Domenico Cataldo's last words were."

Morossi translated.

"I don't remember."

"Try to make an effort," Sedgwick insisted. "Did Domenico say something to you?"

"He said I was only good for pigs," she answered at last, lowering her head. The crowd murmured. The girl lifted her head slightly and again met her parents' eyes.

"This concludes the defendant's testimony," announced Evans.

Now it was the prosecution's turn. McIntyre stood up and addressed Maria. "Why did you continue to see Domenico Cataldo even though you had realized he was a good-for-nothing?" he asked, looking into her eyes.

When Morossi translated, suddenly Maria became very agitated.

"Because he wouldn't leave me alone . . . I loved him. . . ." she answered.

Maria could no longer think clearly and her testimony became confused.

"When we went to Baxter Street, an Italian woman came to open the door. She and Domenico whispered something. I did not want to go in and I ran away."

"But yesterday you swore that the reason you left that house was because you had seen a man, and not a woman as Cataldo had told you. Why did you say this?"

"I don't remember, I ran away."

"How did you meet Domenico?"

"On the street."

"When did he propose to you?"

"The second time we spoke."

"And you didn't think it odd?"

"No. He said he had some savings and that he was ready to start a family."

"The Baxter Street incident happened before or after you went to the bar on Chrystie Street?"

"I don't remember . . . I don't know."

"Yesterday, you stated that it happened before. . . ."

"I don't know. . . ."

McIntyre glanced at his notes and then asked Maria to repeat the story of what happened in the Chrystie Street bar.

"He offered me a soda and put a reddish liquid in the glass. 'Drink, drink,' he said, 'You'll like it, it's good. . . .' I drank . . .

it was dark. When I woke up, he told me he loved me. He showed me his bankbook and told me he would find an apartment and marry me."

McIntyre let Maria continue rambling.

"The first night in the apartment I didn't want to take my clothes off, but he forced me down onto the mattress. 'I promise you, tomorrow I'll take you to city hall,' he told me. The second night, he did it again . . . I was afraid and I was crying. Then, he made me do it every night, sometimes more than once. He offered me money, first two hundred, then three hundred dollars. I didn't want his money. I wanted to marry him. Then I was the one who offered him money: 'If you marry me,' I told him, 'I'll give you all my savings. Then, if you don't want to live with me, I'll go back to my family. . . .' "

The prosecution attorneys consulted each other. McIntyre continued: "Now, let's go back to the morning of April 26. When you pulled the razor out what was Domenico doing?"

"I don't remember. . . ."

"Didn't you tell us he was playing cards?"

"Yes, sir."

"Did you cry after you killed him?"

No answer.

"Did you cry?" McIntyre repeated.

"I don't know. . . ."

"Did you faint?"

"I fell to the ground. . . ."

McIntyre turned to Morossi. "Sir," he said, "Miss Barbella states she does not remember whether she cried, but instead she remembers that she fell to the ground. Please, ask her why then she cannot recollect whether or not she cried. . . ."

Morossi obeyed.

"Someone told me I fell to the ground, and I don't remember having cried," Maria answered.

"Well, do you remember whether you cried afterwards?"

"No, I don't remember, I don't think I did. . . ."

"When you arrived at the police station you saw Agent O'Rourke, the policeman who speaks Italian?"

"I don't remember. . . ."

"Did you see Mr. Ciambelli from the Italian newspaper?"

"I don't know. . . ."

"Did you see him here, yesterday, on the witness stand?"

"Yes, yes . . . there was an Italian, but I don't remember his face."

"Did that man say something to you?"

"I don't know what he told me."

"Did Agent O'Rourke speak to you?"

"I don't remember."

"At that moment, were you crying?"

"I don't know."

"So then, on April 20 Domenico Cataldo told you that he would never marry you. Why didn't you kill him then?"

"Because I never thought of doing it. Never!"

"In your deposition, you stated that you saw Domenico lying on the bed and that you wished he were dead."

"No, I didn't say that."

"You said so at the police station."

"I don't remember. . . ."

"Where did you find the razor?"

The heat was stifling, but Maria was trembling.

Mrs. Foster had closed her fan. The rain had stopped.

"I took it from the chest. I knew where it was because I saw him put it there. The chest was always open and the razor was to the right."

"When did you take it?"

"When he went out. . . . He was going to leave for Italy."

That was when Deputy Assistant District Attorney Lauterbach jumped to his feet. Brandishing the razor, he approached Maria with long menacing strides. Someone in the public protested and the judge struck his gavel.

"Do you recognize it?"

Maria averted her eyes. Lauterbach turned to Morossi and unexpectedly grasped him by the hair, bringing his left hand to the interpreter's throat. Morossi stiffened in surprise. Mrs. Foster looked at Maria's lawyers who watched the scene without intervening.

"Is this how you cut Domenico Cataldo's throat? Is this how?" the lawyer persisted.

Maria burst into tears. "I don't remember. . . ."

"How did you strike him?"

She was shaking with sobs and struggled to breathe.

"Did you pull the razor out in the bar or outside, on the street?"

"I had it in my pocket. . . . He was sitting at the table."

"Why did you cut his throat?"

"I didn't want to do it. . . ." Maria collapsed.

Finally the defense shouted: "Objection!"

Judge Goff told the prosecution to proceed.

"We must not forget," Lauterbach proclaimed emphatically, "that this young woman has killed a man. I have never seen a case in which a defendant has been better treated. This is a court of law; we cannot let ourselves be dominated by sentiment or compassion. Miss Barbella has agreed to testify and she must be treated just like any other witness. The questions are pertinent."

Seated next to the *New York Times* reporter was a doctor by the name of Theodore Scheale.

"I wouldn't be surprised if she had a fit," he remarked. "Has anybody looked into her medical history?"

"I don't think so, and I doubt she understands the implications of what is happening here," answered the reporter, taking notes.

Maria's appearance had changed. Her dark eyes, now swelling, stood out in her stiffened and bloodless face.

"I didn't want to kill him. . . . Often he used to beat me. . . . He wanted me dead," she whispered.

But Morossi did not hear these words. Mrs. Foster tried in vain to catch his eye. In any case, the jury was not really paying attention. Maria's despair increased suddenly. Sensing that something was wrong, Mrs. Foster got up from her chair and moved next to Maria just in time for the girl to collapse hysterically in her arms. It all happened quickly.

"Mrs. Foster, I must ask you kindly to leave the room," Judge Goff ordered. But she did not move.

"Mrs. Foster, I ask you to leave," repeated the judge, so that she had to comply. Some minutes went by, but Maria could not calm herself. Then Goff called a recess. He allowed Mrs. Foster to reenter and to lead the defendant out of the courtroom.

Ten minutes later, the two women returned. Maria was calmer and the interrogation continued, stern and implacable.

"Why did you kill Domenico Cataldo?"

Maria forced herself to look at Lauterbach.

"I did not want to kill him," she repeated.

"What was the reason you cut his throat?" the lawyer insisted.

"I don't know . . . I wanted to marry him, then I don't know what happened. I don't remember."

Lauterbach repeated the question seven times and seven times received the same answer: Maria did not know, could not remember, did not want to kill him, did not know, could not remember, wanted to marry him. So her testimony came to an end.

Goff called a lunch recess. One by one, the jurors retired.

The trial resumed an hour later. The defense called Maria's employer, Mary Tilley, who lived at 18 Howard Street. She testified that she saw Domenico Cataldo following the girl on the street and grasping her by the arm.

"Maria is honest and works hard," she added. "I certainly have no complaints about her."

Pauline Deleva, an old Italian woman who had been Domenico's neighbor, took the stand next.

"Mrs. Deleva," said Evans, "did Domenico Cataldo ever mention Miss Barbella to you? Why is it that you have always known he had no intention of marrying her?"

The woman was about to answer when Goff shouted: "The question is not admissible! This line of questioning is improper because it strengthens the prosecution's case."

"If Your Honor will allow it, we are ready to take that risk," Evans replied.

McIntyre intervened "Objection, Your Honor. As district attorney I am an official of the Court and it is my duty to preserve the rights of the defendant. Attorney Evans is attempting to prove that the crime was premeditated and this is prejudicial to Miss Barbella's case."

Mrs. Foster, who was a veteran of the trial courts, could not understand how such testimony could possibly harm Maria. If anything it would have thrown some light onto Domenico's character.

"Objection sustained," said the judge, and called Evans to the bench. The witness was told she could leave.

"Counsel, is it possible to know your line of defense? You have not enlightened us on this point," Goff said firmly.

"Let us suppose that my defense is based on the fact that Maria Barbella, at the moment she committed the crime, was not of sound mind," the attorney answered sarcastically.

"Therefore the defense is one of temporary insanity? Do you intend to prove it?"

"That is not what I said. Your Honor, is it necessary that this statement be made right now?"

"No. Given the particular circumstances, I want to give you every possible latitude. At the same time, I must advise you that I will have to deliberate on those questions the prosecution will object to without knowing your line of defense. . . . And this may be counterproductive for you."

"Your Honor, the only statement we wish to put forward is that of 'not guilty.' "

"In that case," Goff repeated, "I want it to be clear that the court will have to deliberate on the questions without the benefit that usually results from our knowledge of the defense's thesis."

"We understand," Evans said with finality.

Vincenzo Manguso, owner of the Thirteenth Street bar in which Domenico was killed, was the next witness.

"The night before he died," the man said in Italian, "Domenico Cataldo told me that he had four or five girls better than Maria and that he wasn't going to marry a single one of them. He also said that he had a wife and children in Italy and that he was going home."

Maria's eyes opened wide and Mrs. Foster felt the girl's hand seeking hers out. Morossi translated. The district attorney objected: the testimony was irrelevant and unreliable. Goff agreed, and the statement was struck from the record.

Angelo Piscopo, who lived on the same floor as Domenico and Maria, testified that he had often heard the couple arguing.

"The fights were violent and I often heard the woman begging him to marry her."

Then it was the turn of John H. Gerdes, owner of the bar on
Chrystie Street. He had seen the couple in his establishment,
but did not remember the exact day nor what they had had to
drink. Once more, following the prosecution's objections, Goff
dismissed the witness before he could finish testifying.

Mrs. Foster was increasingly uneasy. Goff was stonewalling
any testimony about Domenico's character. Now, it was her
hand that sought out Maria's.

The next witness was Filomena Barbella. Maria watched her
mother's faded figure settling itself on the witness stand with
Morossi's help. Despite the heat, her head was covered with a
shawl.

"What is your name?" asked Sedgwick.

"Buonsanto Filomena in Barbella," she replied, using her
maiden name first, as was customary in Italy. Her voice was calm.

"What is your relationship to the accused?"

"I am her mother," she answered readily.

"When did you see Domenico Cataldo for the first time?"

"On East Thirteenth Street. . . . Maria was always at home,
until she met him. One day she didn't come back. . . . We
looked all over for her, her father and I. Finally, someone told
us where she was. . . ."

"And what did you do?"

"We went there, her father and I, but only once together.
Her father never returned to that house. He couldn't accept it.
I often went to see my daughter. I was hoping to convince that
man to marry her. 'My son, why don't you marry my daughter,
since you've taken her away from us and dishonored her?' But
he always said: 'I won't marry her. She's poor, what would my
relatives say if I married such a poor girl?' One day he offered
her money. 'Take all you want, but leave me alone,' he told her.
'Honor can't be bought,' I told him. 'You'd better marry her,
otherwise I can't take her back home. Her father doesn't want

her. How can you be so deaf to your own people's customs? Do it for the love of the Virgin Mary Mother of God! Marry her, or she will never be able to hold her head up again!' "

Morossi couldn't keep up with her regional dialect and skipped more than one sentence. Sedgwick then asked her to describe the morning of the murder.

Mrs. Barbella, gesticulating, explained that she had gone to Maria's rooms and found the couple arguing furiously. When she asked what the problem was, Domenico turned on her in a rage. " 'Get out of here!' he yelled at me. 'I don't want to marry her, understand?' Then he ran out. Maria went after him, and I followed her to the bar. 'Don't come pestering me here too,' Domenico shouted when he saw me. 'My son, I am here only to implore you to marry her,' I told him, but he didn't even look up from the cards."

"Was he drinking?"

"A beer. . . ." Filomena did not need any prodding to continue her story. "I kept repeating: 'My son. How much I've cried over what you are doing to my daughter.' Maria was there, behind Domenico, and she had her back to me. She did not turn around. 'You must marry me today,' she told him. 'Leave me alone,' he said. Then he turned to me, laughing, and asked me for two hundred dollars. 'Oh my son, if I had them I would give them to you,' I answered him. 'What do you need all that money for?' "

The jurors were visibly bored by the torrent of unintelligible words. Filomena did not know when to pause for Morossi's translation and more than once he had to take hold of her arm to interrupt her. Then she would apologize and stare into space, fighting to control herself.

"He said Maria did not have the right dress," she continued. " 'If you think thirty dollars are enough, I am willing to go to all my people and raise the money,' I answered him. 'Oh my

son, what are all these excuses, what are you trying to do?' He
was silent. 'I don't want a new dress. You will marry me as I am,
yes or no?' That was Maria speaking. And that was when he
shouted something about pigs. . . . At that moment Mrs. Manguso pulled me aside and I turned to her. 'Filomena, go away,'
she whispered. 'Otherwise this fight will not end. . . .' "

Morossi interrupted her again.

"That was when I heard an uproar. I turned around and saw
both of them going towards the door . . . then they fell,
Domenico was on top of her, but then he got up and ran away.
I can't tell you what I felt. I went outside. I saw blood on the
street and I began to scream: 'He killed her! He killed her!' But
then suddenly I saw Maria in the doorway." Filomena began to
cry, her sobs mingling with Morossi's voice.

"Mrs. Barbella, do you remember having told your daughter: 'Don't kill him in the presence of your mother'?"

"I never said that!" the woman exclaimed with the little
strength remaining to her.

"Did you see the razor in your daughter's hand?"

"I didn't know she had it. . . . I didn't know. . . . I didn't see
anything." The last words of her testimony were drowned out
by a violent fit of tears.

A voice announced: "The court is adjourned until Monday."

During the weekend, Mrs. Foster was upset by an article which
appeared in the World. The headline read: "HER FATE IS
UNCERTAIN." There was a drawing of Maria on the witness
stand, next to Morossi and Mrs. Foster herself.

> . . . Her lawyers drew from her lips the narrative of a poor girl's
> wrongs at the hands of a libertine, up to the moment before she
> killed him. . . .

Artist's sketch of Maria Barbella, The World, *July 11, 1895.*

. . . "It matters not," said Judge Goff, "whether Cataldo was a saint or a devil. The only question before the jury is, did this defendant kill him and kill him with premeditation?"

Mrs. Foster thought the phrase "it matters not" was a bad sign. She was not a judge or a lawyer, but she had made a sort of career within the criminal justice system; she was the guardian of those whose lives "mattered not."

She well knew by now how things went: from a crime, a complex and multifaceted event, some judges and lawyers extracted the part that interested them—the legal formula, the sound precedent. The cruelty of domestic abuse, poverty, and ignorance did not count at all.

An article appearing in *Metropolitan Magazine* described Mrs. Foster as "engaged with gentle compassion in her daily good deeds. . . . An example of blameless charity." "Gentle compassion" was not the phrase she would have used to describe herself, no more than the pseudonym "Tombs Angel." Her sincere desire to remain anonymous had failed, allowing the journalists to cast her as a tabloid saint.

Mrs. Foster might have preferred an institutional role to this saintly reputation. Her activity was not simply limited to sympathy, but a genuine attempt at rehabilitation. She had defended dozens of women, providing them with medical care, vouching for them upon their release. And, until she found them work, she often supported them with her own money. She was filling an institutional void in assisting immigrants and indigent women, and it is perhaps according to the standards of an aid to the state that she deserved to be judged.

Despite the fact that the newspapers cast her as a saint, Rebecca Foster lacked neither enemies nor peers. There were many women who supported prisoners, both privately and for charitable organizations, and their numbers were such that Judge Goff, resentful of such interferences, had begun an investigation. According to him, these women were fronts for bail guarantors and lawyers intent on cheating defendants with vain promises.

"ANGELS FOR MONEY," ran a sensationalistic headline. "Philanthropists preying on prisoners."

"When you made your accusations against the 'Tombs Angels,'" the interviewer asked Goff, "were you thinking of anyone in particular?"

"No, no one in particular," Goff had answered rather evasively. "I am certain harm is being done, but I cannot yet prove it. If, as commissary of Good Deeds, I had the power to decide who should enter the Tombs, the number of so-called 'Angels,' who now have free access, would be drastically reduced."

Whether or not Goff was right, it was true that these "Angels" often embarrassed judges and attorneys. If, for example, a woman was found guilty of prostitution, it could certainly be pointed out that it was a series of men—from the landlord to the policeman, from the juror to the lawyer to the judge—who had come to the conclusion that she was dissolute, rather than a desperate woman who had been forced to walk the streets. Then an intruder would step in and tell all those men that they were wrong, and that she would vouch for the woman they had convicted. This intruder was often Rebecca Salomé Foster. It was impossible not to take her into account: the Tombs Angel had an undeniable knack for distinguishing the unfortunate from the genuine criminal.

But Maria Barbella's case presented a new challenge to Rebecca Foster. For the first time, a ward of hers faced death by the electric chair. This new method of execution had been recently invented by Dr. Alfred Southwick, a dentist from Buffalo.

Back in her room at the Park Avenue Hotel, Rebecca Foster felt powerless. Up to that point the trial had been flagrantly unfair. Even her appearance next to Maria seemed to her as useless as *Metropolitan Magazine*'s idealized portrait: gloved and hatted, she was pictured in the Tombs' corridor, pausing at a cell door, the image of compassion and futility.

That Sunday, unable to go to the Tombs, she remained at home.

CHAPTER SEVEN

$\mathcal{O}$n Monday, July 15, as Maria reentered the courtroom, Detalmo and Cora were still at sea. A storm lasting two days and two nights had slowed down the *S.S. Nomadic*'s crossing.

At two that afternoon, the defense called Maria Poggi, a woman from Ferrandina who had known Maria since she was a child.

"I swear it on my children, she is a good girl," the woman said anxiously, in Italian. "Can you not see it for yourselves?" she cried, pointing at Maria. All eyes turned to her. Morossi translated, and Lauterbach came forward.

"Objection, Your Honor! The witness must keep to the facts."

"Objection sustained."

The woman took a breath and continued. "Mrs. Deleva, Domenico Cataldo's neighbor, told me he was a good-for-nothing. She had seen him come and go with women. . . . She never knew what he was up to. . . ." Without waiting for the translation, Judge Goff raised a finger and dismissed the witness. He no longer seemed to care whether or not the jury heard the testimonies.

John Klein was called. He was a frequent visitor to the Chrystie Street house to which Domenico had brought Maria that first night. As soon as this fact came to light, the prosecution objected, was sustained, and the witness was told he could leave.

The defense had no more witnesses. Goff asked Maria's lawyers to sum up their case, and Amos Evans stood up. He began by once more pleading with the court to reject the first-degree murder charge.

"The prosecution still has not provided any proof that could induce the jury to return a verdict of guilty against this defendant."

Mrs. Foster was baffled. Of course Maria had killed Domenico Cataldo! Who else? Evans was making a fool of himself.

"The preponderance of the evidence shows that the defendant is not guilty of murder in the first degree," he reiterated. "The depositions the prosecution has provided in support of its thesis are, wholly or in part, illegal. Therefore, there have been no valid depositions. I ask the court to advise the jury to acquit the defendant of the charges of first-degree murder and of voluntary as well as wrongful manslaughter."

Only the presence of several courtroom attendants prevented the crowd from exploding. Goff lost his patience, rapped his gavel repeatedly and, shouting, demanded silence. Order was restored. Evans and Sedgwick exchanged perplexed glances, then looked at the judge who returned their gazes with obvious hostility. Without any explanation, he refused to consider their request.

Evans turned to the twelve jurors:

"I beseech the jury to have mercy on this poor girl," he implored, moving toward Maria and pausing in front of her. "She is the victim of an immoral man, a man who seduced

women with promises of marriage, a man who took advantage
of her innocence. His vile betrayal brought her to desperation.
I remind the jury that he also threatened to kill her. . . . The
only possible verdict for Maria Barbella is that of 'not guilty' in
the name of man's honesty and woman's purity." And that was
all. Mrs. Foster tried to decipher the expressions on the jurors'
faces. Not a single witness had mentioned Domenico's threats
toward Maria. How could these men remember something
which had never been said? How could they be persuaded by
such a feeble speech? Their faces showed only an indifferent
attention; they contained no trace of emotion nor sympathy
for Maria.

Assistant District Attorney McIntyre adjusted his bow tie,
cleared his throat, and began to speak.

"I wish it were possible to demonstrate the murder was not
premeditated. The prosecution feels a profound compassion
for this young woman, but no matter how strong the voice of
my and your sentiments, compassion has nothing to do with
this case. No argument has been advanced in favor of Maria
Barbella's innocence: I am obliged to affirm this out of professional correctness and because of the oath I have taken in
accepting my office. It has not been stated that this woman
acted in self-defense. Her attorneys have not advanced the thesis of momentary insanity and, despite their contention that
Maria Barbella is not guilty, they have refused to prove it. They
certainly cannot deny that she did kill Domenico Cataldo. The
juror who violates his oath commits perjury and removes himself from God." He paused, waiting for the threat to sink in.

"The defense's arguments are unjustifiable. There has not
been a seduction, nor the use of drugs. One can only speak of
seduction if it has taken place through violence, or if the
woman is in an obvious state of confusion. The evidence in our
possession does not prove that this happened. If you acquit

Maria Barbella, you will implicitly grant to every woman in this city who has an illicit relationship with a man the right to cut his throat with impunity. Are you, gentlemen of the jury, willing to encourage a conduct so contrary to the principles of our society? I do not wish to persecute a woman, but if you acquit Maria Barbella you may as well abolish our courts of law and do away with the district attorney's function."

It was Judge Goff's turn. He spoke for three quarters of an hour in the stifling heat, forgetting the haste and impatience he had displayed toward the witnesses. Obstinately, he retraced the story of the crime, lingering over the grisly details of the murder. According to him, all the evidence showed that Maria had acted in a fully conscious manner: indeed, she had even been obliging towards Domenico Cataldo. He berated men's excessive indulgence in judging crimes committed by women and asked the jury to set mercy aside and to simply dispense justice.

"It is your duty to accept the judiciary's laws without objection," he stated. "If this crime has been committed with the premeditated intent to cause the death of Domenico Cataldo, the defendant is guilty of murder in the first degree. The killing did not take place in retaliation against betrayal. When Maria Barbella took the razor from the chest, she had a plan in mind. It is up to you to decide what it was."

Morossi did not translate, so few of the Italians present understood Judge Goff's words. The Barbellas were silent and did not seem aware of what was taking place. Maria stared into space. Mrs. Foster held her fan open on her lap. The judge ended his speech with a stern reminder of the sacredness of their oath. His words echoed in the courtroom:

"Your verdict must be an example of justice. A jury must not concern itself with mercy. The law does not distinguish between the sexes. The fragility of the female sex is sometimes invoked to excuse savage crimes. We cannot publicly proclaim a woman 'not guilty' of killing a man solely because this man has proposed marriage and then changed his mind!"

At 6:10 that evening the jury retired to deliberate.

They reached their verdict on the second ballot, in less than three quarters of an hour, but they had to wait for the judge, who had gone to dine at Astor House.

At seven, Maria was at the bar again, with Mrs. Foster beside her. A newcomer might have taken the tall lady, with her chalk-white face and tense lips, to be the accused and the small young woman her faithful servant.

The jurors filed in one by one. The court clerk took the roll call and each man solemnly answered to his name. Mrs. Foster helped Maria to her feet and held her by the waist. The girl was so frightened she could barely stand.

"Do you judge Maria Barbella guilty or not guilty of murder?" asked the clerk.

"Guilty of murder in the first degree." The jury foreman spoke in a voice so low that Judge Goff had to ask him to repeat the verdict. All eyes were on Maria, but her face did not betray any emotion. Evans asked that the jury be polled. Each juror was asked if that was in fact the verdict. Each one answered: "Yes, it is."

Mrs. Foster tightened her grip on Maria's arm. From the front row came the sound of muffled sobs. For a moment after the verdict was rendered, Maria remained the only person in the courtroom who had not understood its meaning.

"Tell the prisoner," Goff ordered. The jurors averted their eyes from the girl. Morossi leaned against the stand with hesitation and whispered the verdict in Italian, but Maria still did not seem to understand. Then she looked at him with dismay.

Goff's voice resounded in the courtroom: "The sentence will be handed down on Thursday."

On Tuesday, July 16, an article appeared in the *Brooklyn Daily Eagle:*

> . . . The American code has triumphed over the Italian. This is the United States and not Italy, and Italians who come here must learn that the stiletto and the razor as instruments of justice are under ban. . . . In Italy a girl who kills her betrayer does right and no one punishes her.
>
> Miss Barberi is the first woman convicted of murder since the electric chair became the instrument of capital punishment.

The evening papers published contradictory versions of Maria's reaction to the verdict. The *Herald*'s headline was: PLACID MARIA BARBERI. *Wholly Undisturbed by Her Conviction and the Prospect of Death.* The *Brooklyn Daily Eagle,* on the other hand, described a distraught Maria: ". . . The convicted murderess rose at 5 A.M. without having slept at all. When her breakfast was served she could not eat . . . and spent the morning sitting on the edge of the cot weeping."

Mrs. Foster arrived at the Tombs at dawn the morning after the verdict. Maria had spent the night and the next morning completely motionless, curled up on her cot. She had not moved even when a young couple armed with drawing pads appeared. Fallon, the warden, had allowed the Van Rensselaers to visit Maria, a concession which was highly irregular and which Mrs. Foster did not approve of. The two artists maintained that a portrait of the girl would increase the public's sympathy for her, but Mrs. Foster suspected that they were bent on exploiting Maria for their own benefit. In any case, Maria was certainly not an ideal model. She was curled up on herself, her head sunk into her lap, looking more like an abstract shape than a person. The couple's drawings did not progress beyond the sketch of a gray mass.

A visit from her mother and her sister Carmela threw Maria into such a state that Mrs. Foster was forced to send them away. The girl then fell into listlessness once more. She did not touch her lunch. But at four in the afternoon, when an elegantly dressed young lady stooped to pass through the small door of cell number 17, Maria at last raised her head and hesitantly extended her hand to the visitor.

"I was in court, and I am here now because I would like to know you better," the woman said in good Italian.

"You speak Italian!" Maria's eyes brightened.

"My mother is Italian."

"When people talk I get scared because I don't understand what they are saying."

Cynthia Westover, one of the few female journalists in the city, had such a gentle manner that Maria immediately felt at ease.

"I only wanted to hurt him a little . . . I wanted us both to be arrested," Maria said suddenly.

"What? I don't understand."

"I only wanted to wound him so that we would both be arrested," she said again.

"Why did you want the two of you to be arrested?"

"I thought he cared for me. We had made some plans, but then. . . ."

"But why did you want to be arrested? Tell me."

"I begged him to marry me, but he was going back to his village and I thought I would die. I decided to make him marry me." A lump rose in her throat and she fell silent for a moment. "Someone told me that I should go and talk to a judge and that he would make Domenico marry me. But how could I do that? Only by being arrested. And if they arrested him, too, he couldn't leave, could he?" Her confidence rose, and with it her speech came more rapidly. "I saw two policemen nearby. I knew that if Domenico and I had a violent quarrel, they would come running to arrest us, especially if there was some blood. I didn't want to kill him!" She burst into tears. "I only wanted him to bleed a little . . . and then I don't remember anything more. He ran into the street. Now the judge will listen to me . . . and he will make Domenico marry me. I went home and I put on my most beautiful dress . . . and then they arrested me." Maria was almost babbling, only half making sense.

Miss Westover was dumbfounded. "Why didn't you say all this in court? Did you tell your attorney?"

"I don't know . . . I don't know. They told me Domenico was dead . . . I couldn't think. . . ."

The matron came in with two glasses of water.

"Did you tell Mrs. Foster?"

"No one speaks Italian . . . I don't remember."

"But there was an interpreter in court. He's Italian. . . ."

"I only know that if you fight, the police come and they arrest you. . . ."

Maria did not seem to understand how serious her situation was. The journalist was dismayed to see how remote the idea of execution was from the girl's mind.

This is what Cynthia Westover wrote in *The Recorder*'s evening edition:

> . . . There is nothing of the murderess in Maria's physical appearance. Her voice is soft and musical; her hair is a beautiful black and combed into a neat coil on top of her head.

. . . If the story be true that killing was the last thing she con-
templated—and her appearance bears it out—it explains why
it was with a certain calm, now easily understood, that she has-
tened to her room and put on her best dress, for was she not
going before the judge to tell her story? And perhaps the good
man would then and there make Domenico marry her.

This explains why she was under no apparent stress when
arrested. Her only object was to make a fight big enough to
attract the attention of two men whom she thought were policemen not far away. Now they had come and she was content.

The blood on her hands did not frighten her, for she had
planned to draw blood; that, she said, was to ensure her arrest.

She did not know that Domenico was dead; her only fear
had been that they might not be taken before the judge who
was to make things all right.

The Italians all think she is justified.

Lawyer Amos Evans, who defended her, said that she has
never told him the story of her intention to inflict merely a
slight wound on her betrayer, thereby bringing him and herself
to court. In his opinion the killing was done while the woman
was in a frenzy.

Mr. Evans has an unfavorable opinion of Judge Goff's
charge to the jury and said that he drove them to it, like sheep.
He left no other verdict possible. It was the same as a peremptory charge, and those jurymen believed they would be guilty
of perjury if they did not convict her.

Mr. Evans made a startling statement: "I know on absolute
authority that before such a verdict was returned, those jurymen one and all entered into a solemn compact with each
other to recommend Maria Barbella to executive clemency in
case of sentence. This shows beyond doubt that they wanted to
bring in a second degree verdict but were frightened by Goff's
iron-clad charge. . . ."

After the reporter's visit, Maria again withdrew. From the hall-way, the other prisoners heard her crying. Some of them were young and, like Maria, seemed out of place in the prison. A Mrs. LaGrange, charged with arson, spoke Italian. The matron on duty asked if she would help calm Maria, so Mrs. La Grange, along with five other young women, went into cell number 17.

"I was in a different cell yesterday," Maria said as soon as she heard Italian being spoken. "Why did they move me here?"

Mrs. La Grange answered with hesitation: "Because this is cell number 17, the lucky one . . . Didn't you know that?"

At that moment steps were heard, and a small group of mis-sionaries from the Bleecker Street Episcopalian Mission appeared in the doorway: a priest, tall and clean-shaven, and three pretty girls in white dresses and straw hats. They arranged a harmonium in the hallway. One of the young women sat down at the keys, while another handed Maria a piece of apple pie. The music began and a simple evangelical hymn filled the prison.

At the same time, in the blazing glow of the sunset, the steamer S.S. *Nomadic* was making its majestic entry into New York harbor. The ship was three days late and an anxious crowd waited at dock 39.

After Detalmo and Cora had stepped ashore and passed cus-toms, they found out from their cab driver that Maria Bar-bella's trial had ended that very day, and that Maria had been found guilty of murder in the first degree.

CHAPTER EIGHT

$\mathcal{D}$etalmo and Cora were staying at the Savoy, a newly-built hotel on Fifth Avenue and 59th Street. With its Renaissance facade, marble floors, walls and stairways of precious wood, statues and frescoes framed by palms and flowering plants, the Savoy resembled a lavish aristocratic palace. The couple occupied a suite that was an exact reproduction of Marie Antoinette's boudoir in the Trianon at Versailles.

At nine the next morning, Wednesday, July 17, a street carriage stopped in front of the Tombs. Cora descended and quickly walked up the stone steps of the dismal building. She was nervous: she had never entered a prison before. She announced herself to the guards as "Cora Slocomb," omitting her married name and title. A matron led her into the narrow windowless room where she was to be searched. Cora opened her purse and unbuttoned the light beige linen jacket of her redingote outfit.

"Should I take my hat off?" she asked uncertainly.

"Yes," answered the matron.

Cora complied, trying not to spoil her hairdo.

"I imagine you're here to see that poor Italian girl."

"Yes, of course."

"Mrs. Foster is waiting for you upstairs."

Cora followed the matron up a freezing flight of stairs. The prison's climate seemed to be completely removed from the summer season outside. Cora's striking appearance caused a commotion as she walked down the hallway in the women's wing: some of the prisoners even rose from their chairs. Mrs. Foster came out of one of the cells and moved forward to greet her. The two women had not met before, but had already discussed Maria's case on the telephone, and Mrs. Foster had filled Cora in on the trial proceedings.

"My God, she's small!" was Cora's immediate thought when she entered the cell and saw Maria for the first time. The girl, wearing a loose shift, was seated on the edge of her chair, nervously twisting a handkerchief in her hands. Cora noticed that Maria's right shoulder was higher than the left, a consequence of all the hours spent sewing. It made her think of her lacemakers, back in Brazzà, and of how their posture would also alter with time.

Maria straightened and shook the lady's hand. Instead of sitting down, Cora knelt at the girl's feet so that she could look her in the eyes.

"Good morning," she said in Italian. "I was born in America but I live in Italy. I am an immigrant, too, although I crossed the ocean in the opposite direction to yours."

Maria was upset. What did this beautiful lady want from her? She did not know what to say.

"I didn't want to do it, madam . . . I loved him very much . . . only . . ." she whispered.

Cora, surprised by Maria's soft tone, understood immediately that the girl would confide in her if she were encouraged to talk about Domenico.

"Tell me. What did he look like?" she asked accordingly.

"He had wide shoulders and a beautiful mustache. He was intelligent and knew many things. He knew how to read books. . . ."

Cora listened, ill at ease. These were not the words of a repentant murderess, but those of a young widow in mourning.

"He was not lazy and worked hard. . . . He had saved enough money for a barbershop." As she spoke, Maria emphasized her words with brief hand gestures.

Cora watched her, reflecting on how unfair the press had been in describing: a thickset girl, with a jutting chin and a big head. In actuality, Maria was pleasant-looking. Of course, her complexion was very pale, but it had been more than two and a half months since she had breathed any fresh air.

This meeting was decisive for Cora. Maria's case could be summed up with a single, simple question: Did the girl really intend to merely wound Domenico Cataldo? The answer lay in Maria's character, which the lawyers and Judge Goff had deliberately tried not to understand. Cora observed the girl in front of her, listened carefully to her words, and believed that Maria had buried the memory of that terrible murder in some corner of her consciousness, that she had forgotten everything. It was at that moment that mere interest became total commitment. The juridical quibbles, the police reports, and the journalists' arguments—which had divided Cora's mind—gave way to what she now felt that she understood about Maria's psychological state. She did not need any more evidence that Maria was not responsible for her actions on the morning of April 26.

Cora told Mrs. Foster that she was ready to do everything in her power to help the girl. Mrs. Foster assured her of her unconditional support. She was well versed in the ways of lawyers, courtrooms, and legal questions. Cora had persuasive powers and connections in high places. Their alliance was a natural one.

There was no time to lose. They had to obtain a reversal of the court's verdict right away. Maybe, if they acted quickly enough, they might be able to block Goff's call for the death penalty. Sentencing was scheduled for the following day.

Before leaving Maria, Cora gave her the most encouraging words she had heard so far: "You will have the best protection that money can buy. . . ." Then she hurried back to the hotel where Detalmo was waiting for her. They immediately contacted Horace Russell, a prominent retired judge and family friend. The conversation was brief and to the point. Russell arranged for Cora to meet one of his former protégés, the brilliant criminal justice expert Frederick House. House was committed to social causes: if he were to decide to take on Maria Barbella's case, his fee would be flexible.

Since Cora had agreed with Mrs. Foster that she should first speak with Amos Evans, Maria's attorney, they went together to his office at 309 Broadway.

Cora abstained from remarking on Maria's deplorable defense. Fortunately for all concerned, Cora had not yet read of the questionable relationship between Evans and Goff, as revealed in the morning edition of the *Italian Herald*. According to the article, Evans had ardently supported the so-called "Goff Petition," which called for the magistrate's election as chief justice of the New York criminal court, with a salary increase of three thousand dollars a year. It was suspected that Goff had assigned Maria's case to Evans—rather than to a better-known attorney—to return the favor.

Evans did not seem to share Cora's urgency or even her belief that the sentence could be suspended. He advised patience: an attitude the two women found unacceptable.

"Maria should not have been convicted of premeditated murder," he said. "But that is how it went, and I'm sorry. However I believe that if a petition were to be started, many signatures could easily be gathered. . . ."

"I'm afraid I must tell you, Mr. Evans," Cora interrupted him, "that I am not as optimistic. I can assure you there are many people out there who would be delighted to see an Italian immigrant go to the electric chair. Although it is my intent to seek clemency, I am convinced the girl should be retried, taking all the elements into account. Now, if you please, will you be so kind as to explain the steps necessary to file an appeal?"

Evans's arrogance was annoying, and the heat added to Cora's irritation.

"I will proceed in the customary manner," Evans explained. "On Friday I will officially file the documents. It is my duty not to leave anything to chance. All the signs point to an immediate acquittal." Cora and Mrs. Foster looked at each other with disbelief. What signs?

"I have engaged a private attorney for Miss Barbella," Cora announced matter-of-factly. She was certain House would take the case. How could he refuse?

"Who is it?" asked Evans.

"Frederick House. You will meet him tomorrow morning in court," she added confidently. Mrs. Foster was impressed with her assertiveness.

Evans did not seem at all ruffled. "I know his reputation and will do everything possible to cooperate with him."

After a hasty good bye, the two women took a cab to the offices of Friend, House & Grossman. House and his partner Emanuel Friend welcomed them cordially. Cora did not need to introduce Mrs. Foster, because the two men recognized her instantly.

Lengthy explanations were unnecessary; the men had followed the Barbella case with interest, and House admitted that he had been present in the courtroom throughout the trial.

Young and clean-shaven, House dressed informally. His hair was parted on the side. Behind the small, metal-rimmed glasses, his eyes shone with dynamic energy. He seemed to possess both a steady character and a healthy nonconformism. Cora was reassured by this first impression.

"There certainly was something murky . . . don't you agree, Mrs. Foster?" Friend asked, speaking of the trial.

"Yes, undoubtedly," she replied. Friend was short and much older than House, but he had a certain charm.

"I have a question for you, Mr. House," said Cora. "Why do all the newspapers refer to Maria Barbella by the name 'Barberi'? The *New York Times* was the only one to use her correct name at first, and now it, too, is conforming."

"Frankly, I thought her name was Barberi. . . ." said Friend, baffled.

"No, her name is Barbella," Mrs. Foster explained.

"It happens often with immigrants, and of course the press does nothing to help. Mistakes have a strange longevity. Rather than correct them, the majority of men would rather transform them into law. . . ."

"Would you agree to represent Maria Barbella?" Cora interrupted him, impatiently. "Other considerations aside, I am entirely opposed to the death penalty and would like this to be made clear."

House became serious. "On this point, madam, my partner and I both share your opinion."

"I am ready to begin a campaign for justice for Maria Barbella straight away. I have many influential friends, not all of them opposed to the death penalty, but I am determined to help this girl."

House liked the energy emanating from Cora's voice. He answered without hesitation.

"We are delighted to accept. To tell the truth, this case justifies our profession. We will not expect a fee, madam, apart from the trial expenses."

Cora and Mrs. Foster exchanged a satisfied look.

House then pointed out that the State of New York granted only two days between the verdict and the actual sentencing, so there was no time to seek out new evidence to attempt a suspension. It was too late.

"The sentencing is set for tomorrow morning, isn't it?"

The women nodded. House reassured them that both he and Friend would be present in the courtroom the following day. The two women parted. Mrs. Foster, who lived just two blocks away, walked home, and Cora returned to the Tombs.

She found Maria sitting in the hallway. The matron told her that, for the first time since Monday night, the girl had finished her meal. Cora sat next to her, and all the other prisoners stared at them.

"I imagine you know that tomorrow morning you must go back to court," Cora said, going straight to the point.

"Will Mrs. Foster come with me?"

"Of course, and I will be there too. I will sit in the front row, so you will be able to see me. You will have two new lawyers."

"New lawyers?"

"Yes, attorneys Frederick House and Emanuel Friend. They are good people; you must not worry about a thing. I have come to tell you that you must ignore what the judge will say tomorrow."

"I don't understand what the judge says."

"I know, but don't even listen to what the interpreter tells you. It won't be easy, but you must try. I will be there with you, and I am your friend."

"But you are American, aren't you?"

"Yes, but now I am Italian. I left my country eight years ago."

"I left my country three years ago," Maria echoed. "Now I am American. Have you ever been to Ferrandina?"

"Not yet . . ."

"It's near Matera. Domenico was from Chiaromonte. He said he was going back home and that he was not going to take me with him. . . ." Maria looked at her hesitantly. Cora wished her goodnight with a kiss, making a sign of the cross on her forehead.

"I always do that to my daughter before she goes to sleep," she whispered to her before leaving.

That day the *World* published an editorial entitled: "Should Maria Barberi Die?"

. . . There is no doubt of the guilt of Maria Barberi. But there are still some points in the case which were not brought out in the trial. These points, involving the question of the condition of her mind at the time of the crime, were not alluded to in the trial. In other words, the girl does not appear to have been properly defended.

She is poor, helpless, and ignorant of her rights. No brute beast brought to the block for slaughter could be more unconscious of the proceedings than this poor creature has been. Under these circumstances her case was left entirely in the hands of a lawyer appointed by the court. Without wishing to do him an injustice, he seems to have hurt the case more than helped it.

Legally and technically this may be a fair trial. But when a human life is at stake, technicalities which suffice to acquit do not suffice to condemn. . . .

By the time Cora reached her hotel, the *Recorder* was printing its morning edition. The front page headline read: "HOPE FOR MARIA. COUNTESS SAVORGNAN VISITS HER IN PRISON." How the newspaper had found out about Cora's visit was a mystery, as was its use of the name "Savorgnan." Detalmo and Cora rarely used their full last name, "di Brazzà Savorgnan," and they were registered at the Savoy simply as Count and Countess di Brazzà.

. . . A new and powerful friend appeared yesterday morning in the person of Countess Detalmo di Brazzà Savorgnan. Her intimate friends in the city are the Vanderbilts, Iselins, Couderts, and other wealthy families, whose influence, if it were aroused on behalf of the poor girl, would be very potent.

The Countess, who speaks Italian fluently, will try to get a mammoth petition for a pardon started and she will have no trouble in getting it signed by the leading business and professional men in this city. It is almost certain that the great public will join in. Her heart seems to have quite gone out to the poor girl. . . .

CHAPTER NINE

On the morning of Thursday, July 18, Cora entered the Tombs with a large bouquet of red roses.

It was nine o'clock, and a large crowd had already gathered in front of the courthouse. The sentencing to death of a woman was a sensational event.

Few women had been convicted of first-degree murder in New York State. In the previous ninety-five years, only five executions of women had been recorded, all of them by hanging. The first of these cases was Margaret Houghtaling, who was killed in October 1817, six weeks after she was convicted of killing her son. She asserted her innocence to the end. A few years later, another woman confessed to the crime on her death bed.

Elizabeth Van Valkenberg was the second woman to die in this way, hanged in 1846 for poisoning her husband. In 1849, it was the turn of Alice Runkle from Utica and, in 1852, of Anna Hoag, both also hanged for poisoning their husbands. In 1887, Rezelena Druss was executed for having shot her husband, whose burned and mutilated body was found in a marsh. Hanna Southward, convicted in 1889 of the murder of a man who had betrayed her, died of tuberculosis before she could be executed. In 1890, the Italian Chiara Cignarale shot her husband to death on Third Avenue; her death sentence was commuted to life in prison in the Auburn penitentiary.

After 1889, the method of execution changed. Dr. Alfred Southwick had invented the electric chair and patented it with the State of New York. On January 1 of that year, electricity took the place of the noose and, by the end of 1890, a death chamber had been built at Sing Sing.

The first experiments with electricity as a means to kill were carried out on a horse. Electrodes were applied to its forehead and a rear leg, just above the fetlock. Then a 1,200-volt current was unleashed. Southwick immediately afterwards cut open the animal's windpipe and inserted a tube connected to a pump. For half an hour he tried to induce artificial respiration, with no reaction from the horse. Experiments were then conducted using other animals: It was thus discovered that a jolt of 500 volts could kill a dog or a calf weighing 75 pounds.

On March 29, 1889, in Buffalo, New York, a grocer by the name of William Kemmler came out of his house and calmly told his neighbors: "I killed my wife. Yes, and for that they will put the noose around my neck." He was wrong. Instead, he became the first man in history to die in the electric chair.

The newly founded New York Electric Club began a campaign against the electric chair in the press and the courts. These supporters of electricity did not want to see it degraded. They argued that no known electric apparatus could generate enough voltage to kill a man with the certainty and respect for human dignity guaranteed by the scaffold.

Detalmo di Brazzà, a scientist as well as an enemy of the death penalty, had followed the Kemmler case with misgivings. He saw it as the decisive test of the dawning industrial society.

The U.S. Senate formed a commission to find more humane forms of capital punishment. The commission also recommended that criminals' bodies be autopsied and that executions and burials not be open to the public. Among those who appeared before the commission was Thomas Alva Edison, whom Detalmo had visited several times at his laboratory at Llewellyn Park in New Jersey. At that time Edison was running a full-fledged campaign against alternating current (AC) and its principal proponent, George P. Westinghouse. Edison's tactic was to exploit the public's fear of AC, saying that not only could the high voltage burn the filaments in light bulbs, it could also damage people and objects. New York City was then trying to run its suspended high voltage cables underground, partly to prevent the fatal accidents of the past.

Speaking before the commission, Edison warmly—but not without ulterior motives—recommended that AC be used for executions in the electric chair. In November 1886, Westinghouse had installed an alternating current generator in Buffalo, providing energy for domestic use that was less expensive and more efficient than Edison's direct current (DC), which did not cover as long a distance. Orders for Westinghouse's dynamo went up and Edison feared losing his principal market, New York City. If Kemmler were to be executed using a Westinghouse dynamo, thought Edison, that machine would forever have a negative association.

On August 6, 1890, at 6:35 AM, William Kemmler took his seat on the electric chair. The top of his head had been shaved, and openings for the electrodes were cut in his shirt and trousers. Turning to the Buffalo deputy sheriff, Kemmler said: "Joe, stay until the end. Don't let them experiment with me more than they need to."

The chair was bolted to the floor and built of heavy oak. A square structure, with a high slanting back and wide armrests, it had a headrest, straps, and adjustable electrodes: metallic disks measuring about three inches in diameter, covered with a sponge layer. The spinal electrodes jutted out horizontally, and the head electrode descended from the ceiling. The electric cable ran along the floor, protected by a wooden strip.

The dynamo and the engine were in one of the prison laboratories, a few feet away. The voltmeter, the switch, and other instruments were in an adjacent room. Communication between the control room and the dynamo room took place with electric bells.

When Kemmler entered the death chamber, the prison warden introduced him to the spectators, who sat in a semicircle around the electric chair. His last words were, "Well, I wish you all good luck in this world."

Following the warden's orders, Kemmler took off his jacket and sat down on the chair. Leather bandages encircled his forehead, and his arms and legs were tied with straps. Noticing that the prison employees were nervous, he told them to take

Woman in the Death Chair, The World, *February 1896.*

their time and to make sure everything was in place. He pressed his back against the spinal electrodes; then, turning to the warden, he said: "Sir, you'd better adjust the skullcap. It's not fastened well."

The mask that was placed over his face left his lips and nostrils uncovered. The electrodes were moistened with salt water.

The electrician, E.F. Davis, the first electric-chair executioner, wore a double-breasted business suit and a black felt hat. At 6:40, he closed the circuit and a 1,450 volt current passed through.

Kemmler's body gave a tremendous heave against the straps. Muscles contracted, and his throat turned a vivid red. A puff of smoke rose from his head and with it the smell of burnt flesh. The man moaned: he seemed to be trying to breathe. Then he remained motionless. Dr. Spitzka, a neurologist, waited seventeen seconds and then announced: "This is fine. Switch the current off. He's dead."

"There we go!" exclaimed Dr. Alfred Southwick. "This is the conclusion of ten years' work and study. From this day on we live in a more advanced society."

While the physicians congratulated each other on the experiment's success, Dr. Louis Balch, the public health director, cried out: "Look at that wound!"

At the moment of contact, one of Kemmler's fingers had scratched off a piece of skin at the base of a thumb. The gash was pulsing blood.

"Turn the current back on immediately," shouted Dr. Spitzka. "He's not dead!" The Associated Press journalist fainted. The Erie County district attorney, who had convicted Kemmler, fled the room in horror. Davis closed the circuit. A few more seconds and Kemmler was finally dead.

The autopsy report revealed that Kemmler's pupils remained dilated after death. The eyes had star-shaped fractures in the crystalline lenses. The high body temperature of 138 degrees was retained, as in a thermos, because the blood had stopped circulating. The cardiac wall had ruptured, and the heart and lungs were engorged with blood. When the scalp was sliced off, it could be seen that the summit of the cranium had withered. There had been capillary hemorrhages at the base of the third and fourth cerebral ventricles, as well as in the gray brain matter and in the marrow. The flesh, at the contact points, was scorched. Within three hours, *rigor mortis* had completely set in.

The Westinghouse Company spent thousands of dollars in an attempt to prevent the application of the new death penalty directives. The best lawyers were hired to prove that death by the electric chair was not instantaneous, since the victim's muscles continued their spasms after the current was switched off. But nothing could be done.

The world press positioned itself with the detractors of the new method of execution. The *New York Sun* suggested that "civilization find other ways with which to manifest its progress." The *World* proclaimed: "The single quick pull of the rope around the neck is doubtless better than this passage through the tortures of hell to the relief of death." The *London Standard* asserted: "The age of the stake is in the past; the age of electricity too will pass."

Despite the *Herald*'s attempt to keep the story of Kemmler's execution alive, it was forgotten within a few days, due to a lively debate over whether the body of former president Ulysses S. Grant ought to be transferred from New York to the Washington National Cemetery.

A year later, four executions on the same day, July 7, 1891, renewed the press's interest. The Sing Sing warden barred reporters from the death chamber. One of the four men put to death was Japanese, and the press stressed the fact that he died a "pagan," despite the proselytizing efforts of the Tombs chaplain, the Reverend Law, who had been a missionary in Japan.

A campaign against the electric chair increased the newspapers' circulations, but it also caused a backlash. A New York County jury indicted nine publishers (including the *Herald*'s Gordon Bennett and the *World*'s Pulitzer) for violating the Electrical Execution Law, which regulated capital punishment via the electric chair, and which allowed the publication of only the essential details of executions. All the publishers were arrested, and their bail was set at five hundred dollars. Once it was paid, however, the debate died down and other news took up the front pages. Thus, the electric chair entered into the history of New York State, and Westinghouse came to be considered the cocreator of the new method of putting criminals to death.

Six years after the advent of the electric chair, a woman was about to be sentenced to it for the first time.

The temperature had dropped during that night in July, and a slight haze veiled the sun. Detalmo was waiting for Cora in front of the Tombs. She had refused to hand over the red roses to the guards, insisting that she wanted to give them to Maria personally. Their fragrance had invaded the tiny cell.

As soon as the courthouse doors were opened, the throng pushed and shoved its way into the courtroom. The security guards had been increased. The doormen tried unsuccessfully to shoo away the Italians who had not made it inside, and the hallways were filled with clusters of people animatedly discussing their compatriot's fate. Cora and Detalmo reached the courtroom through a private doorway. Outside, on Franklin Street, another great crowd had gathered in the hope of glimpsing the prisoner as she crossed the Bridge of Sighs.

At ten o'clock, Judge Goff came out of his private chamber. Maria's father was at the far end of the courtroom, along with his eldest son, Giuseppe, and Father Ferretti from the Church of the Transfiguration. Maria's mother, her sisters, and her younger brother had not been allowed to enter.

Under her mauve-colored veil, Cora, who sat in the front row, carefully surveyed the room. A sapphire pin gleamed in the middle of her high collar. Next to her sat the actress Cora Brown Potter, her cousin; two rows back the prominent suffragette Mary Livermore could be seen. She had managed to be present, despite her old age and failing health. Also in the room was Rosalie Low, one of the few women attorneys in New York.

At 10:20, the court clerk called Maria Barbella to the bar. The public suddenly fell silent. The girl was dressed in black and wore a large flowered hat. Her face was pale and her lips almost violet. As she approached the bar, Sheriff Tamsen entered and came to her side.

"Will you tell us your name?" the clerk asked her through the interpreter, posing all the ritual questions. Then Assistant District Attorney McIntyre began to speak:

"I am here in compliance with the law," he said. "Despite my reluctance, I ask the court to proceed according to the code. Miss Barbella was summoned to trial on July 11, and from that date until the 15th of the same month, this court and the jury have studied the evidence against her. The defense has been heard. We know that everything possible has been done. Attorney Evans has had his client's mental health evaluated and was assured that at the moment of the crime she was of sound mind. . . ."

Cora squeezed her husband's arm. The mental health exam was an outright invention.

"The defense has done everything in its power to elicit the jury's understanding," McIntyre continued. "The accused has been competently defended, and now the lawfully prescribed sentence must be handed down to her."

There was no translation. Suddenly, Amos Evans rose out of turn and loudly requested a postponement of the sentencing.

"Despite the fact that I did everything in my power on behalf of Miss Maria Barbella, someone has intervened on her behalf and has hired private counsel. Attorneys House and Friend are present in the court, and I ask therefore that the sentencing be postponed for one week so that we can adequately prepare for argument."

House was clearly taken aback. He had told Evans that a last-minute intervention would be a waste of time and would only prolong the girl's ordeal. He was certain that it was better to follow the regular appeal process. But Evans still hoped to remedy his mistakes and save face in the courtroom. At this point House was compelled to make a diplomatic statement.

"Attorney Evans's hands were tied," he said. "He was unable to call this city's prominent experts to his aid. Miss Barbella therefore did not benefit from testimony which could have saved her. Because this young woman is now in the shadow of death, all we ask is a reasonable and lenient adjournment. The people of New York will not be harmed by it, nor will the course of justice be impeded."

"It is not a matter of leniency," John Goff replied. "I am here as an administrator of the law, and independently of how unpleasant the exercise of my function may be, I must acquit myself of it in a correct and impartial manner. A postponement of the sentencing would accomplish nothing but the introduction of elements of uncertainty in the administration of the law. The request is denied."

House was unable to contain himself: "How terrible to think, Your Honor, that had someone else been seated in your place, the answer might have been different!" His words echoed through the crowd. Goff's gaze became icy and his gavel rapped brusquely on the table.

"If I could discern the slightest advantage to the defendant," he answered, "I would grant her the deferment. The arguments you have put forward in favor of an adjournment of the sentencing are inconsistent. The law sanctions a complete review of all trials through the Court of Appeals. Therefore I intend to pronounce the sentence immediately."

The clerk asked the girl to stand up: Maria obeyed, uncertainly. Solemnly Goff pronounced the sentence. "Miss Maria Barbella was tried and convicted of the crime of murder in the first degree, and a jury of more than average intelligence faithfully weighed the evidence brought forward. . . . The jury manifested sympathy in her regard. They rendered a verdict in accordance to the law. . . ." Sentence by sentence, the interpreter repeated the words in Italian, but Maria seemed indifferent.

"It is ordered that the New York sheriff transfer her this very day to the custody of the warden of the state prison of Sing Sing, and that from this day forward she be held in isolation. It is also ordered that she be allowed to see no one, except the prison guards, her immediate relations, a priest, and her attorneys until the week of August 19, when it is ordered that the warden of the state prison inflict upon her the penalty of death in the manner prescribed by the laws of this state: execution by electricity."

Morossi shouted the lines. When he proclaimed "execution by electricity" the crowd gasped collectively and Maria collapsed. Sheriff Tamsen came forward, approached the judge's bench, and received the death warrant from Goff's hands: it was decorated with a silver seal and tied with a blue ribbon.

House jumped to his feet and loudly demanded that his client be allowed to remain at the Tombs at least three more days.

"I would be delighted to grant your request, but I cannot do so," Goff replied. "The Tombs warden, Mr. Fallon, declines all responsibility towards the prisoner unless Sheriff Tamsen provides a detail for her. And the sheriff is unable to do so. Request denied."

House was indignant.

Mrs. Foster led Maria out of the courtroom.

While Cora rushed to the Tombs, Detalmo remained with Frederick House, who was besieged by reporters on every side. Exasperated by the judge's decision to send the prisoner to Sing Sing right away, House stated that he considered the woman's immediate transfer a cruel and inhumane act.

"I have just accepted the case and I need to spend some time with my client. However, the sheriff does not intend to assume further responsibility. I am surprised that a man can be so ruthless. His conduct certainly seems despicable to me."

It was, in fact, customary for a judge to accept an attorney's request to spend some days conferring with his or her client. Emanuel Friend supported House's view of Goff in the pages of the *Sun:* "It was a histrionic display of a harsh and unyielding justice."

Cora, meanwhile, having said good bye to Maria, was leaving the Tombs. At the prison entrance she met Mrs. Giampiccolo, the girl's aunt, who was on her way in to visit her with Sedgwick, Evans's assistant. Before undergoing the usual search, the attorney, almost jokingly, asked the woman if she were carrying any weapons. Without discomfiture, Mrs. Giampiccolo extracted from her bodice a stiletto at least nine inches long. The guards blocked her and she began to shout in Italian as loudly as she could: She always had a dagger with her, for defense. . . . She didn't know it was against the law. . . . She did not mean anyone any harm. . . .

The *World*'s morning edition ran a front page article by the well-known journalist Arthur Brisbane. *THE BARBERI CASE. Sentence of Death Must be Imposed Upon the Girl Today. BUT WILL IT BE CARRIED OUT?*

. . . When a State like this makes up its mind to kill a young woman weighing 105 pounds, speaking no English, understanding nothing of her rights, badly defended and ill-fitted to cope with 6,000,000 people, the case is interesting. . . .

I had the pleasure of talking to Miss Barberi in the Tombs prison yesterday. . . . I told her through a translator that killing by electricity demanded the assistance of doctors, and I ventured the assertion that it would be hard to find any American doctor willing to make himself the executioner of a woman. I don't know whether she understood me.

In the first place, as you will perhaps admit later on, Miss Barberi ought not to be killed even if the killing could be done neatly and modestly. But it can't be done modestly.

The law permits the killing by electricity of any woman who commits murder. But the law does not permit any warden, sheriff or doctor to outrage a woman's modesty, and that nullifies the permission to kill.

If Miss Barberi is to be killed by electricity she must be brought in the presence of several men, with her head shaved and one of her legs bare to the top of her thigh. She cannot be killed with her legs decently covered, because if her skirts were down, the electrode might make them catch fire. . . .

The State of New York, "by the grace of God free and independent," will not parade this young woman with one leg bare before a company of scientists and then kill her. The contest between her and the State of New York is not an equal one. She has never been free or independent. She was born a slave. Happy the murderess who can speak the language of the country in which she murders. . . .

CHAPTER TEN

*M*aria Barbella was registered at Sing Sing as follows:

1895. Miss Marie Barberi
July 18.   Received from New York.
          Sentenced July 18—Execution. Verdict: murder 1st
                           Hon John W. Goff
          Who arrested you? Don't know.
          Born: Italy
          Age: 22
          Occupation: dressmaker
          Complexion: dark
          Eyes: hazel or gray
          Hair: dark brown
          Stature: 4.11
          Weight: 105
          Read: yes, a little
          Write: yes, a little
          Habits: beer very moderately
          Tobacco: no
          Single
          Resided when arrested at 13th St. New York City

Mother: Mott St. #136. Philomena Barbera
Medium-sized head with dull expression
Hair black and grows low
Large eyes. Eyebrows arched heavy dark
Small pug nose. Rather large mouth with corners
    turned down
No marks on face or hands. Rather full bust
Small build. Arms and hands plump. Good teeth
Scar on right arm above the elbow

The prison employee who registered Maria, doubly mispelling her name, noted an apathetic expression. Perhaps Maria was exhausted after her journey upstate. She had been on display for hours.

Handcuffed, she had boarded the Fourth Avenue streetcar at one o'clock in the afternoon. Mrs. Foster escorted her, along with deputy sheriffs Schneider and Kelly. The prisoner had not been assigned a special convoy, and Mrs. Foster was furious. Was exposing the girl to such humiliation a part of the sentence? On the other hand, Maria seemed not to notice she was on public transportation. The passengers stared at her as she clung to Mrs. Foster, her lips moving silently in prayer.

"Me *there?*" asked Maria when the streetcar reached Grand Central Station. She could barely walk. The throng in the great entrance hall parted for the captive and her escort. A newsboy hawked Maria's story to a row of men waiting in line for a shoeshine.

On the 2:05 to Ossining, Schneider gave Mrs. Foster permission to remove the prisoner's handcuffs. The train reached Ossining at about 3:00. Only the railroad workers witnessed Maria's transfer to the special vehicle from Sing Sing. The trip up the hill was brief, and soon the carriage entered the penitentiary's imposing cast iron gates. Maria couldn't manage to walk, and

Sheriff Schneider had to carry her inert body into the warden's office.

Although he was considered a lover of discipline, the Sing Sing warden, Omar V. Sage, was of a far kinder disposition than his Tombs colleague. A little over sixty, Sage was an honest and loyal man. He had been at the penitentiary just three years. Formerly a detective in New York City, by virtue of his rank as National Guard colonel he had been nominated warden of Sing Sing. The prisoners did not despise him, because he did not despise them.

Sage lived with his wife and two daughters inside the prison walls. Their large brick house had three rows of balconies, a facade covered in thick ivy, and a magnificent view of the Westchester forests and the Hudson River winding as far as the eye could see.

Schneider set Maria down on a little couch in the office. She seemed cold, and Julia, the warden's wife, covered her with a shawl.

Judge Goff's hasty decision to have Maria transferred immediately had not only prevented her from consulting with her lawyers, but also caught Sage unprepared. As she was the first female convict held at Sing Sing in eighteen years, and the first there on death row, Maria presented the problem of female surveillance: he certainly could not put her with the men. While waiting for two female guards from Albany, the girl was temporarily assigned to a Mrs. Vincent, who had been recruited on short notice.

"Miss Barbella has no idea what the procedures are," Mrs. Foster explained to the warden. "She is certain that she is to be killed immediately. If I could, I would like to stay here tonight." Sage gratefully gave the Tombs Angel his permission, and his wife offered her help.

"Mrs. Vincent will do the day shift," the warden explained. "However, until the other two arrive, I am forced to have our guard Talcott watch her, and I don't like to do that to a woman."

Meanwhile, on the third floor of the infirmary building, a group of inmates was busy preparing a cell for Maria's solitary confinement. Finally word came that the work was completed. Mrs. Foster helped the girl off the couch and led her out, with Talcott and Mrs. Vincent escorting them.

Maria was walking slowly and uncertainly. It took a long time to cross the huge courtyard. On the way up the stairs to the third floor, she stopped at every landing to catch her breath, like an old woman. Then there was a long hallway. Two prisoners in the infirmary managed to catch a glimpse of her through the open door of the dormitory. On reaching the cell, Maria stopped in her tracks and refused to continue. She was convinced that it was the death chamber.

The two women went in before her, and only then did the girl take some hesitant steps. The cell contained two wooden chairs, a stool, a table, and an iron cot. The matron sat on one of the chairs. Mrs. Foster took the stool. Maria stood, staring at the remaining chair. Was that the one with the electric current? She looked at Mrs. Foster suspiciously and at Mrs. Vincent with terror. When the matron pointed at the chair, Maria darted into a corner. The two women exchanged looks silently; then Mrs. Foster, sensing the reason for Maria's anguish, sat down on the empty chair, and then returned to the stool. The girl approached slowly, touched the chair fearfully, moved it toward the middle of the room, and finally sat down.

Mrs. Foster spent a sleepless night. She could hear Maria's subdued crying, while the guard Talcott paced the hallway in his heavy boots. She began to think about the other prisoners in solitary confinement.

Six of the eight death row cells were occupied. The last arrival was Vincenzo Nenno, an Italian immigrant who had slaughtered his wife in front of their two children. After the crime, he had made the children walk around the room until their footprints had covered the whole floor with blood. Amos Evans had been his defender, and his execution was set for August 12.

The other five cells were occupied by Feigenbaum and Richard Leach, who had poisoned their wives; a man called Caesar, who had killed his girlfriend with a butcher knife; and a businessman by the name of Tuckewitz, who had murdered his partner.

Mrs. Foster knew their stories well. Appeals had been filed by all except Leach and Nenno; barring an intercession by the governor, they were to be executed within a few days.

Leach was thickset and a perennial joker. He always asked for stewed potatoes because, he said, fried foods made life shorter. The warden gave in to his requests.

Caesar had a beautiful voice and with his warm baritone had sung gospel songs for the entire night preceding the sensational execution of Dr. Robert Buchanan, which had just taken place.

Robert Buchanan had been a physician, and his second wife was a wealthy heiress twenty years older than he. She died suddenly on April 22, 1892, in their New York home. After the funeral, the doctor moved to Nova Scotia, where he remarried his first wife.

In New York, the rumor spread that the heiress had been the victim of a cruel hoax by her husband, who was determined to get his hands on her fortune. The body was exhumed and an autopsy confirmed these suspicions. Buchanan had tricked the coroner; following a lethal dose of morphine, the dead woman's pupils would have dilated, so the doctor had used a small quantity of atropine to limit that effect.

His trial had caused a sensation. After several legal appeals, Buchanan was finally electrocuted on July 1, while Maria was still at the Tombs. Anna Buchanan had gone to the governor's mansion in Rhinecliff, New York, at dawn on the day of execution, in a desperate and useless attempt to convince him to spare her husband's life. Buchanan's last words to the warden were: "I am entirely innocent of the crime for which I am about to die. There was no more morphine in that woman than there is in you at this moment. I suppose I am not the first innocent man to be executed."

Buchanan's body was exposed to the public at 127 Varick Street in New York. The July 3 *New York Times* wrote:

> . . . It is estimated that nearly 5,000 people passed around the coffin and looked upon the features of the murderer.
>
> The greatest crush of spectators came at noon, when the factories and stores in the vicinity released their help for lunch. Workmen came in large groups. Some attempted to climb into the room through the windows. Others scaled a fence and tried to enter through a rear door. All were driven back, and formed a line, extending far down the street.
>
> The undertaker stationed himself at the entrance and, to quiet the crowd, occasionally shouted: "Take your time! Take your time! Everyone will have the chance to see the body!"
>
> "Why don't you charge a quarter for admission and retire on the proceeds?" asked one. . . .

The death row inmates could talk to one another from their cells, but on the third floor of the infirmary, Maria was completely isolated. Her relatives would not be able to visit her often. Judge Goff still had not approved Cora and Mrs. Foster's request for permission to visit the girl.

After her sleepless night next to Maria, the Tombs Angel got ready to leave. She hugged the girl and tried to reassure her once more, whispering that God was on her side; that she was not alone; that she was protected by people who would not let her die; that she should do nothing but eat, sleep, and keep strong.

Maria was left alone. She was shaking with cold, despite the stifling heat inside the cell. She spent the first two days glued to the chair that had frightened her so much at first. Small as she was, her feet did not reach the ground and hung inertly in their black felt slippers. Every noise made her tremble under her dark tunic, and she jumped whenever she heard the sound of steps.

She murmured "thank you" for the bowl of chicken soup, "thank you" for the plate of stewed beef that came directly from the warden's private kitchen, but the food was returned untouched. Maria slept very little and thanks only to the sleeping pills the prison doctor gave her. Early on Saturday morning Mrs. Vincent, who had agreed to watch Maria only temporarily, changed her mind and thought it her duty to stay. The warden cabled to Albany that only one other female guard should come.

Mrs. Zimpcamp arrived on Sunday, during the visit from Maria's relatives. Mrs. Barbella had brought a basket of shiny red apples, which the entrance guards promptly confiscated. Mother and daughter could speak, but all physical contact was forbidden: a guard sat between them. Gesturing, Filomena told Maria that her name was in all the papers, efforts were being made to save her, and so on. The most important information was that her new lawyer had filed a request for appeal and that this meant an automatic suspension of the sentence.

"It means they won't kill you just yet," explained her older brother, Giuseppe. "They can't do anything to you. They'll keep you here, but they won't put you on the electric chair."

"Your father received five dollars from the *New York Times*," announced her mother.

"Yes," her brother confirmed. "A company called Flandrau sent the money. . . . They build carriages in Broome Street. The newspaper sent someone with an envelope to Mott Street. Papa says he will use the money to come visit you."

Mrs. Barbella was excited. "Papa was going to Broome Street today to thank them . . . you know, they're not even Italian. . . ."

Maria did not speak and gazed silently, now at her mother, now at Giuseppe.

On the previous day, in Amos Evans's office in New York, a journalist was interviewing Cora in Frederick House's presence. Her statement was published the next day:

. . . "We propose," Countess di Brazzà said, "to ask Governor Morton to grant Maria Barbella a full pardon. The good people of this city are full of sympathy for this poor girl. . . . If she had merely cut off the man's ear instead of his throat, we would have him in the dock now and send him to prison for having abducted the girl. Women have a hard enough fight to maintain their virtue, and it is time the new woman arose and asserted herself. . . ."

"We want to shower upon the Governor such a mass of names in petitions for pardon that he must act. We want the press to help. If the press can interest the great mass of people, I can work the racket among the 400—pardon me for the slang, but I believe that is how you would put it. I am going now to Newport to see my society friends to get names and help.

"This, I believe, is something which should be done by Americans, therefore I have not gone to the Italian ambassador, Baron Fava, to get his help.

"I am an American who married an Italian. I was an emigrant from America to Italy. Maria Barbella is an emigrant from Italy to America. I feel that we are in equivalent positions and I must help her."

On Sunday, July 19, as thousands of people read Cora's interview on the front page of the *Sun,* Mrs. Vincent noticed a slight unrelated change in the prisoner. Maria was almost smiling. The guard was surprised to notice how white and regular her teeth were.

Maria ate all of her breakfast and then raised her eyes and looked around her room. It was infinitely bigger than her cell at the Tombs. She stood up and paced the walls to measure it. The room was about fourteen square feet, the same size as the two rooms she had shared with Domenico Cataldo put together. There was a real bed with a comfortable mattress. She had not slept in a real bed since she left home to live with Domenico, five months before.

There was even a rocking chair; it had been there all along, but she now noticed it for the first time. She sat down and began to rock herself, back and forth, back and forth. In a short while she fell into a deep sleep.

CHAPTER ELEVEN

*C*ora's printer worked day and night on the petition she and Frederick House had written. Just four days after Maria's sentencing, dozens of boxes, containing 13,000 copies of the document, arrived at Evans's office.

The text read as follows:

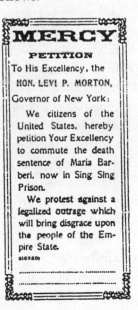

MERCY

PETITION

To His Excellency, the
HON. LEVI P. MORTON,
Governor of New York:

We citizens of the
United States, hereby
petition Your Excellency
to commute the death
sentence of Maria Bar-
beri, now in Sing Sing
Prison.

We protest against a
legalized outrage which
will bring disgrace upon
the people of the Em-
pire State.

Each copy of the petition was sent with a covering note from Cora:

> I kindly ask that the petition be placed in prominent places so that as many as possible may have the opportunity to sign it. Not only the quality of the names of the supplicants, but the quantity will impress His Excellency. No one in this case is too humble or too poor to help save a human life.
>
> As the time is short, I urge all those who take an interest in the girl to do everything in their power to facilitate the gathering of names. As soon as the slip is filled, it should be returned to Mr. Amos H. Evans, 309 Broadway, New York City.

In a July 19 interview with the *Recorder,* Frederick House said he was certain the Court of Appeals would agree that Maria's trial had contained many irregularities. But he did not reveal his grounds for appeal. "They will be strictly juridical ones," he said, "and they will have no relationship to the efforts now under way to obtain her pardon." Above and beyond the legalities, he knew very well that a massive press campaign was a vital element of the defense.

The Savoy Hotel soon became Cora's campaign headquarters in the battle to save Maria. The entire hotel was mobilized: The manager put a room at her disposal free of charge, and the employees spent much of their free time circulating petitions among the guests, delivering messages, and even helping with the correspondence. The Underwood Company sent a typewriter and a secretary, and the improvised office was soon flooded with visitors and phone calls.

The campaign for Maria's life awakened great interest among journalists, who followed Cora wherever she went, even forcing their way into the hotel to interview her. The press's intervention transformed Cora's intent to save Maria Barbella from the electric chair into the first nationwide American campaign to abolish the death penalty. Preachers of every stripe soon found in the young Italian immigrant's predicament a parable for their sermons. Cora and Detalmo followed the press campaign in several New York dailies.

On July 20, the *Herald* ran an editorial which caused an uproar because of its radical feminist ideas. The author was Nicola Gigliotti, an Italian woman.

... What, in civilization's name, is this "marriage" for which women kill their lovers when they cannot obtain it, and from which so many fly, once having obtained it? The answer is simple. ... It is only a relic of barbarous slavery—a modified form of the ceremony of banging the purchased "wife" unconscious and carting her into the hut as eternal chattel. And the same modified form will continue as long as women sell themselves for wealth and position—for even a home and a name!

Who armed Maria Barberi? Centuries of this inhuman, one-sided prejudice are what have caused prostitution in our cities, opened divorce courts and blinded us with the bondage of custom to the real ugliness of marriage.

But without what is called scornfully "free unions" female individuality cannot be attained. With a continuance of marriage, man must always be socially, economically and legally the woman's superior—a position which should be decided solely by character. ...

Had Maria fearlessly entered into a free union with her lover, instead of succumbing to the bait of "marriage," she would have had no cause for the shame which drove her to her frenzied act. ...

Feminists did not need Gigliotti's strong opinion to rise up. Maria had been in Sing Sing just a few hours when women began to make themselves heard. The feminist elite, made up of talented writers with a large and international public, came forward to support Maria. Mary Livermore, Elizabeth Cady Stanton, and Susan B. Anthony took the lead.

Mary Livermore, who was a rigorous Calvinist feminist, as well as a teacher, journalist, and orator, published an article in the *World* showing both her compassion for Maria and her uncompromising defense of all women. The tone was combative, rather more like that of a correspondent from the front lines of a cruel war than that of a reporter.

> . . . When a woman undertakes to avenge her innocence she is condemned to death. And yet they say that women have their rights! I, for one, cannot blame Maria Barberi. If the law will not protect women—and it won't—they must protect themselves. I would have done what she did myself. I say now, as I have always said, that if a man had the temerity to ruin a daughter of mine, I would strike him dead without hesitation. He would not occupy the same planet with me.

Elizabeth Cady Stanton was a brilliant scholar and the most ardent supporter of women's right to vote. At the 1848 Seneca Falls convention, she had stated that women's suffrage was the key to more concrete and decisive reforms. In a July 19 article in the *World* she wrote, in her usual persuasive style:

> . . . Every sentence and every execution I hear of is a break in the current of my life and thoughts for days. I make my son the victim. A woman knows the cost of life better than a man does.
>
> No woman has ever had a fair trial, nor will she have until she is tried by a jury of her peers. Laws are made by men, administered by men and executed by men. The courthouse

is packed with men. Maria Barberi was arrested by a male officer, locked in a prison by a male jailer, prosecuted by a male lawyer, convicted by a male jury, sentenced to death by a male judge, under a law passed by a male legislature, approved by a male Governor, and all elected male voters. She is to be electrocuted by a male warden, her body dissected by a male surgeon, and finally dumped by a male undertaker in the Potter's Field. She had no voice in legislature halls or at the ballot-box in shaping the laws under which she was sentenced to die.

Women have been denied their rights and privileges long enough. Ordinary men do not weigh our feelings carefully. The jury who convicted the poor Maria Barberi were not capable of judging the motives which actuated her crime. They know nothing of the feelings of outraged womanhood. What could this poor helpless creature do in her own defense?

Susan B. Anthony, president of the Woman's Suffrage Association, had been arrested twenty years earlier for daring to vote. Her July 27 piece in the *New York Herald* was perhaps the most balanced and convincing:

My opinion is and will always be against murder, whether by the individual or the State, but I am especially opposed to the State murdering a young woman who cannot understand our language and for a crime that is often condoned in a man. . . .

The law refuses to punish the man who, under promise of marriage, robs the woman of her chastity. But when the forsaken creature takes vengeance, the New York law consigns her to a most ignominious death, for women in the State of New York have no political peers among men save those inside the state prisons and lunatic asylums.

All decency and justice is outraged at the barbarism of judicial murder of man by man in accordance with his own man-made laws, but when he proceeds to perpetrate the atrocity upon the head of woman, all nature revolts and cries: "Hands off!" at least until women are enfranchised and together with men shall decide what shall be law and who shall execute it. The whole state of affairs, the two moral codes, the foraging upon the poor, ignorant women—a mere harmless pastime for men—and then consigning their victims to shame and death, all cry out for power in the hands of women to make, shape and control their own moral code, not only, but that of men also. Things are surely all one-sided now. I hope that the governor will commute the girl's sentence and that the law for judicial murder will be annulled by the next legislature.

Many other prominent women expressed their ideas in the press in more or less the same terms. These included Mrs. Ulysses S. Grant, Elizabeth Grannis of the National League of Social Purity, Mary Ormsby of the Peace Society, and the actress Lillian Russell. Harriet Lincoln Coolidge wrote that, because Maria was brought to America as a minor, she should be pardoned and sent back to Italy to start a new life.

The *World*, under Charles Chapin's editorship, became the main forum for Maria's detractors, but the other major dailies also opposed both Maria's pardon and the feminist campaign. On July 25, an unsigned letter appeared in the *Herald*.

This movement in favor of the condemned murderess, Maria Barberi, is criminal, for if it succeeds it will have the effect of driving other fallen women to the appalling crime of murder. And should we, as Christians, encourage others to follow in her path? I would ask mercy for this sinner by begging that her sentence be commuted to forty years' imprisonment, but I would not outrage law and order by asking for clemency.

That same day, the *Herald* ran an article titled: *IT IS A DIVINE COMMAND. Reasons Why Maria Barberi's Life Should Not Be Spared:*

Among the persons who demand a commutation of punishment or even a full pardon for Maria Barberi must be a large number of professed Christians who forget that we have no right to criticize, far less to set aside the divine command that those who take life, except in some cases different from this one, shall lose their life: no exception is made in favor of woman, and the Saviour expressly stated that the law must be observed.

Does Maria deserve as much compassion as is shown to her? "We should be merciful and forgive," some say. Did she show mercy, did she forgive? . . .

That in the past women were denied much that is now properly accorded to them is no reason why a woman who has fearfully violated divine and human law should not be punished for it exactly as would be a man. While, lastly, a seducer is to be abhorred, it must not be forgotten that Maria had no need to allow herself to be seduced.

The *Tribune* published a letter objecting to that newspaper's hostility toward Maria:

Sir: . . . That you should favor execution of poor Maria Barberi is not surprising. . . .

I beg of you to do all you can to save her life. A man ruined her; men tried her; a jury of men found her guilty, and a man sentenced her to die!

Buchanan, for a deliberately planned murder of a woman for money, had three trials and two years of life before he suffered the penalty of his crime. But then he was not an Italian immigrant. . . .

Brooklyn, July 20, 1895, E. E. Chatfield

Following this letter was the paper's reply:

The *Tribune* has not taken a stand in favor of the execution of Maria Barberi as this discriminating reader suggests. It simply advised that for the sake of enforcing the law upon the violent element of her countrymen, already too prone to take it into their own hands, the Governor should not be "overhasty" in granting a commutation of the death sentence. With relatives of the girl going about with concealed stilettos, it will be a good thing to delay action for a time and give them a chance to think over the serious consequences of taking a life.

On July 22, the *New York Times* also attacked Maria Barbella:

. . . No weaker argument could be imagined than that put forward by the people who are endeavoring to secure a pardon for the woman convicted last week of murder.

. . . Why should this poor creature be killed, they ask, when men are allowed, almost every week, to punish conjugal infidelity with death? In other words, because one great wrong exists, a survival of barbarism, a second should go unpunished! That juries will acquit men who, for a certain provocation, slaughter their wives, is a disgrace to our civilization and proof of its incompleteness. The abuse, however, is one to be remedied not by duplicating it through the extension to women of the same license. . . .

It was clear that the press was ranged against Maria and that this opposition would hurt her case. Cora examined the situation. If public opinion was influenced by the press, which was owned by publishers and run by editors, it followed that she ought to turn to them directly: Maria's fate was partly in their hands.

Detalmo could not accompany Cora on her rounds to the newspapers. He was distracted by other concerns: the solar spectrum, the possibility of oxygen in the sun, and the spectra of elements. He was scheduled to travel upstate to visit his colleague Daniel Draper, brother of the celebrated astronomer Henry Draper, who was married to Cora's cousin. The Draper brothers had built a colossal reflecting telescope with which Daniel had taken a photograph of the moon fifty-one inches in diameter, the largest ever made. The family-owned meteorological observatory in Hastings-On-Hudson was a scientific shrine. Before leaving, Detalmo made sure that Cora was not going on her round of the newspapers alone. Rebecca Foster would go with her. Detalmo had no intention of discouraging his wife, but he was certain that not all the editors would welcome her and that some would not take her seriously.

On the morning of July 23, Cora and Mrs. Foster set off on their public relations mission in a rented carriage. Their first stop was the *Herald,* whose luxurious new headquarters were located at the corner of Thirty-fifth Street and Broadway. The building was an exact reproduction of an Italian palazzo, even though the architects of McKim, Mead and White had taken the liberty of placing an enormous clock flanked by a statue of Minerva over the entrance. Under the colonnade, knots of people gathered at the large windows to watch the rotary presses, which were in constant motion as they printed, counted, and folded ninety-six thousand newspapers an hour. It struck Cora as an odd coincidence that Detalmo's cousins owned the building next to the

Palazzo del Consiglio di Verona, in Italy, which had served as the architects' model.

The editor, G. G. Howland, was not in. The two women were led into an office. Around them, the newsroom was in a paroxysm of activity, with people coming and going, typewriters in full swing, frantic delivery boys, and endlessly ringing telephones. The local news editor, who was following the Maria Barbella story, entered abruptly and shook hands with both women. He was a little over thirty and wore a white shirt with rolled-up sleeves.

"How can I help you?" he asked.

Cora made the introductions.

"Oh yes!" he exclaimed, sitting down at the desk. "You're here for the Mott Street murderer. Why so much fuss over this Italian?"

Cora was annoyed. "I must confess, sir, that your question surprises me greatly." She looked at him sternly in the eyes. "It seems I have a mistaken impression of your publisher. I thought James Gordon Bennett had a favorable opinion of Italians. He sails every year on his yacht between the Riviera and Capri, enjoying the hospitality of Italian friends. . . ."

The editor seemed confused. "In Italy he is on holiday. In America it's a different story. . . ."

"Oh, I understand now," Cora retorted sharply. "It is obvious that your newspaper subscribes to the idea that all the Italians in America belong to the Black Hand. . . ."

"Not all, madam, but most of them. . . ."

Cora tried to keep calm. "For your information, the Black Hand includes only a small percentage of the Italian immigrant population. In any case, if they don't defend themselves, no one in this country will do it. I am absolutely convinced of that!"

"Unless they are so fortunate as to find an ally such as yourself, madam," he answered aggressively.

"Precisely," she replied. "In Dante's *Inferno,* with which you are no doubt acquainted, the hottest place in hell is for those who, in a time of crisis, remained neutral." Cora stood up to leave. "I wish you good luck, sir. It must not be easy to face such responsibilities."

Park Row, in the business sector, was known as "Newspaper Row." The park was dominated by the World Building's dome, a lesser version of the one at Saint Peter's in Rome. The small building which housed the *Sun* was adjacent to a taller one which would soon be occupied by the *Tribune.* The *New York Times* building was the highest and widest. Rows of windows of every width and style, Romantic, Gothic, and Baroque, covered the entire facade. An American flag flew from every rooftop.

Cora and Mrs. Foster began with the *World.* As soon as they announced themselves, they were taken to the city editor, Charles E. Chapin, also known by the nickname "Pinch." His paper had not been particularly kind to Maria. Surprised by his friendly welcome, Cora addressed him diplomatically.

"I must congratulate you, Mr. Chapin, on your coverage of the Barbella trial," she said, before going straight to the point. It was not the moment to take him to task for the many factual inaccuracies she had read in his reports. "I am certain that you are aware of the gravity of the situation: If something is not done, the poor girl will die," she said assertively.

Chapin nodded and unexpectedly began to criticize Goff's behavior and express concern for Maria. He congratulated Mrs. Foster on her charitable works and Cora on her courageous intervention. His convincing manner baffled them. Maybe he had had a change of heart during the night. They were nonplussed, but also enormously relieved because the *World* had a very large distribution, especially its Sunday edition.

Mrs. Foster left the office first. Cora was about to follow her, when Chapin took her by the arm and whispered insinuatingly:

"I could be very useful to you, madam. Your lacemaking business would benefit greatly from the space I could dedicate to it in my newspaper. . . ."

Cora did not know how to respond.

"However, madam, time is money. Don't you agree?"

"Of course . . . everything is money," she said, "more so in this country than in Italy." The conversation had taken a demeaning twist, but she let him continue.

"Everything has a price, madam, and you know I could do wonders for your cause. . . . But I need your cooperation."

Charles E. Chapin was for sale.

"I sincerely hope you will do so," she answered, trying to disengage herself. "After all, a life is at stake. As far as my cooperation is concerned, I will always be at your disposal for any information you may need." And she left.

Mrs. Foster was not surprised at Cora's story. Chapin did not have a good reputation. But the paper's owner, Joseph Pulitzer, was deaf to the complaints about Chapin's character and to the rumors about his professional ethics: he may have been an unpleasant man, Pulitzer rationalized, but he was an astute editor and his articles sold papers.

Cora and Mrs. Foster continued their rounds: They went next to see Charles A. Dana at the *Sun,* then to Charles Miller of the *New York Times.* At the *Tribune* in Nassau Street, they met with the reporter Emily Crawford, who took an interest in Maria's case and promised to ask her managing editor, Whitelaw Reid, to let her follow the story.

It was late afternoon when the two women crossed the Brooklyn Bridge to canvass the *Brooklyn Daily Eagle* headquarters. By the time the carriage returned across the great bridge, the pinnacles of Manhattan were silhouetted against a glowing sunset. The hands of the huge clock on the Consolidated Gas Company tower read a few minutes before seven.

Night had fallen when they finally reached the *Recorder* at 15 Spruce Street. This daily had supported Maria from the very first: it had even published its own detachable petition, designating a whole room for the collection of the hundreds of letters and signatures that had arrived in response.

In reaction to the public interest in Maria's story, the paper had written:

> . . . Maria Barberi must be saved! And saved she will be. The chief magistrate is not possessed of that insensibility which could strap a woman to an electric chair and kill her.
>
> Thousands of petitions to the Governor were cut out from yesterday's paper and started on their errands of mercy. Solid men of business added names, which if signed to checks, could be worth fortunes. Men and women sojourning at the watering places secured hosts of signatures.
>
> The Countess awoke yesterday in Newport to find herself famous. Her noble act has awakened a quick response in the public mind. All day yesterday letters poured into the office of Lawyer Evans, asking for pardon slips, and expressing the appreciation of the Countess' work. . . .

Cora and the Tombs Angel had had a hard but productive day. Although rebuffed by the *Herald* that morning, Cora managed later to contact its publisher, Gordon Bennett, in person. Within forty-eight hours the newspaper changed its editorial line on the young Italian immigrant awaiting execution.

In the storm of conflicting opinions that had gathered around Maria's case, very few voices stated an opposition to the death penalty in itself. During a conference on criminal justice that took place in Rome that July, the American delegates had been the most fervent supporters of capital punishment, surpassing even the French in their zeal. Although lacking any democratic basis, the belief that legalized homicide was efficient seemed deeply embedded in American society: only three states, Michigan, Wisconsin, and Maine, had at one time debated a halt to executions. The punishing of one murder with another was considered almost a divine right.

America thought Italy a backward country. But in 1786 Grand Duke Leopoldo of Tuscany was the first European leader to declare that legalized homicide was not a deterrent to crime and should be abolished forever. In his territory, for a quarter century, justice was meted out mildly and crime did not increase. The resumption of the death penalty took place under Napoleon. In 1830 in Florence, when a convict was taken to the gallows, the streets were deserted: the citizens had all gone to church to pray.

Compared to the Tuscan citizens, those of New York cut a barbaric figure; like cannibals, they had flocked to view Dr. Buchanan's body, scorched by the electric chair.

Cora and Detalmo could not reconcile America's reputation as the home of science and abolitionism with these anachronistic, barbaric leanings. Their opinion coincided with that of General De Lafayette: "Until the infallibility of human judgment is proven, I will struggle for and demand the abolition of the death penalty." Realizing that belief in capital punishment was deeply embedded in the American consciousness, they were cautious about discussing it with their acquaintances. The supporters of the death penalty were often influential citizens, pious Christians dedicated to charity. What use would it be to tell them that murder was usually committed on an impulse, while crimes against property were premeditated? What use would it be to refer to the most recent national statistics, which showed that the executed were almost exclusively disenfranchised, without proper defense, and often not of Anglo-Saxon origin?

Cora considered the death penalty a powerful instrument of repression against minorities. At any given period in history, murderers seemed to come from those groups that were striving to carve out an autonomous existence for themselves within society.

When a journalist from the *Reporter* asked him whether he believed in the death penalty, the famous American judge Noah Davis answered with bitter irony: "Of course, of course; it's the most capital thing in the world! If it were not for capital punishment, I would expect to be murdered before reaching my home tonight."

In Paris, a few months before Maria's tragedy, the controversial trial of Emile Henry took place. He was charged with the bombing of the Terminus Café. When the judges sentenced him to the guillotine, Henry turned to them and said:

"My crime is a reaction to all the murders the government commits every day. Who gives you the right to take the life of your fellow citizens?" Georges Clemenceau, who had been following the trial, stood up and said: "*Malheureusement, il a raison.*" ("Unfortunately, he is right.")

There were supporters of the death penalty who were convinced that certain people do not have the right to live. Others said it was too expensive to keep convicts in prison for life. Omar Sage, the warden of Sing Sing (who was opposed to the death penalty), estimated that it would take five thousand dollars a year to keep Maria Barbella in prison. The main guard, Mrs. Vincent, was paid one thousand eight hundred dollars a year, and her assistant, Matron Zimpcamp, received a salary of one thousand dollars.

CHAPTER TWELVE

Thirty miles from New York, on the east bank of the Hudson River, where three hundred years earlier the Sintsink Indians' smoke signals rose, stands the massive hulk of Sing Sing state penitentiary. The long building of rough gray stone was completed in 1828 by an army of convicts. They had quarried the stone on the spot, transported it, broken it, mixed it with debris and iron slag, and piled it stone upon stone.

The main building had not changed at all over time. Not a ray of sunlight had penetrated those walls in over sixty years; they oozed with dampness every summer. The crimes the prisoners committed in Sing Sing were often more savage than the ones for which they had been incarcerated—born as they were of absolute desperation and impotent rage against their harsh jailers. Suicides averaged one a month. Of these deaths, the outside world knew nothing.

The day began with a head count at 6:00 in the morning. Half an hour later, a bell rang and the inmates went to empty their slop pails in an open sewer. At seven, they were marched into the mess hall, where they were fed a breakfast of prison hash mixed with potatoes or cereal. The midday meal consisted of a piece of meat with bread and coffee; there were never any fresh fruits or vegetables. At six they ate a light dinner. Sleep was next to impossible: the New York–Albany railway line ran under the southern entrance gate, and the train's rumble, magnified by the tunnel, shook the stone walls.

This was life at Sing Sing: If a man had to serve a one year sentence, he spent 5,380 hours in a dark cell and 3,380 hours sitting on a bench during the day.

In 1892, when Omar V. Sage became warden, the prison was still functioning like a medieval institution. Horrified by the barbarous conditions, Sage made some changes: Criminals are not beasts, he believed, but men who have deviated from the right path. His style was strict and unyielding, but never needlessly cruel or inhumane.

The inmates were no longer forced to attend Sunday services. Except for those on death row, they were allowed to write as many letters as they chose, as well as notes of complaints and suggestions to be put in a special box. Smoking was allowed, although not in the cells.

The 1,403 inmates had not been told of Maria Barbella's arrival, but the news traveled fast: a young woman had entered their hideous world. No one was allowed to see her, and yet the mere idea of her presence caused a disturbance throughout the prison. Her fate became everyone's concern. The presence of a young woman on death row was something special: it awakened in the prisoners memories of mothers, sisters, wives, and lovers. Many of them, like Domenico, had savagely mistreated a woman. But this was different: a woman was about to be executed. Instantly, Maria became a Joan of Arc, and no inmate doubted her innocence.

The rumor spread that she was beautiful. Many messages to Maria were put hopefully into the complaint box, but they remained undelivered. The men who had prepared Maria's cell and made her the rocking chair had done so with care. Maria's every word or gesture soon made the rounds of the prison. Her state of mind, her health, every item of news about her was thoroughly discussed. Everyone knew she had been allowed to wear her own clothes—which her mother had brought—and that she always wore black. When her guard Mrs. Vincent asked why she did so, Maria answered, "Me dress black for Domenico . . . He live, he die, same me dress black."

In a July 24 interview with the *Herald,* Sage stated: "Her behavior is blameless. She is a model prisoner."

It was not difficult to imagine what lay behind Maria's "blameless behavior." The girl was completely isolated, not only from the world but also from the prison life, and spent her days rocking in her chair, as if that movement kept her company. She hardly spoke, not even to complain of the stifling heat that tormented the other prisoners. Under her calm and infinitely patient demeanor lay a dreadful thought: the chair, that chair which could kill her, was lurking in some corner of the building, maybe very close to her. Even remembering Cora's reassuring words before she left the Tombs gave her no relief.

"I told Maria the prison is in the country, near a beautiful river," Cora told the *Sun.* "That poor girl was so nervous and exhausted I feared she was going to die before reaching Sing Sing. I also told her I had been sent by Queen Margherita, and I asked her to have faith in me. Maria embraced me and said she did truly trust me."

Segregated from everyone and everything, terrified at the prospect of a foul death, Maria let her mind wander in a labyrinth of illusions.

"Maria is not always conscious of having killed Cataldo," Mrs. Vincent confided to the *Recorder* on July 30. "Sometimes she says he is dead, but does not think he was murdered. Here at Sing Sing we are all convinced that she was not herself at the time of the killing."

"Do you like Mrs. Zimpcamp, the new matron?" Mrs. Vincent asked Maria one day.

"She's nice, but she never . . . she never sleeps," Maria answered. Unaware that she was under round-the-clock surveillance, the girl was wondering why the matron stayed awake at night.

"He angry to me," she added in her warm voice. "But I no care for that, only say 'me marry' and he say 'tomorrow, tomorrow.' He no dead."

"He no dead." This was a refrain that everyone, including Julia Sage and her daughters, soon got used to. Only one other idea was as persistent as the thought of Domenico.

"Me dream," she told Mrs. Vincent one morning. "Me back home . . . in Ferrandina. . . ." The fantasy of her native village in Italy was a recurrent one. For Maria Barbella, the world was reduced to the hope of seeing Domenico Cataldo and her native country once again.

One evening, the *World* ran a startling headline: "MARIA BARBERI IS PREGNANT!" The telephone in Sage's office rang incessantly. Other newspapers demanded details: was she five months along, or close to giving birth? Would the prison physician, Dr. Ervine, deliver the baby? "THE FIRST CHILD BORN AT SING SING!" announced the *Herald*. The story raised questions that had never been considered before. How could a pregnant woman be executed? Did the law on capital punishment take these circumstances into account? And what about the execution of a woman who had just given birth? Under what law could a newborn be deprived of its mother?

The truth was that the *World* had invented Maria's pregnancy outright. The press was obviously determined to exploit her case to the fullest. While the news was traveling, Sage called Charles Chapin. He was told that the information had been received from credible sources close to the girl, but Chapin refused to reveal them.

For at least a week, the press continued to profit from their falsehood. Maria did not know about the rumor, nor about the anguish it caused in the dank rooms of the Mott Street tenement, where a small wax candle in a glass of water burned for her night and day beneath an image of the baby Jesus. Maria's parents were given the news when a journalist from the *Recorder* came to their house to deliver a six dollar contribution from an anonymous reader. When the newsman came in, Mr. Barbella was sewing—he had finally found some work—and Filomena was ironing with a coal iron. At the announcement of Maria's alleged pregnancy, Filomena could not prevent herself from crying out. She assumed it was a lie, but she was aghast at the thought that everyone was going to believe it.

"Have you paid your rent?" asked the reporter.

"Yes," answered a young boy who appeared suddenly. "Oh yes, last month the lady in black from the Tombs paid it. This month it was paid by the lady in white from Italy."

Meanwhile Rebecca Foster had obtained permission to visit Maria from Judge Goff. There were no limitations, and Cora could visit as well.

On Thursday morning, July 25, Mrs. Vincent told Maria in an official tone: "The Countess di Brazzà will be coming to see you this Sunday."

When Cora and Detalmo, on their first trip to Sing Sing, entered their train compartment, everyone turned to stare.

Cora carried a canary in a cage. Canaries had become a fad ever since a German bird breeder had written in the *World* that they not only courted and kissed each other, but could even learn to speak. Cora thought a bird would be good company for the girl, so she telephoned Sage and requested permission to bring one. The warden was reluctant at first, but eventually gave in. So the canary, along with Cora and Detalmo, found itself on the train to Ossining and, although it didn't talk, its nervous chirping attracted everyone's attention.

The couple stayed at the American Hotel, a charming establishment on Ossining's main street. The owner was happy to welcome them and proudly pointed out that his hotel had been the first in the country to circulate the petition for Maria among its guests. In the dining room that night, Maria Barbella's case was the main topic of conversation, along with proposals on how to prevent train robberies, which had become extremely common: a gang had recently held up the New York–Albany express.

The next day, Cora spent two hours with Maria in her cell, reading her passages from articles written about her in Italian newspapers. The girl was surprised to see her own name in print and traced the large letters with her finger. Cora's calm voice gave the printed sentences an almost magical spell.

Meanwhile, Detalmo, who did not have permission to visit Maria, had the grisly privilege of visiting the death chamber containing the electric chair. Sage threw the switch, and Detalmo heard the crackle of electricity as it coursed through the apparatus.

On Monday, July 29, the day after Cora's visit, a great change took place in Maria's cell. Julia Sage came in, followed by an inmate carrying a large square of glass and a tool kit. The man went to the cell's only window, giving Maria a long, searching look. Then he removed the windowpane, which had been painted gray—death row prisoners were not allowed to look outside—and substituted it with the transparent one. Sunlight invaded the room and Maria ran to the window. Fascinated by the glow of the setting sun over the majestic river, she remained there, staring into the vast summer landscape. The sun slowly vanished and darkness came, and still she did not move.

CHAPTER THIRTEEN

*I*n Washington, the possibility of Maria's execution was keeping the Italian ambassador, Baron Fava, awake at night. The telegraph line with Rome was buzzing.

In New York, the Italian Consulate at 24 State Street was under siege by journalists. On July 23, the Italian Consul General, Giulio Branchi, let reporters from the *Recorder* into his office. Asked whether his government would intervene in the matter, Branchi answered: "No, my government has decided it would be disrespectful to this country to intercede with Governor Morton. When Italians settle here, they must behave themselves and must expect to be treated as United States citizens would."

The consul thought that, had the murder been committed in Italy, the girl would have been treated very differently. The *Corriere Lucano*, a newspaper from Maria's region, would have given the incident no more than a blurb, and readers would have pondered the case no longer than it took to read about it. Probably, the story would not even have spread to the rest of Italy. What impressed Italians was not Maria's crime but the punishment, which they thought was shocking.

"In our country," explained Alberto Degli, the vice-consul, "Maria Barbella would have been sentenced to three or four years in prison, nothing more. Never would it be suggested that the girl had deliberately planned the murder. In fact, had Maria not sought vengeance, a male relative might have done it for her, to safeguard the family's honor."

"To tell you the truth, I don't believe she's guilty," the consul general continued, "and I will tell you why. When a girl of her social background is jilted, her first thought is that another woman intends to steal her man. So she has a single wish: to disfigure him so that the other woman won't want him anymore."

Branchi was certain that, were the appeal to be granted, the retrial would "delete the infamy of premeditated murder, which unfairly compromises the reputation of all Italians, here and abroad." Concerning the death penalty itself, the Italian position was unequivocal: executing a woman was an ignoble act.

"The legalized murder of a woman, in our time, would constitute a shame from which the State of New York and the United States would never recover," he added. "However, in this country an appeal is very expensive. The Countess di Brazzà is doing the impossible and my government is grateful to her. Personally, I think Maria Barbella should seek clemency without appealing her case."

Cora was more optimistic than Branchi. She was determined to obtain a retrial and was willing to finance the entire appeals process, as well as the public education campaign. But not everyone understood her and some of her friends were mystified. What could motivate her to dedicate so much time, energy, and money to the fate of a stranger? Others still, like Chapin, doubted the honesty of her intentions. Was she using the case to advertise her lacemaking schools, or out of a desire to see her name in print?

"That which people criticize today, they will imitate tomorrow," Cora was fond of saying to show her contempt for such base insinuations.

The *World* tried to undermine Cora almost daily. On July 19, the paper employed the old trick of mixing accurate and inaccurate information:

> The statement was publicly made that the Countess di Brazzà is ready to aid the murderess with money, and will ask her friends to do the same. The countess now declares that she has been misquoted. . . .

Cora was, in fact, helping Maria financially, but what she asked of her friends was only that they try to exert their influence over public opinion.

Another article in the *World* on July 25 attacked her more indirectly:

> The *World* has learned certain facts of importance in connection with the Barberi case. It states them here without quoting its authorities for reason of propriety, but it states them as facts.
>
> At the time the sentence of death was passed upon the Italian girl it was understood in official circles that there was to be a commutation. The governor was to be petitioned to change the sentence, not as a condonation of the crime but in recognition of the mitigating circumstances of the case.
>
> On receipt of such petition, whether signed by one citizen or ten thousand, the governor would have sent it to Judge Goff with a request for his opinion as the law requires.
>
> The judge would have replied with a clear-cut declaration that while the law required a verdict of murder in the first degree, the circumstances made the case precisely one of those in which the ends of justice would be best served by the exercise of executive power to save the woman's life while protecting the community against her passions by locking her up.

Upon this the governor would have commuted the sentence, and the law would have been satisfied.

Unfortunately, indiscreet zeal secured new counsel for Maria Barberi. The new counsel filed a notice of appeal. . . . It is one thing for a governor to interpose between sentence and execution, and quite another to take the case out of the hands of the courts. . . .

The same hysterical zeal has seriously embarrassed the governor's action on another level: he has no sympathy with the contention that the woman's crime is justifiable. . . .

It is a pity that counsel and sympathizers have not let the case alone. . . .

Detalmo saw the accusation of "hysterical zeal" as a direct slur against his wife.

Meanwhile, the *Sun* dispelled the rumors that large sums of money were being raised with the announcement that "the Countess di Brazzà wants it to be known that money is not necessary for Maria Barberi's appeal."

On July 29, a stranger gave the Savoy Hotel doorman a letter addressed to the Countess di Brazzà. The typewritten message was anonymous and to the point:

> *Dear Countess:*
> *Desist at once all further involvement in the Barberi case. Make a public statement announcing the closing of your pointless campaign.*
> *Act within two days or you will be forced to act.*

Cora was not afraid. Rereading the note, she was certain that the unknown author was only trying to intimidate her. Whatever her opinion of it, the threat was significant: The campaign for Maria had inspired a wave of hatred and resentment. But against whom? Was Cora the target or was it Maria herself? Was the author of the note a strong enough supporter of the death penalty to resort to murder in its cause? Was it a matter of intolerance toward Italian immigrants? Was it an attack on feminists? Cora could not answer any of these questions.

"I am a stranger in my own country," she sighed. But she did not consider for a moment abandoning her battle for justice, not even when, that afternoon, another warning arrived: It was an exact copy of the first letter.

In response, Cora gave a statement to the *Herald* in which she denied certain false rumors and defended herself from the accusation of "hysterical zeal." With calm determination she explained that before intervening on Maria's behalf she had patiently awaited a sign that it might be possible to obtain justice for the girl. She had even asked to speak with Judge Goff, who had declined to meet with her. She had begun her campaign after all else failed.

According to the law, an appeal had to be filed before the first day of the month of the execution. The unusually speedy sentencing, which had set an execution date of August 19, provided only eleven working days in which to file. Nevertheless, Cora had let three days lapse during which the bureaucracy could have stopped her campaign.

Once the movement to save Maria began, it acquired a life of its own which the justice system—and politicians—simply had to take into account. Cora told the papers:

> . . . From Texas to Massachusetts have already come news of
> mass meetings, and from Maine to California requests for slips
> [petitions]. . . .

America is above all things a government for the People and by the People, and what man or woman would dare to obstruct our highest aspirations for good?

We demand mercy for Maria Barbella and all unfortunates, and shall do so as long as there is need for it.

The threats continued: two more arrived the following day, one in the morning and one in the evening. The hotel lobby was always so busy that it was impossible to identify the mysterious messenger. The last letter was found near the revolving entrance door, on the morning of July 31. It contained the dramatic phrase: "Today is the last day."

Detalmo had had enough. He asked his wife to remain in her room with Mrs. Tingley, her secretary. He forbade her to answer the telephone or open the door, and gave the doorman orders not to allow anyone or any phone call through. Then he set off to see the newly appointed police chief, Frederick Grant, who was a friend.

Son of former President Ulysses S. Grant, Frederick was one of those men who place friendship above not only political advantage but also professional foresight. To the dismay of his Republican colleagues, he was taking a big risk in defending a police captain accused of corruption. The Republican party was girding itself to reclaim the presidency from Grover Cleveland, who was facing domestic and foreign crises. At home, unemployment, labor strikes, and an invasion of immigrants boded political change. Abroad, in Cuba, an insurrection had broken out, and a confrontation was brewing with the British over Venezuela. The possibility of war had caused a furor on Wall Street. It was no time for carelessly damaging the Republican cause.

Detalmo showed Grant the threatening letters, speculating that the author was a lunatic not worth worrying about. But

Grant answered: "My dear friend, a madman is more dangerous than a criminal. I will immediately arrange for your wife to
have adequate protection. Beginning tomorrow, one of my
men will be at her disposal twenty-four hours a day."

The next morning, New York policeman Joseph Petrosino
became Cora's bodyguard. A thirty-five-year-old Italian from
the province of Salerno, Petrosino's powerful build was evident
under the dark gray suit he wore when escorting Cora. But
since his first day on the force, twelve years earlier, he had been
the shortest policeman in New York: he measured just five feet
two inches. He did not have a beard and his face was disfigured
by smallpox. Although his bulldoggish appearance did not
inspire confidence at first, it was eventually impossible not to
admire his indomitable courage. His beat was the Mulberry
Bend neighborhood, where he had earned a reputation as the
Black Hand's archenemy. Petrosino's aim was to destroy it, and
he went about the task with unyielding persistence and great
ability. He was familiar with the crime syndicate's rules and
methods, its membership and hierarchy both in America and
in Italy. He had an uncanny ability to anticipate its moves. He
was a fluent speaker of several southern Italian dialects and
knew the taverns of Little Italy as well as a farmer knows his
fields. He had made an art of his detective work.

Petrosino questioned Cora for more then two hours about
the anonymous threats. He wanted to know exactly when she
had arrived in town; what she had done every hour of every day
since; the names of all the people she had talked to—when,
where, why, and whether in person or on the telephone; which
means of transportation she had used, horse carriage, or train—
why, when, where, and with whom, and so on. So much had
happened in those few days that Cora's memory faltered, but
Petrosino did not give up. He did not take notes, but he sat
motionless and attentive, looking at her seriously and taking in

every detail. In the end his only comment was: "I will get to the bottom of it. It will only take me a few days. . . ."

From that day on, Petrosino was always at Cora's side. He followed her with such discretion that she often forgot he was there near her, never losing sight of her. Cora and Detalmo were bewildered: when did he find the time to investigate the mysterious threats? Petrosino himself was a mystery. They concluded that his function was solely to protect them. But one morning, Petrosino unexpectedly announced: "I think I am on the right track."

CHAPTER FOURTEEN

$\mathcal{T}$he summer of 1895 was marked by an exceptional heat wave. While the immigrants of Little Italy spent most of their time in the street, escaping their suffocating tenements, many of the rich flocked to Manhattan Beach, where they displayed their indifference to the searing sun with a bright parade of boaters and parasols.

Manhattan Beach, which ran in front of the stately summer homes of Sheepshead Bay, represented the triumph of the entrepreneurial genius of the financier Austin Corbin. He had built the Marine Railway, connecting the beach to the Long Island Railroad, thus making it easy for New Yorkers to visit his hotel and gamble at the nearby racetrack, which he also owned. It was at his hotel that Cora and Detalmo stayed for a short while. They listened to glide waltzes, strolled on the broad seaside promenade, and dined with friends across the bay, but above all they made that holiday resort a launching pad for the Maria Barbella campaign. Manhattan Beach was the haunt of New York's high society, including a solid sector of the press, the government, and judicial circles, and Cora's combative spirit finally met its match in this large company of influential people.

The *Herald* confronted former senator Thomas Platt, but not before Cora had spoken to him. "I feel the deepest compassion for Maria Barberi," he told the reporter. "Last Friday I was in the company of our governor, and I heard him express his anxiety for the girl."

Interviewed on the boardwalk, former New York governor Roswell Flower concurred. "While I believe in capital punishment," he told the *Recorder*, "I am also convinced that certain situations call for mercy. Men who have committed crimes of passion with less provocation than this poor woman has endured have not been sentenced to die. If I were still governor I would commute the sentence or even, if possible, grant her a pardon."

Austin Corbin himself wrote Governor Morton a letter: "I am under the impression that for the people of our state, the Maria Barberi affair is more important than any other case: If this woman were to be executed it would be difficult to cancel the disgrace that would fall upon us all."

New York's Episcopal leader, Bishop Henry Codman Potter, was related to Cora: His son James was married to her first cousin Cora Urquhart, who had left society circles for an acting career. Potter became one of Maria's supporters and raised his authoritative voice in her defense. He stated to the *Brooklyn Daily Eagle* that "Maria Barberi had been induced to the crime by a social code different from ours. This constitutes an excellent motive for clemency." At the same time he warned the public against "those who exact revenge on their own." And as his interviewer wrote: "With Bishop Potter clemency means commutation and not the full pardon that Countess di Brazzà and many other women hope for."

In the *Sun*'s editorial, the bishop took a stance more favorable to Cora's position.

. . . Asked what he thought should be done with Maria Barberi, he replied: "Why, I thought everything was already being done for the poor child. I don't think her sentence will be carried out."

"And regarding the justice of the sentence?"

". . . Surely responsibility does not rest equally with the cool, deliberate wrongdoer of mature years and this childish, ignorant, hot-blooded Italian girl. . . ."

The Bishop spoke most cordially of the Countess di Brazzà and her efforts to save the girl. . . .

Having already secured the support of a former senator, a former governor, and a bishop, Cora was on the hunt for even more illustrious names. Robert Green Ingersoll, known as the "great agnostic," had already contacted her.

Ingersoll was a lawyer and a philosopher. His speech at the 1876 Republican convention in Cincinnati did not assure James Blaine's presidential candidacy, but his eloquence made him famous overnight. His orations always drew a crowd, especially in his native state of New York. Having followed Maria's trial closely, Ingersoll had done some careful research before stepping into the fray. He wrote in the *Recorder*:

I do not believe that ever before in the history of our country has public opinion through the press been so forcibly agitated over any one case as in this of the Italian Maria Barberi. People have comprehended at last, perhaps unconsciously, the profound truth of the ancient philosopher: "Homo sum et nihil humanum alienum a me puto." In my opinion the acting parties must be reversed—that is, the alleged victim must be considered the real criminal and the alleged criminal the real victim—just that and nothing more. It is therefore a question of justice and not of mercy; and if justice the woman cannot obtain in our honorable country, then let her have mercy!

It was probably Ingersoll's statement that made Maria's case one of national importance. By the beginning of August, the Barbella affair was known and discussed in cities all over the United States. Liberals and Catholics, feminists and leaders of society, pragmatic reformers and true romantics, all maintained that Maria should live. Through letters to Governor Morton and an avalanche of editorials, the nation harshly criticized the State of New York.

The racial aspect of the case roused Italian-Americans. A letter arrived from Galveston "in the name of the Italian-American residents of Texas":

> We the undersigned, assembled in a mass meeting, solemnly state that Maria Barberi's sentence constitutes a ferocious absurdity . . . that if such a crime had been committed by an American woman they would have made a heroine of her; that in executing a woman not responsible for her act, the United States would lose the esteem which the civilized world has granted. . . .

The Italian-Americans of Patterson, New Jersey, organized a benefit performance of "The Harp Player" by the Vittorio Alfieri Theater Company, and the famous actress Lina Lodigiani played the leading role.

The *Tribune* received a letter from Hartford, Connecticut, written by a bedridden invalid who specified that he had lived three years in Italy. He strongly defended Maria's actions and "was using an inkwell which had belonged to the great Giuseppe Garibaldi" to write the letter.

Governor Morton's desk was covered with protests against the death penalty, such as one from Newport, Rhode Island, signed

Charles Stanzone: ". . . May your pardon of Maria Barberi be the death sentence of that most outrageous remnant of a barbaric age, an indelible stain in our civilization: capital punishment."

There were also those who held rather extreme opinions on Domenico Cataldo's behavior toward Maria. In a letter to the *World,* R. H. Nott of Brooklyn stated:

> The fact is that the girl was betrayed under promise of marriage, a crime for which under Jewish law the criminal was taken outside the city walls and stoned to death, but a crime for which the nineteenth-century law gives no commensurate redress. . . .

The *Washington Post,* the *Hampshire County Journal,* and Boston's *Arena* all took Maria's side.

The former governor of Kansas, John St. John, expressed his opinion to the *World* in the form of a question: ". . . Had Maria been the daughter of a millionaire, would she have been sentenced to die?"

A Catholic priest, the Rev. J. M. Lucy of Little Rock, Arkansas, promoted a petition that was signed by people throughout the state, including Governor Clarke.

Former Supreme Court Justice Lyman Brinkerhoff of San Francisco told the *Recorder:* "In my state the girl would be in no danger whatsoever. In traveling across the continent from the Pacific coast, I heard the case discussed in the compartments. Not a single soul was against her."

Europe did not remain silent. Its protests usually had a note of chivalry. Viscount Jardy de Montracy wrote from Paris: ". . . If a man comes into my house at night and robs me, I have the right to kill him, but if a villain robs a woman of her virtue, she has no right whatsoever against him!"

Some letters were quite moving. "I'm amazed that men could convict under such circumstances," wrote a woman from

Kentucky. "It could not happen in my state. I will walk my feet
sore getting signatures. . . ." And a seventy-year-old woman
from Brewster, New York, offered to march all the way to
Albany to beg for the governor's pardon.

From Fort Scott, Kansas, came a strange proposal addressed
to "the Governor of Sing Sing":

> . . . I am against capital punishment. If the laws of your state are
> so strict that they demand the blood of a helpless woman, I pro-
> pose that the State of New York provide a passage for me to Sing
> Sing, and that I may be permitted to fill the doomed woman's
> place. Thank God I have an immortal soul that the laws of New
> York do not control, so I fear not what men can do. . . .

On August 1, the *Herald* announced:

> The Countess di Brazzà has received a contribution of $11.
> The countess insists that there is no pressing need for money,
> and is anxious to know whether the donors wish its return or
> its presentation to the girl's family. However, she states that the
> Barberis are not at present subjects for charitable gifts.

Despite Cora's repeated statements on the subject, money continued to flow in from all sides. George Pullman, the industri-
alist, donated sixty dollars and fifty cents, but the most
conspicuous amount came from the famous Broadway pro-
ducer Steve Brodie, who sent one hundred dollars. The money
was given to Maria's family.

The *Herald* unexpectedly ran a front-page article titled
"WORK OF MERCY BY A COUNTESS." The piece praised Cora's
initiative and courage as well as the sheer number of things
she had been able to accomplish in such a short time. It
quoted her:

It's simple, [Cora had said] persons of every walk of life have helped me. I have not been at all alone in this. I could mention hundreds of names of women and men who have come to Maria's rescue devoting time, money, and ideas to her situation. . . .

But the barrage of national attention seemed to have hardened Cora's opposition in New York. These detractors were convinced that, had common citizens not interfered, the criminal justice system would already have arrived at its own form of clemency.

Frederick House published a rebuttal in the *Herald:*

We would refuse to withdraw the appeal even if the governor in person demanded it. In any case every conviction of murder in the legal history of New York has always been followed by an appeal. There is no precedent for a lawyer abandoning a client in the hope of securing a commutation of sentence, and the suggestion is nothing short of an abomination. . . .

Asked to specify the first trial's irregularities, House gave a detailed answer: "In the first place, the defense was not allowed to corroborate the defendant's version, which was subsequently attacked. If the court had decided that Maria's story did not require validation, how could it then with integrity allow it to be attacked? The defense's witnesses were dismissed without being heard. We could invalidate Maria's conviction on the basis of O'Rourke's testimony alone. He described an alleged confession which was secondhand and acted as his own interpreter. The defense objected to evidence based on hearsay. Again, the girl was not allowed to call witnesses who could corroborate her story, while everything that tended to support the evidence against her was readily accepted."

Asked why the temporary insanity defense was not used, House answered simply: "There was not enough money for such a defense. Evans was appointed by the judge himself, and a temporary insanity defense is usually very expensive."

House's next words piqued the reporter's interest: "We are preparing Maria Barbella's case in all haste and intend to file it immediately before the Court of Appeals, which will not be in session until October 1. We have in our possession startling new evidence which will give a decisive turn to the matter. I cannot say more at the moment, but I am certain the press will uncover these astonishing and previously unheard-of facts."

In the meantime, Maria's detractors, too, had been busy and had come up with a seemingly airtight argument against her. The twin sciences of phrenology and physiognomy were at the height of popularity and were accepted blindly. Phrenologists believed the individual personality to be legible in the morphology of the skull. More often than not, however, these diagnoses were based on hindsight. Nelson Sizer, editor in chief of the *Phrenological Journal,* provided the *Herald* with a comparative study of the heads of the suffragette Susan B. Anthony and Maria Barbella. Sizer showed that both women had very strong features; however, while the Italian girl's cranium was "grotesquely asymmetrical," Susan B. Anthony's was not. The expert's catalogue continued with a description of Maria's "enormous" lips and "jutting" cheekbones. In Sizer's opinion, "the crudeness of her traits on the whole" confirmed her "lack of culture and refinement in the social, moral, and aesthetic sense."

According to him, Maria was passionate rather than sentimental, inclined to impulsive acts and, if provoked, could react "like a trap snapping shut when the fox steps into it." Sizer added that, had Maria used poison to kill Domenico, "it would have been more difficult to prove her guilt, because this method requires an intellectual subtlety completely foreign to the woman in question."

The phrenologist then turned his attention to the circumference of Susan B. Anthony's occipital bone.

The size of her head would convey an imperfect notion of its value: This woman has a brain with a purpose from which she never swerves. . . .

She is violent in defense of her principles. Her iron determination is shown by the length of the line from ear to ear to the top of the head, and by the extent of the chin downward and forward. The breadth of the chin, the squareness of the bones, the direct blue gaze, all contribute to the pronounced power of her brain. . . .

The signs of connubial sentiment are wanting in the lower back of the head, in the eye, and in the center of the upper lip. Her mouth is set and firm.

Her maternal instinct is directed to the whole race, not to the joy of having children. Her universal form of love is further indicated by the absence of that graceful curve near the outer mouth of the upper lip, which is the characteristic of the typical feminine mouth. . . .

Maria Barbella had never heard of the legendary Susan B. Anthony, whom the press called "the murderess's supporter" and who defended Maria with all the "iron determination that her jawbone betrayed." Nationwide, suffragettes, whatever the size of their skull, were following her example.

"Day after day, the cause of women's suffrage receives what are, and rightly so, mortal blows at the hands of its own supporters," read an editorial in *The New York Times*. "To anyone who believes in the rule of law, the recent public statements made by those who support the cause of women's suffrage demonstrate once more that women should never be granted political equality."

"And what of men's right to vote?" wrote Ellen Battelle Dietrich from Cape Cod in reply. "No one speaks of it, despite the Brown case in Kentucky, which is scandalous at the very least."

The recent Brown case involved a man who had killed a couple in a jealous act of revenge. The judge and jury knew the motive, and yet it was deliberately not mentioned during the trial.

"The essence of Americanism is that no government is just which does not rest upon the consent of the governed," Susan B. Anthony declared. "We do not punish infants and idiots for murder, for we understand that such culprits should be judged according to their knowledge, freedom, and responsibility. But our laws condemn women to the political status of infants and idiots, and punish Maria Barberi in a way that is not inflicted on a man as guilty and dangerous as the murderer Brown."

The August 8 *New York Times* disagreed with her:

. . . Let us suppose the position reversed, that the woman, after having maintained with the man relations that were proved to exist, had broken these relations, and it was the man who thereupon turned and killed her. Would there have been a movement for his pardon on the part of any distinguished representatives of the male sex? Clearly not. The movement for the pardon of Maria Barberi is distinctly incompatible with the demand for equal rights and equal privileges for each sex, for it is a movement for the pardon of a woman under conditions which would not give rise to a movement for the pardon of a man as a man. It is a distinct infringement of the principle that what is sauce for the goose is sauce for the gander. . . .

The story of the young woman languishing in Sing Sing had also captured the imagination of painters and artists. Among them was a successful playwright of the New York Yiddish theater, Moishe Ha-Levi Ish Hurwitz.

A shrewd self-promoter, talented improviser, and master fundraiser, Hurwitz was the P.T. Barnum of the Yiddish stage. To publicize an opening in 1888, he had choreographed a pageant with knights on horseback, orchestras, singers, and multicolored floats that went from the Lower East Side to Poole's Theater at Astor Place. Thousands of New Yorkers turned out in the August heat to watch it. The "Professor" himself, as Hurwitz was called by his entourage, led the parade in a top hat and wide sash, living up to his reputation as the Lower East Side's most elegant gentleman.

As far as Maria's story was concerned, Hurwitz intended to follow his usual working method of gathering material, waiting for his subject's notoriety to reach its peak, then quickly adapting it for the stage. The finale would match the current of public opinion: indignation if the sentence was carried out, or indignation if it was not.

In an article titled "MARIA A FREAK BY PROXY," the *Herald* suggested ". . . that should Maria Barberi be pardoned, she will center upon a professional career as a dime museum attraction. Managers of such concerns find that crime has an immediate money value. . . . She would find her rival in wax. . . ."

The *Herald* was right. Wax figurines of Maria were ubiquitous: The curiosity shop at Macy's, the amusement park of Coney Island, even the Bowery were invaded by life-sized replicas of "Maria the murderess." Maria didn't know that outside the cell she shared with Cicillo, her chirping canary, she had become as famous as a Broadway star.

CHAPTER FIFTEEN

*W*hile Maria's celebrity grew and House prepared his case, Police Lieutenant Joe Petrosino continued to shadow Cora, befriending Detalmo in the process. Detalmo had a human warmth which even the habitually withdrawn Petrosino could not ignore. The two men made an odd pair: one a tall worldly man who enjoyed being taken for Count Leo Tolstoy; the other a short, unmistakably southern Italian with a large head and bulging muscles.

Petrosino intrigued Detalmo with his stories about the Italian underground. From New York to Chicago and New Orleans, he knew all its haunts and ways. "There is no single organization operating in the name of the Black Hand," he explained. "The reality is one of many competing clans at war with one another. The notion of a single organization is a device for disseminating panic, nothing more." Petrosino also confirmed Detalmo's opinion that men who left southern Italy to settle in America were rarely criminals at heart. They did not intend to become gangsters. Used to hardship, they were prepared to take any job and be exploited at half wages in order to send money home. They also sent euphemistic letters: bricklayers wrote that they were *"costruttori di palazzi,"* "builders of palaces." It was not easy for immigrants to adapt to the life of exile, but it took severe mistreatment to push them to criminal behavior.

"This is why Pasquarella set up her organization," Petrosino told Detalmo. Who was Pasquarella? Detalmo had never heard of this woman from Marcianise, near Naples, who presided over a secret world. She was in fact the "the grandmother of organized crime," the forerunner of Al Capone, Lucky Luciano, Albert Anastasia, Frank Costello. Her official business, a horse stable, occupied an entire block on Park Avenue between 108th and 109th streets in Manhattan.

"Pasquarella never sleeps," said Petrosino. "She spends the night in the basement of her stables, taking care of her real business. She is the queen of organized crime and is constantly surrounded by ten bodyguards." A tall redhead, Pasquarella led a small army of men trained in the use of knives and other weapons. She commanded them with an iron fist. The tenets of their organization were loyalty and silence. Members were expert in the use of arms, in the discreet art of picking pockets and stealing wallets, in breaking into safes and cleaning out houses without leaving any telltale clues. "Until recently she had no competition. She was the boss," Petrosino continued. "But now she's in for trouble. Someone else has moved in on her territory." The intruder was Don Giosuele, already known as "Zio Mico" (Uncle Mico). Petrosino knew everything about him, his "life, death, and miracles," as Italians say. The Black Hand was conceived in Don Giosuele's establishment on First Avenue, between 109th and 110th streets, a typically small and airless saloon like the one in which Maria had slashed Cataldo's throat.

"Crime always leaves a trace," said Petrosino, explaining his craft to Detalmo. Petrosino's art lay precisely in the ability to follow a trail and neglect no detail. He was a master of disguises and could take on many identities. If necessary, he would pose as a hobo and live for long periods in the streets; or he might work as a laborer in a factory, or assume the look of a starving peasant just off the ship, searching for work. He could play the roles of bootblack, coachman, priest, or even gangster, a role which came easily to him.

In his search for the author of the threatening letters to Cora, Petrosino had taken on yet another role. Having followed several blind leads, including a fruitless search for Domenico Cataldo's relatives—his brother Louis, the streetsweeper, had vanished—Petrosino concluded that the Black Hand was not involved. So, following an intuition he'd had since Cora had told him of her meeting with Charles Chapin, the editor-in-chief of the *World,* he had gone undercover as a reporter into the *World* newsroom.

One morning, Petrosino called Cora and Detalmo. "The author of the letters is Charles Chapin. I can prove it." The policeman had found out that the letters had been written with the typewriter Chapin kept at home: the paper, the typeface, and the ink corresponded exactly.

The two were speechless. What could possibly have been his motive? "Envy, malice . . ." Petrosino speculated. "I can arrest him immediately. . . ."

Cora and Detalmo looked at each other. "No, better ignore the whole thing," said Cora resolutely. "Chapin's arrest would deflect attention from Maria's cause. And then, I certainly don't need any more publicity and gossip about me."

Petrosino accepted her decision reluctantly. As the case would remain officially open, he was free to continue guarding Cora, a rather pleasant task. Chapin would probably not go further with his crude intimidation tactics.

Since Domenico Cataldo's death, there had been no shoeshine stand at the corner of Elm and Canal. The Italians in the neighborhood superstitiously avoided that place. In any case, no one seemed to miss Domenico, and someone had drawn a black cross on the spot where his chair used to be.

The people of Little Italy followed Maria's story with avid curiosity. At night, especially on Mott Street, men, women, and children sat on the steps of their squalid tenements and listened to the latest developments as if it were a fascinating romance novel. Those who knew English were asked to translate the daily news articles. In the weak light of an oil lamp, one read while the others listened carefully, trying not to miss even the smallest detail. Now and then, the story would be interrupted by lively discussions.

Those hot evenings spent listening, discussing, and weighing Maria's fate alarmed witnesses who, fearing arrest or any involvement with the law, had held their tongues throughout the trial. But now the scheduled date of the execution was near. No one in Little Italy, not even Maria's family, had really understood that the request for appeal acted as a stay of execution, and everyone was certain that Maria would soon be dead.

One morning, a man limped into Frederick House's office and shyly introduced himself. Mr. Vicenzo Salvato was an Italian shoemaker, lame and widowed, with a small shop in a Spring Street basement. In faltering English, he told House the story of his daughter Cristina.

When she met Domenico Cataldo, Cristina was fourteen. She took care of the house, and Cataldo seemed to show up every time she went outside on an errand. She ignored him, but his requests became ever more blatant. When she began to run away every time she saw him, Domenico changed tactics. He took it easy. He stayed away for a bit, letting her think he had vanished, then would reappear. He told her she was the most beautiful girl he had ever seen, and one day convinced her to go for a walk with him. They strolled to Battery Park, where he pointed to an island in the distance and said: "Let's go to Staten Island." Cristina let herself be swayed: she had always wanted to ride the ferry. During the voyage, as the island of Manhattan faded into the distance, the girl panicked, but Domenico reassured her. He took her to a house where there was food and wine.

Her father looked for her everywhere. He did not turn to the police because, like many of his fellow immigrants, he was afraid of them, and in any case he was sure they would not have paid him any attention.

When Cristina returned the next day, he knew something terrible had happened and was able to elicit the whole story. Desperate, he went on a frantic search for Cataldo. He found him at home. He begged Cataldo to marry his daughter, but the man threw him out roughly.

Cristina Salvato was not the only victim of Domenico Cataldo. The shoemaker named at least five more girls, all underage, who had fallen victim to the licentious shoeshine man.

"Se Maria not kill im, somebody need kill im. For this he like go back to Italy. Se no killim yet becose people afraid man protect da Black Hand," he said, in a mixture of Italian and rudimentary English.

The next day an anguished woman came to the office. She was slim, blonde, and neglectful in her appearance. She refused to reveal her name and insisted on seeing House. When told that he was out, but that his colleague Friend might be able to see her, she disappeared as quickly as she had come. The secretary related to House that he had not been able to see her face, because she had spoken through a black veil, holding a dusty fan open in front of her mouth. "She must have been about thirty, her accent did not sound Italian, but I think she is," he concluded.

"She'll come back," remarked House. House was right. The woman reappeared the following day. This time she lifted her black veil, revealing an angelic face with porcelain skin and nervous blue eyes. Her worn, once-white lace blouse was now an indefinite color, and her parasol was torn in several places. House let her speak without interruption.

"My name is Antonia Turini," she began. "But please don't tell anyone I've been here. Domenico Cataldo was my lover. He had a way with women I can't explain. He could make them laugh, tell them what they wanted to hear. It happened a week or two before Maria went to live with him. He was not my first lover. I was not an ingenue and I knew his reputation. . . ."

At this point her story took an ominous turn. "I stopped at nothing. I became an instrument of his will to get rid of Maria. The girl wanted to get married and he was certainly not the type. I knew that, too. But she kept insisting. He thought if we drove her mad she would kill herself, and that is what he tried to do . . . drive her insane. He was sure that Maria, sooner or later, would throw herself in the river. Every time I met her in the street, I followed her and told her how Domenico laughed at the idea of marrying her. 'Domenico says you're not even good for cleaning the floor,' I whispered to her. 'You're so insignificant he doesn't know how he ever thought of speaking to you. That's right, and he says you were the one who went after him . . . and he was drunk that day . . . if he'd been sober, he would have died rather than go with you.' Maria never reacted, she didn't say a word and walked on. He was sure that she would eventually kill herself. It was just a matter of time. Instead she killed him, and now I must thank her for it. My life is what it is, but at least he's not around anymore."

House was wondering why Maria had never mentioned those incidents to anyone. That alone could have saved her. Had she really lost her mind after killing Domenico?

The American justice system was a mystery to most Italian immigrants. They found it inconceivable that witnesses were

DOMENICO CABALDO

*Domenico Cataldo, from a newspaper sketch
at the time of the first trial.*

sometimes detained, while defendants could get out on bail.
For these and other reasons, including fear of the Black Hand,
yet another witness had stayed in hiding. Nando Tavolacci,
former owner of the Tavolacci Bar, had not even followed the
newspaper accounts. Since that fateful day when he sat down

to play cards with Domenico Cataldo, he had tried in every way to ignore Maria's case. Nando had sold the bar on East Thirteenth Street to the Mangusos sometime before the murder, but he continued to go there. He was such a regular customer that it had not been necessary to change the small sign at the entrance that said "Tavolacci."

At the time of the killing there were four people in the bar: the proprietors, Vincenzo and Caterina Manguso; Maria's mother, Filomena Barbella; and Nando Tavolacci. During the trial, the Mangusos and Filomena had been considered prejudiced witnesses, and Nando was never even mentioned.

"The true story of the murder has not been told," Mrs. Manguso told House. "Nando Tavolacci knows it, and knows it all. Two days after Maria's arrest, he confessed to me that he had all the evidence. That's what he said before he disappeared. . . ."

House said he would ask the police to track down Tavolacci. But Caterina Manguso objected: "We're looking for him. We don't need help from anyone; we know how to make our people do what's right."

Sure enough, Nando was found two days later. He was not inclined to see the lawyer, but he went. While he revealed what he knew, he perspired and stammered as if he were signing his own death warrant. House's reassurances did not comfort him, and neither did the promise that he would not be arrested. He did not fear arrest but something far worse, and he insisted that his name and address be kept secret.

Within a couple of days the press uncovered Nando's story, which House had refused to divulge to the *Recorder*. A *Herald* headline read:

WITNESS TO MARIA'S CRIME READY TO TESTIFY THAT CATALDO PUT HIS HAND UPON A STILETTO. FEAR HAD KEPT HIM SILENT!

. . . Maria has repeatedly asserted that at the time she entered the saloon where Cataldo was on the day of the crime, he was seated at a table playing cards with another man. The stranger disappeared. This man, whose name and whereabouts Lawyer House is not ready to make public, was found by George Borcia, a barber of No. 283 Bowery. This witness to Maria Barberi's vengeance tells a story which, if true, makes the unfortunate woman's act one of self-defense.

. . . The man says that he distinctly saw Cataldo put his hand quickly into his breast pocket when the woman approached, and that a few moments before, he had seen the handle of what seemed a stiletto protruding from his pocket. Whether Cataldo succeeded in drawing the knife or what became of it, the witness does not know, but he positively asserts that what he says is true. . . .

The *Recorder* instantly published a highly melodramatic version of the same story:

. . . Cataldo was done with her. He tired very quickly of his victims. He wished for a fresh one every month. He had tried by all his demoniacal ways to shake her off—he had treated her with brutality, had sent her insulting messages through his latest mistress, had openly laughed in her face when she begged him to marry her. But she, constant to the single thought that he must make good her name, still pursued him. He would run away from her, go back to Europe, and then return quietly, hoping to escape her by keeping away from his old haunts. . . .

When Maria came in to make her final appeal for justice, Cataldo saw her coming, and the stiletto in his vest pocket glittered as his hands instinctively sought its handle. The man, sitting with him at the table, took one look at the girl and dropped the cards from his hand. Her eyes were glaring wildly.

Like a flash, Cataldo was on his feet, stiletto in hand, but before he could strike, a razor had slashed his throat. He ran out and up the street, and did not pause until he reached a pile of beer kegs at the corner, where he tottered and fell and died. . . .

Cataldo himself told the man that Maria was crazy. Out of his lips, which are now dead, came the evidence on behalf of the girl who slew him. . . .

The stiletto, which Cataldo dropped when he staggered out of the room, disappeared. . . .

The *Recorder* had gone too far. No witness had ever testified that Domenico had drawn the knife or brandished it after jumping to his feet. Cora did not appreciate this awkward attempt to plead Maria's case. The new information was valuable enough: there was no need to embellish it. The knife had been mentioned in the police report, and therefore the arresting officers O'Reilly and Hay knew of its existence. Consequently, Goff and McIntyre also knew about it. But during the trial there had not been the slightest hint of it.

It was a colossal oversight, more than enough to declare a mistrial and prove the negligence of all the participants. It was the small error that can compromise an entire operation.

Cora thought Maria's initial defense team only incompetent, but Detalmo was not as indulgent. If his admiration for the United States had never lacked strong reservations, his talks with Petrosino had made him think that a kind of grand conspiracy was responsible for the Italians' ill fate. The image of New York as an ideal melting pot in which different races could merge was false: The city was in the grip of nothing less than a conflict between armed factions. Detalmo ironically compared it to Napoleon's occupation of Italy. The Italians in New York had taken a long voyage to find even more unbending masters, to become subordinate to Irish and Jewish immigrants. Despite their reputation as criminals, Italians were, in many ways, the most docile and exploited immigrant group. An 1890 study noted that "in the poor neighborhoods [the Italian] is welcomed as the tenant who will give the least problems. . . ." In other words, thought Detalmo, the Italian behaves exactly in the manner of one who is content to live in a degrading condition and be exploited.

While the social mechanism was unable or unwilling to protect Maria, the machinery of death proved to be quick and efficient. Circumstances such as the accused's state of mind, the abuse she had suffered, her illiteracy, and crucial evidence, such as Domenico's knife, had been sifted out of the trial testimony and then discarded as though utterly insignificant.

CHAPTER SIXTEEN

*T*he discovery of new evidence in her favor caused Maria's detractors to attack her even more vehemently. An August 3 headline in the *Brooklyn Daily Eagle* declared: "MARIA BARBERI NOT AN INNOCENT." The paper minimized Nando Tavolacci's revelations about the stiletto, stating that McIntyre had kept those aspects of the story under wraps in order not to "place the girl in a worse light than necessary."

Maria was described as a loose woman who had had many lovers, the implication being that she killed Domenico for money.

> . . . The crime occurred among a class with whom the officers of the law are much more familiar than are the sentimentalists who have made the outcry. . . . It would have been wise to investigate a little before they started their crusade. It was Davy Crockett who said: Be sure you're right; then go ahead. But Crockett was not a woman.
>
> Mr. McIntyre is convinced that a new trial would show the woman in a much worse light than the first one did. . . .

In response to a flood of letters, the governor's secretary Ashley Cole made a statement to the *Tribune* and the *World:* "In my long experience I've never seen such an overwhelming expression of public opinion. A sensational craze has pervaded the whole country from Cape Cod to the Golden Gate," he said. "However, the lack of knowledge regarding the real facts of the tragedy, the woman's motives, her age, and her social condition, is astonishing. Thousands fear that she is to be executed in two weeks, and a great many reporters believe the condemned woman to be a child of fifteen. It is necessary to make it clear once and for all that Governor Morton cannot intervene on this question until a decision is made regarding the appeal, and that these solicitous letters are useless. . . ."

The *Brooklyn Daily Eagle* informed its readers that "among the letters was one from the Countess di Brazzà." On the envelope were the words "personal" and "urgent" in capital letters.

While the governor kept silent, his wife, in an interview with the *Herald,* declared herself "absolutely in favor of Maria." Cora was greatly heartened by this, as she knew the woman had great influence over the governor. News from Washington also renewed her optimism. President Cleveland had just commuted the sentence to death by hanging of Thomas Taylor, convicted of killing his wife.

Taylor had declared himself insane, but the jury believed he had accidentally shot his wife during a suicide attempt. Because the District of Columbia did not recognize different degrees of murder, the judge was forced to sentence him to death.

President Cleveland had accepted a petition for commutation by numerous prominent citizens with the statement that ". . . In deciding this case, I cannot depend on the theory of insanity or that of premeditated murder. . . . This commutation is granted because there is not sufficient evidence for premeditated murder. I believe that, on the basis of the facts which have been put forward, it can legitimately be deduced that the discovery of his wife in flagrant adultery could have altered Taylor's mind to such an extent as to induce him to take her life in a moment of blind rage."

On the wave of enthusiasm generated by the positive outcome of the Taylor case, mass meetings in favor of Maria were organized in various cities. In Boston, two thousand people filled Faneuil Hall, holding signs calling Maria "a victim of ingenuity and true love." In New York on August 1, protesters filled Germania Hall at 291 Bowery. The hall was festooned with American flags of every size. "It was a most unusual assembly, a unique case in the history of this state," wrote the *Recorder*. "Despite the heat, people flocked in long before the appointed time."

Cora was not present at the Germania Hall rally. She was at Sing Sing. The warden had allowed her to bring Maria a white kitten Detalmo had found while on a walk to Grant's Tomb on Riverside Drive. Cora went with Mrs. Foster and, as always, Petrosino. When the women entered Maria's cell, the kitten, after a fearful glance in the canary's direction, jumped into the girl's lap.

The next day, at noon, the twenty-one-year-old daughter of General Daniel Flager, commander in chief of the military supplies section, went to the Washington police and said: "I've come to turn myself in. I have just shot a Negro."

Like the other youths in the neighborhood, Ernest Green was attracted to the laden fruit trees in General Flager's vast garden. One morning, the boy put a hand through the iron railing to take a fallen apple. A pistol shot rang out. Ernest tried to run, but another shot felled him. The first .32-caliber bullet had struck him in the back. The second had punctured his lungs.

Having confessed to murder, Bessie Flager was sentenced to three hours of jail time and a five hundred dollar fine. The fact that she was even arraigned caused an uproar in Washington. The press immediately took her side, commiserating with her shock upon learning the boy had died. In the end, they wrote, it had been an unfortunate accident, although it was difficult to explain how it had happened.

The case contrasted sharply with Maria's. While Bessie Flager once more took up her place within Washington's high society, Maria Barbella faced death. Cora shook her head and remarked: "The United States are like a painting whose bright colors disguise large areas of shadow. . . ."

The deadline for the presentation of Maria's petition to Governor Morton was set for August 5. Throughout the night of August 4, volunteers of every age and class canvassed Manhattan to gather the largest possible number of signatures. Every method was fair game: people were stopped on the street, signs were posted on shop windows, petitions were placed near cash registers in department stores. In Amos Evans's office, which had come to resemble a post office, another group of volunteers sorted the signed petition slips—150,000 in all. The inalienable right to petition, sanctioned by the Constitution of the United States, was not often put to use. The flood of signatures now proved that the public had been deeply affected by the Maria Barbella affair and had not hesitated to use that form of civil protest.

"The law is not fast-paced," House told the *Herald.* "It took a month just to obtain a transcript of Maria's sentence. If a new trial takes place, we will present all the new testimony and the girl will certainly obtain a light sentence, if not a full pardon. If, however, the court were to uphold the previous verdict, the new evidence will be submitted to the governor and the girl's life will depend exclusively on his willingness to grant executive clemency. Meanwhile, Maria can do nothing but wait patiently."

At 11:03 on the morning of August 5, Emanuel Friend was on the train to Albany, on his way to the governor's residence, where he would hand in the official petition and all the signatures. That day, in Sing Sing, thirty-one-year-old Richard Leach and the Italian immigrant Vincenzo Nenno were executed. Unaware of this, Maria sat on her rocking chair near the window, stroking her white kitten. When the train passed, the girl did not even lift her head.

CHAPTER SEVENTEEN

*I*t was a difficult decision for Cora and Detalmo, but the responsibilities of home called: they had to return to Brazzà. The month of September brought intense activity, due to both the grape harvest and increased production at the lacemaking cooperative. And they missed their daughter, Idanna. Detalmo was also anxious to install his new invention: a pump which would bring running water from the spring to the house and stables. He had shown it to two prominent American companies, and they had made him some interesting offers. Cora did not want to abandon Maria, of course, and there was still a cardinal to recruit. Cardinal Gibbons of Baltimore, Cora's spiritual advisor and family friend, was about to return from an audience with Pope Leo in Rome. Both Cora and Detalmo thought that his support was worth a short delay in their departure. When they finally managed to connect with his eminence, Cora felt that the infrastructure they had built for Maria Barbella would stand without them. House, Friend & Grossman had her case in hand; Mrs. Foster's frequent visits, the attention of Matrons Vincent and Zimpcamp, and the concern of Mrs. Sage assured that Maria was well looked after; the editor of the Italian newspaper Cristóforo Colombo had offered to pay for Maria's relatives' monthly travel to Sing Sing; and even Father Ferretti of the Church of the Transfiguration was planning to visit her.

Finally, toward the end of August, Detalmo and Cora set sail for Italy. Joe Petrosino had insisted on accompanying them to the last and stood on the wharf, hands in his pockets, watching the steamship making its way out of the harbor.

The American press quickly lost interest in Maria, and her world shrank again to one room. But news of her situation regularly reached Brazzà. Rebecca Foster wrote weekly. Cora liked to translate these letters and read them aloud to the lace-makers, who followed the story of their compatriot in the New World as though it were a serial romance novel. One week they learned of her insomnia, the next about her night-mares. They were incredulous at first, but Maria's legal odyssey was an American story they could compare unfavorably to those told by the *padroni,* the labor recruiters who enticed Ital-ians to emigrate.

Evocative lithographs of steamers and ocean liners bound for New York or Buenos Aires decorated the walls of many a tavern, and the peasants were fascinated by them. According to the *padrone* who hawked steerage tickets on these ships, any intelligent man willing to work could make a fortune in those far-away lands. Now the women of Brazzà knew a case history which they could juxtapose with the *padrone*'s promises of broadcloth suits and gold chains. For the Brazzà lacemakers it was a revelation to learn that, in America, a prison cell was preferable to the living quarters in certain neighborhoods.

The first news from Sing Sing was not comforting. "Blood, blood," Maria cried out in her sleep, according to Julia Sage. "She has stopped smiling once again. Sometimes she kneels on the bare floor and prays. My husband allows her to go to church. She sits behind the altar, where no one can see her, and listens to the inmate Charles Douglas playing the organ."

"She is obsessed with Cataldo and misses him," wrote Matron Vincent. "But I think it's not him she really misses but rather the great love story she thought she had found. When she speaks of him she always says 'my Domenico,' but she never alludes to the way in which he died."

One day they heard that Maria's appeal had been filed in Albany, and then came a long letter from Julia Sage saying that Maria was better. It contained a surprising postscript: "I learning to read. Also write. Thanks. Love. Maria Barbella."

The girl had been transferred from her room in the infirmary to more permanent quarters. She now had a small apartment with a private toilet. Her sitting room, where she sat in her rocking chair during the day, contained a cane-seat steamer chair, a four-legged stool, and a table. The bedroom had two cots, a washstand, and a chair. Although she no longer had the river view she loved, she was definitely more comfortable.

Maria's meals, unlike those prepared for the other inmates, came from the infirmary, and sometimes even from the warden's own kitchen: beef stew or mutton on Thursdays and chicken on Sundays. Maria had never before eaten as well as she did now, under sentence of death.

The two matrons took turns watching her under the constant vigilance of a prison guard. Julia Sage visited her once a day, not only out of concern but also because she liked the girl's company. In one of her letters to Brazzà, she remarked that the descriptions of Maria did not do her justice. She thought Maria had a natural charm and kindness.

When she received visitors, Maria unconsciously adopted the manners of a hostess. An observer might have been struck by the girl's dignity as she welcomed Julia Sage by kissing her hand and inviting her to sit down in her cell as though it were an elegant drawing room. One evening, her dinner came while Mrs. Sage was still with her. The girl shyly offered her a cup of tea, which was accepted. Soon that became a ritual.

Unlike during the first days of her detention, Maria now asked for news of people she knew. She would inquire, for example, about Bessie, a girl she had met while at the Tombs, after whom the kitten had been named. Bessie had a similar story. She had shot the man who had seduced her with promises of marriage, blinding him for life. When Julia Sage told her Bessie had been acquitted on grounds of temporary insanity, Maria's answer surprised her: "Maybe now he'll marry her." To which Mrs. Sage answered cautiously: "But he's blind and cannot support her." Maria said impassively: "It doesn't matter. It's Bessie's turn to work and take care of him."

Maria was never idle, and crocheted with such speed that Julia Sage could barely keep up with her requests for cotton and wool. She made scarves for the other inmates and for her visitors, as well as doilies for the warden's home.

One day Mrs. Sage asked whether she had ever studied English, and Maria said she used to have a "children's book." So the woman decided then and there that she would teach her, and had a grammar, a notebook, a pen, and an inkwell brought in. On alternate days, Julia Sage gave her one-hour lessons. Matron Vincent looked over Maria's work and made conversation with her on such simple subjects as the relationship between Bessie the kitten and Cicillo the canary. The warden's daughters, Elizabeth and Mary Sage, who were about the same age as Maria, helped her with her spelling and accent. They forbade her to speak Italian, and soon Maria was able to tell little stories about Ferrandina and its customs in English.

She told how her native village had no running water—just like Mott Street—and how she would follow the women to the public fountain near the cemetery, carrying an earthenware pitcher on her head. She described the women who did the laundry on stone slabs, thirty at a time; as they scrubbed and gossiped, a man watched over them from above, regulating the facility like an umpire.

She told of her ocean crossing and her first sight of the New World. On deck, a voice had shouted, "Look! Liberty! La Libertá!" She didn't know what it meant and had wondered whether the person was pointing to the city in the distance, to the big sky above, or to the huge iron bridge over the river. Not until she met Domenico did she discover that Liberty was the name of the great statue anchored like a ship in the harbor.

Maria complained only of the lack of fresh air. "How I would like to go for a walk. . . ." she would often say, looking through the bars at the warden's garden, but she was forbidden to go out.

Julia Sage also wrote Cora that her husband was going through a difficult time: John McKane, the former Coney Island boss convicted of electoral fraud and a prisoner at Sing Sing, was dying of kidney failure. The fatal illness did not move the governor, who had rejected a petition for his pardon.

In October, Rebecca Foster wrote to Cora that the Court of Appeals had met after its long summer recess, but the clerk, Parks, did not know when Maria's case would be taken up. House did not tell his client that she might be in isolation for a long time to come.

On October 18, Julia Sage forwarded a second brief letter from Maria. Like the first fateful news Cora had received six months earlier, the message arrived in the midst of a happy occasion: Detalmo and Cora's wedding anniversary. The estate, Brazzà, was open for one of those special garden parties that lived on for days afterwards in the region's gossip. The guests boated across the small lake, which was densely surrounded by willow trees, and then circled the tiny island with Idanna's imposing doll's castle in the middle; they played tennis on the only court for miles, admired the collection of African heirlooms, visited the inventor's workshop, strolled in the botanical garden, or climbed among the medieval ruins buried in vegetation.

Maria's message read: "Dear Signora. I love you very much. I dream you not come back. What will happen to me? Come see me soon. Your girl, Maria Barbella. P.S. I kiss your right hand."

A few days later Cora left for Ferrandina. She had located the town on an atlas and called its mayor, requesting a meeting with him before winter set in. The mayor had answered with a telegram: Due to the lack of hotels, he would be honored to have her as his guest and would give her a small apartment inside the town hall. It was not luxurious, but the women of his family would be at her service.

Cora set off alone, not knowing that her fame preceded her. The village of Ferrandina had followed Maria's story in the local press and through letters that came from Little Italy. Cora's objective was to gather information about Maria: perhaps someone would remember her, and the defense lawyers could find a good character reference useful.

She did obtain a certificate, sealed by the municipality and signed by the mayor, which attested that Maria did not have a criminal record at the time she left the country, already a young woman. Her visit to Ferrandina also contained some surprises. She found out that Maria's uncle Giovanni, the blacksmith, was a known drunkard. Her mother suffered from fainting spells and was once "possessed by the devil." An exorcist had been called from Matera to "free" her.

It seemed that, on her mother's side, Maria's family had several cases of epilepsy and mental instability. The father's side was less troubled. Everyone remembered Michele Barbella as devoted to his work and family, a man who had known little good fortune and many hardships. Cora even obtained the names and addresses of three immigrants from Ferrandina living in New York who had firsthand knowledge of Maria's family history on her mother's side.

At the end of October, there were still no new developments in the Barbella case and the press was silent on the issue. The newspapers had focused on the forthcoming marriage of Consuelo Vanderbilt and the Duke of Marlborough, which would take place in November. It was the first time that a British duke was to marry in an American church.

The major crime story of the day concerned one Herman W. Mudgett, alias H. H. Holmes, "the greatest murderer in the history of America." He was charged with killing at least twenty people over a period of twelve years. "The devil only knows how this individual could dismember and burn innocent children . . . For my part, I cannot begin to imagine it," District Attorney Graham had said at the trial, which was held in Philadelphia.

On November 5, election day in New York state, Mrs. Foster went to Sing Sing with the entire Barbella family: mother, father, the brothers Giuseppe, Carlo, and Giovanni, and the sisters Antonia and Carmela.

Maria stood at the door to her cell, which was decorated for the occasion with a bunch of roses from Sage's garden. The conversation was in Italian. Mrs. Foster had brought her a fashion magazine, a copy of *Uncle Tom's Cabin* by Harriet Beecher Stowe, a box of pretty stationery, and some crochet thread. Filomena gave her daughter a family heirloom, her own terra-cotta handwarmer. Thanks to a special permit, Maria was allowed to take leave of her relatives with a kiss.

That night, for the first time in her life, Maria fell asleep while reading a book.

On November 17, a telegram from New Orleans brought to Brazzà the news of the sudden death of Cora's uncle, Robert Day. His wife Sallie, who had gathered hundreds of signatures for Maria, was perhaps Cora's most intimate friend. According to the *Daily Picayune* the death was accidental: hearing someone prowling on his property one night, Robert had left the house holding a rifle. He tripped and a shot went off, hitting him in the chest. Cora knew, however, that her uncle Bob had committed suicide and she could not imagine a motive: he was a respected and happily married man.

In December, Julia Sage wrote that, according to House and Friend, the Court of Appeals would not consider Maria's case until after Christmas.

That year, the Brazzà Christmas tree was over eleven feet high, and Cora had it placed in the entrance hall. As was the tradition, all the peasants came to the villa with their families, and everyone received a present.

One peasant was distraught over the loss of a cow during a storm. Cora bought a cow and tethered it to an oak tree behind the house. Then she tied a string to one of its horns and ran it to a branch of the Christmas tree, attaching a little card with the man's name on it. She did the same with her daughter Idanna's presents, which were scattered all over the house and the garden, so that the girl had to follow the strings to discover all her treasures.

At the Sing Sing Christmas dinner, the 1,403 inmates ate a total of 1,900 pounds of chicken fricassee with bread and potatoes. Before marching back to their cells, each received some lemon crackers and two cigars; those who received Christmas boxes from home were allowed to take them into their cells.

The happiest inmate of all was a young man by the name of George Nesbitt. He was in prison for having presented a bad check for $750 to the Kenmore Hotel in Albany to pay for a $600 bill, hoping to pocket the change. After six years of free room and board, his Christmas gift was a pardon.

The Convent of Mercy in New York sent Maria a large box of cookies, which she shared with her fellows on death row.

Julia Sage came into the girl's cell with a huge bunch of mistletoe and gave her Cora's present: an Alençon point lace blouse made at Brazzà. Maria threw her arms around her and kissed her. Ignoring the cold, she took off her loose-fitting woolen shirt and put on the delicate blouse, buttoning all the buttons. It fit her perfectly. She went to the window and admired her own reflection through the bars.

The prison resounded with Christmas music and singing. Almost all the inmates took advantage of their holiday right to sing in their cells. Some were practicing for the five o'clock concerts that were scheduled for both chapels. Admission was free to the public. As it was an all-inmate performance, some asked that only their initials be listed in the program, fearing someone in the audience might recognize their names.

The organist, Charles Douglas, convicted of the rape of his neighbors' thirteen-year-old daughter, was considered Sing Sing's musical genius. Bach and Albinoni were played in the Catholic chapel. The Protestant program opened with the overture to Boilieu's *Baghdad Caliph,* followed by the romantic melody *Come Where My Love Lies Dreaming,* and the comic opera songs *The Man Who Broke the Bank in Monte Carlo* and *Woman's the Cause of It All.*

At the end some transparencies were projected. The first read, "Merry Christmas." The next one asked: "What's wrong with the warden?" followed by the answer: "Nothing." At that point applause broke out, and all eyes turned to Sage.

The men and sole woman on death row were not allowed to come out of isolation to go to the concerts. Maria stayed in her rocking chair, deep in Uncle Tom's adventures. It took her half an hour to read one page, and she often asked for Mrs. Vincent's help. Finishing the book was a task that would take a long time, and certainly there was plenty of that.

CHAPTER EIGHTEEN

𝒜lmost ten months after Maria's sentencing, the press finally remembered that a woman was still on death row at Sing Sing. At ten o'clock on the morning of April 7, 1896, the Court of Appeals in Albany met to review Maria's case before Judge O'Brien. Assistant District Attorney John Lindsey, representing McIntyre, attorneys Frederick House, Emanuel Friend, and the newcomer Edward Hymes were present. The 28-year-old Hymes was already renowned in New York as one of the first attorneys to introduce psychiatry into his law practice. House was proud to have him on his defense team.

The only two members of the public in Albany that day were Cora and Detalmo, who had returned to the United States for the hearing. Judge John Goff was absent and had not even sent a representative.

The men on both sides squared off across a long rectangular table on a raised platform. House had before him the bulky transcript of Maria's trial. He apologized for any inconsistencies in his references: he had only been able to obtain a complete transcript a few days earlier and it was riddled with mistakes. The judge adjusted his glasses and shook his head. Such a delay was unheard of: Goff's hand was evidently behind it. House articulated his defense on fifteen points, detailing the multiple errors and inconsistencies in the first trial. It took him eight days to present his case, and Cora and her husband did not miss a single session. During the weekend of April 13, Judge O'Brien wrote his 6,000-word opinion on House's exposé. A harsh criticism of Judge Goff emerged:

"A careful review of the record persuades us that the principles of fair trial have been widely violated. The jury's most important decision was that concerning the woman's state of mind at the moment of the crime. The defendant had the right to make use of whatever testimony was legitimately relevant to the case in question." And finally O'Brien berated the extremism of Goff's charge to the jury: "The judge convinced the jury that, in order to reach a verdict, it was sufficient to consider only the woman's act at the moment in which it was committed. However, in so doing, all the events and circumstances of which the murder was but the culmination, were systematically ignored. That charge was a grave error on the part of the court."

On Tuesday, April 16, on the basis of the omitted testimony and Judge Goff's lack of impartiality, the Court of Appeals granted Maria Barbella a retrial.

Elated, Cora telephoned Sing Sing immediately. Sage, however, hesitated to give Maria the good news, as it also meant that she would have to return to the Tombs. The girl's happiness would be tempered by a difficult separation and by the frightful prospect of another trial. Cora took the first train to Sing Sing and, along with the warden's wife, told Maria what had happened.

The girl did not react and stood silently looking out the window. "I don't want another trial. Better die now," she said finally.

Julia Sage assured her the new trial would be easier than the first. "You must believe me," she insisted. "I would not lie to you. You might even be acquitted."

"This time you will not need an interpreter," Cora told her. "Your English is so good that you have nothing to fear. You only have to tell the truth and be yourself." Cora was right. Maria by now spoke a passable English, made almost musical by the sweetness of her voice. And the time spent at Sing Sing had changed her: she had become more poised and self-possessed.

"You must forgive me if I seem ungrateful," Maria then answered. "I know that if a new opportunity is granted to me, it is only thanks to the countess. But I am so frightened and I don't remember anything. If now I can speak English, I must thank Mrs. Sage and all the others who have had the patience to teach me. But I am so afraid," she repeated. "Will Mrs. Foster be with me in court again?" Cora assured her that she would, and this seemed to calm her.

But that was not all. In pained tones, Julia Sage told her of the upcoming transfer. "The only drawback is that you will soon have to leave us," she said quietly. "You will have to wait for the new trial in the Tombs." It was the last thing the girl wanted to hear. She had become used to life at Sing Sing, to the daily visits from Mrs. Sage, to the matrons, the warden, and his daughters. Leaving seemed unimaginable. She had been so comfortable at Sing Sing that the idea of being on death row, with the electric chair nearby, had become almost unreal.

"This is a penitentiary," Mrs. Sage explained. "We can only keep those who have been found guilty, not those awaiting a verdict. That is the law."

"When will they take me away?"

"You will travel to New York on April 26," answered Mrs. Sage.

Maria was pensive for a moment. "That's the day my Domenico died," she then whispered, lowering her eyes. It was true. A whole year had passed.

Ten days later, on the anniversary of Domenico's death, Detective Sergeant McNaught from the central office in New York arrived at Sing Sing with attorney Emanuel Friend. The warden was out, so the court order for Maria's transfer was given to Hickey, his secretary.

When Maria entered the office, Hickey, who had not seen her since the day of her arrival, could not believe how much she had changed. Slim and erect, Maria had lost some of her shyness. She wore a smart burgundy redingote suit with black grosgrain borders, which Cora had brought her from Europe, and the Governor Morton pin her little brother Giovanni had given her. Her hair was gathered in a graceful chignon and topped with a black felt boater that tilted elegantly on her head.

Then came the moment for good-byes: Maria embraced Mrs. Sage, who repeated that she would visit her soon and that Mrs. Foster was waiting for her at the Tombs. Maria shook hands with all the men present: the secretary (to whom she handed a note for the warden), the general staff, and the prison guards, all of whom she thanked for their kindness. Then she picked up the shining brass canary cage and left. As she was about to get into the carriage, Dr. Ervine, Sing Sing's physician, suddenly appeared and kissed both her cheeks. Maria asked him to look after her kitten, Bessie, who had been in hiding for two days.

"It's spring," said Maria jokingly. "She's tired of prison. But I'm sure she'll come back, and then the Sages can keep her and maybe change her name to Maria."

They reached Ossining in time to catch the 5:40 train to New York.

"MARIA BARBERI IS BACK IN THE TOMBS!" announced *The New York Times*. "Her nine months' stay at Sing Sing have cost more than any comparable detention of any other prisoner in the United States. . . . Nothing is known as to when the girl's new trial will be held."

Maria's return reignited the debate about her case. In an April 29 editorial, the *Brooklyn Daily Eagle* came to John Goff's defense:

> . . . Roughly put, the Court of Appeals decides that Maria Barberi was wrongly convicted and must be retried. If retried, her conviction of murder in the first degree will nowhere be expected and her acquittal on the grounds of insanity will be looked for. If this defendant was insane, she should never have been placed on trial. That grave error is a severe reflection upon the office of the district attorney, and on that office alone. . . .

The *Herald* analyzed Maria's anomalous position: she was about to go to court to affirm her innocence for a crime of which she had been previously convicted. The prosecution would of course cross-examine her on the basis of her testimony at the first trial, and Maria would either have to pretend she had forgotten all of it or say that her confession had been coerced. The paper also noted that jury selection was going to be difficult. It would not be easy to find twelve New York men who had never heard of her case.

Meanwhile, Maria was asking herself how long she would have to stay in the Tombs. Except for Matron Smith, all the faces were new to her. Slowly her depression came back, along with the nightmares that woke her. But this time she did not give in; she did not want to disappoint her friends, and so she clung to her crochet and her books. She had begun Jules Verne's *Around The World In Eighty Days,* and often looked at an illustrated book of American landscapes. And when she had opened her suitcase at the Tombs, she found a leather-bound prayer book: a present from the Sages.

Maria spent her days in the corridor, with a book open on her lap and Cicillo's cage at her side. The other prisoners envied her the little bird and began a movement to demand "a-canary-for-all-or-a-canary-for-none." Mrs. Foster interceded on her behalf with the new warden, Van Der Carr. Fallon had recently been ousted: His much-rumored cruelty had finally been exposed that January, when twenty of his prison guards made public a list of his malicious and brutal acts.

Maria was allowed to keep Cicillo.

CHAPTER NINETEEN

*W*hile Maria was being lifted in her imagination by Jules Verne's hot-air balloon, Detalmo was presenting his latest invention to the New York scientific community. The last decade of the nineteenth century was also the beginning of the era of thermodynamics. The carburator had recently been invented. The Lumière brothers had just patented a 35-millimeter moving picture projector and film. Aviation was making its debut. Inspired by Verne, a Russian visionary was even talking of outer-space travel and was attempting to calculate the velocity necessary to escape from the Earth's gravitational pull. Compared to these two adventurous spirits, Detalmo was certainly a more practical thinker.

Detalmo's impatience with postal delays in Brazzà had led him to transform the mailbox. Because his correspondence was slowed by letter sorters, he thought of mechanizing them. But it never crossed his mind to propel the letter sorters into the stratosphere or the ocean depths.

For an entire week in April, in the lobby of the Savoy, Detalmo demonstrated his mail registration machine. The public queued up during lunch hour to get a look at the Count di Brazzà, who stood next to what looked like a wooden desk.

On top were a slit for a ten-cent coin, one for receipts, and one for letters. On the side was a lever. When the inventor put a coin in, a registration coupon would come out of the top. When he inserted the letter along with the coupon, the lever moved. With a scientist's concentration, he pulled the lever; a bell rang and a receipt came out.

The entire operation took no longer than ten seconds for each client. Placed in any hotel or commercial building, the machine could be accessible round the clock. *Scientific American* called it "a great step forward in the efficiency of communications." The April 25 edition of *Illustrated American* dedicated an entire page to it, including a photo of Detalmo, in a pin-striped suit, seated next to his invention. "The count is currently working on the automatic register," read the text.

Rebecca Foster cut the article out and took it to the Tombs. Maria read every word, consulting her dictionary often. She did not understand much of it, but she proudly hung the picture of Detalmo alongside one of Cora on a wooden panel.

Count Detalmo di Brazzà with his postal machine.

At that time, however, it was not the postal registration machine that commanded public attention, but a more grisly apparatus that several jurisdictions were considering as a possible substitute to both the electric chair and the scaffold. Invented by George Jeremiah, a young blacksmith from Columbus, Ohio, the machine could break a convict's neck following more or less the same principle as that used by housewives to wring a chicken's neck. It combined the features of the Spanish garrote, the scaffold, and the electric chair in a single unit: Its inventor assured all that it was absolutely painless and much more cost-effective than the other instruments of capital punishment. The victim sat on a heavy wooden chair, the body tightly strapped in and the head secured to a head clamp. A heavy iron cap was lowered onto the head and firmly adjusted, while a wide strap held the neck to the block. At the moment of execution, a spring was released that made the head clamp rotate downward violently. The pressure would break the neck of any man weaker than an ox, without mutilating the body. The chair then extended into a stretcher for convenient postmortem, and the body could be returned to the relatives almost intact.

Due to stories such as these, Maria's friends were reluctant to let her read the newspapers. She had begun to ask for them, not out of interest in world events, but in the hope of reading news about her case which she suspected was being hidden from her.

With the passage of weeks, Maria even began to doubt that the Court of Appeals had actually granted her a new trial. Could she trust them? Long sleepless nights left her dazed. She was overcome by fear: of the future, of people, even of the guards pacing the hallway. Sometimes her head ached as though each strand of hair were a needle piercing her scalp. She often lost sensation in her hands and feet, hallucinated, heard screams. One day she saw Domenico coming toward her: he wore a hat, his mustache was freshly-trimmed, and his hands were in his pockets. He bent over the mattress to take her . . . No! . . . She was on a metal cot, Cicillo was still there, and her head did not hurt anymore. Maria touched the damp wall. Everything returned to normal when Matron Smith turned the key and light filtered in through the open door. Outside was the hallway, with all its chairs and the women who cursed, complained, waited. Soon Mrs. Foster would come, maybe with the news that the trial was set for the next day.

Mrs. Foster and Cora were convinced that Maria would not be capable of coping with the prospect of a long period of confinement. So, at the question: "When will my new trial take place?" they answered invariably: "Soon, maybe even next week." But the truth was that Maria would probably have to wait for months, until the fall. The prosecution was preparing its case with utmost care.

The time had come for Cora and Detalmo to return to Italy once again. They had gone to the Appeals Court hearings. He had obtained his patents, and Cora had been able to interest a Boston publisher in her new novel. Their daughter's birthday was approaching. Not that Idanna was ever left alone: Surrounded by aunts, uncles, cousins, the lacemakers, and her governess, she was certainly in good hands. The couple was convinced that for an only child, the affection of several people was healthier than exclusive parental love. Even so, they had decided they would not travel without her in the future.

Before leaving, Cora wanted to make sure that Governor Morton had reviewed all the petitions he had received, and that he would be inspired to make use of his executive privilege and grant clemency if Maria were to be found guilty a second time.

Cora telephoned Ashley Cole, the governor's secretary, to arrange a meeting before her departure. Cole asked whether anyone would accompany her. "Only my husband," Cora answered. A few minutes later, the secretary said the governor had agreed to meet with her and the Count di Brazzà, as long as the matter was kept absolutely secret. He ordered her to travel incognito and to get off the train at Croton-on-Hudson. At exactly 9:15 P.M., a carriage would take them to a hunting lodge in the woods of Ellerside, the governor's country estate. The door would be left unlocked and they were to enter without knocking.

Amused, Cora and Detalmo followed the instructions and so arrived at the hunting lodge. Ashley Cole was waiting for them in the small entrance hall; he led them into a drawing room, where they settled in two dark leather armchairs in front of a large fireplace. The wood-paneled walls were lined with stuffed trophies whose glass eyes seemed to stare at them menacingly. They waited under the fierce gaze of a Bengali tiger, slightly unsettled by such a display of human cruelty. They both abhorred the killing of animals for sport and even Detalmo's brothers, explorers in African jungles, despised sport hunters. The fifth rule of Cora's lacemaking cooperative was: "Treat all creatures of flora and fauna with kindness and fairness. Do not destroy, unless for survival or to protect the weak."

A few minutes had passed when a dachshund came trotting in, followed by Governor Levy P. Morton. A former vice president of the United States, Morton had been elected governor of New York the previous year, supplanting twelve years of Democratic rule. Tall and imposing, he was cleanshaven, which was unusual at the time. His thick gray wavy hair was parted on the left side. His wide tie was held by an enormous pearl and he wore a signet ring on his right hand.

The visit almost ran aground in formalities. The governor kissed Cora's hand in the European manner and complimented Detalmo on his postal registration machine. The brandy ceremony was followed by the pipe-lighting ceremony. There seemed to be no way to shake Morton's placid affability. How was their trip to New York? When were they leaving for Italy? Was Cora by any chance related to Joshua Slocum, the great navigator?

"Most likely," she answered, curbing her impatience. The names Slocomb and Slocum probably had the same origins, but it was impossible to know for sure, because fires had taken their toll on family records. The governor began to comment on a recently published book, *Sailing Alone Around the World,* which told of Slocum's adventures on his small boat, the *Spray.*

After an hour of this gracious conversation, Cora and Detalmo finally succeeded in shifting the topic to the purpose of their visit. The governor seemed rather cautious. When Cora expressed her fears about the new trial and alluded to the petition, Morton was quick to say he could not promise anything, but added that he approved the decision to grant the appeal. Despite the governor's lack of commitment, Cora was gradually reassured. Everything would work out for the best, said Morton as he took their leave.

On the 11:30 train back to New York, Cora and Detalmo discussed the strange visit and came to the conclusion that the governor was on their side. Two days later they embarked on an Atlantic crossing once again. Cora was in good spirits throughout the voyage.

In May, Maria disappeared again from the pages of the newspapers. The bass drum of the press beat to the rhythm of those headlines with which journalists claim to write their "rough draft of history":

May 22, 1896: CHEIRO THE RENOWNED PALMIST AT THE WHITE HOUSE reads the President's wife's palm. In the afternoon he is granted the honor of reading the palm of the president himself. He predicts that a son will be born to President and Mrs. Cleveland.

May 30: THOUSANDS TRAMPLED TO DEATH. MAD STRUGGLE OF 500,000 PEOPLE FOR BREAD AND GIFTS DISTRIBUTED IN CELEBRATION OF THE CZAR'S CROWNING.

June 21: More than 50,000 opium users live in the United States and the number is set to double within the next five years. Despite the fact that it is illegal, opium can be bought at the pharmacy without prescription.

July 1: Harriet Beecher Stowe, author of Uncle Tom's Cabin, died yesterday at noon in Hartford, Connecticut. She was 85 years old.

July 12: THE BERTILLON SYSTEM FOR THE IDENTIFICATION OF FEMALE CRIMINALS TO BE INTRODUCED AT SING SING. "Problems with the prisoners may arise," Warden Sage has stated while assisting at a practical demonstration of the method. "In order to be a valid identification, the Bertillon system requires a precise knowledge of the female anatomy, and we do not have a female physician here."

July 27: VIOLENCE BY TURKS AGAINST ARMENIANS CONTINUES. Reports of brutal bloodbaths come from Armenia. A handful of Armenians captures the Ottoman Bank in Constantinople and holds it for an entire day, while armed Mohammedan mobs slaughter all the Armenians they could find.

The bicycle craze continues with unabashed fervor throughout the United States and Europe.

Anton Chekhov went to Jasnaja Poljana where he was surprised to find Count Tolstoy bathing in a stream with his white beard floating on the surface. Chekhov then sat on the bank, while Tolstoy immersed in cold water, spoke to him of the book he has just finished: *Resurrection.*

Lieut. Robert E. Peary of the United States Navy returns from Greenland. To Mr. Peary is due the credit of being the first man to equip an Arctic expedition with a midwife and a baby carriage.

August 11: Professor Otto Lilienthal is killed in a glider crash in Germany, just after the success of his new flying machine on which he made long low flights with winds blowing up to twenty yards per second.

August 19: The engagement of the heir to the Italian throne has been announced. Prince Victor Emmanuel is to marry Princess Helena of Montenegro.

September 18: CONCERT FOR TOMBS PRISONERS. The women sat in the first hallway facing the central gallery where the musicians took their places. Among others, music by Hammerstein's Hungarian band was played.

September 21: Two hundred Indians slain to avenge a woman's murder. The Mill Creek Tribe in California was Massacred in a Night by Two Intrepid Hunters.

October 3: NEWS FROM THE TOMBS. At Last the Law Will Drag Forth a Prisoner for Trial. The City Prison Crowded to Suffocation by Persons Waiting Justice. A Vicious system at Fault.

Maria Barberi Will Finally Be Tried After Passing Almost Two
Years in Jail.

The reporter from the *World* found Maria in her cell, busy
reading a letter from Cora. Next to her was Cicillo's cage, and
on the table lay a cross beside a leatherbound prayer book.

Matron Smith told the journalist that Maria was a model prisoner. "Only once did her temper flare, when some women made
snide comments about her crime. Fortunately the Tombs Angel
was here and managed to calm her. Otherwise she's one of the
quietest and kindest young women we've had in this prison."

The reporter was appalled by the living conditions at the
Tombs, where men were packed three to a cell. On the day of
his visit, fifty mattresses were being distributed for extra bunk
beds. He wrote:

In the Tombs today there are 100 more prisoners than a year
ago. . . .

. . . Maria Barberi suffers perhaps less than the average prisoner because she occupies the position of a "star." Miss Barberi
is a "star" because she crept behind her Mulberry Bend sweetheart as he sat playing cards and killed him to "avenge her
honor." By this she became sanctified in the eyes of the evan-
gelists, and her condition was the signal for a storm of indignant protest. . . .

The circumstances under which Miss Barberi will appear in
court this time are different from those that confronted her
when she stood trembling and weeping before Judge Goff.
Then she was a frightened creature, unable to speak in any
tongue but her own, stupid in a blind, stubborn way.

Now she's a pretty woman, whose eyes flash with spirit, able
to express herself clearly in English. . . .

It is indeed difficult to recognize Miss Barberi in the grace-ful woman who yesterday stood before the matron's desk acting as an interpreter for an Italian prison mate. She became pale and serious only when she was told that she would be called for trial on Monday. But then she said: "I'm ready."

"Do you ever think of Cataldo?"

"I do . . . I love him. . . ."

"Love him? Why?"

"Why? He had lovely eyes, eyes that hold you. He came like the sun into my life and offered me what I thought was a decent future. . . ."

The trial did not begin on Monday, October 5. It was post-poned at the last minute to Tuesday, November 17.

CHAPTER TWENTY

*M*aria's second trial lasted twenty-four days, with sessions also held at night. Cora was absent throughout, but Rebecca Foster was always at the girl's side.

As anticipated, jury selection had not been easy: in a pool of fifty-two men, neutrality was scarce. One man was dismissed because he openly admitted he had a very low opinion of women. Assistant D.A. McIntyre rejected another because he knew Friend, the defense attorney. Albert Isler opposed capital punishment for women: rejected. Charles Fisher doubted Italians could be trusted: rejected. Charles Kurtz stated his inability to convict anyone at all of first-degree murder. Frank Klein, Isaac Epstein, Otto Schmidt, Michael Maloney, and Charles Carey all opposed the death penalty. Eugene Goenick believed all forms of punishment were useless. John Lapazo was struck because he was Italian and Jacob Steuhl because the tenants in one of his buildings were Italian. Robert Wood did not like Italians, nor did Henry Flackersenhaar, a Second Avenue grocer.

"Why not?" asked House.

"Well, they cut into my business," answered Flackersenhaar.

After two grueling sessions of twelve hours each, a jury was finally selected. They were twelve white men, who appeared to be neither chauvinistic nor overly gallant, neither racists nor avowed egalitarians. They were men who felt neither resentment nor compassion when they read the newspapers. There was a tailor, a silk merchant, a hatter, a milkman, a florist, a restaurant manager, a shirtmaker, a fabric and haberdashery merchant, a hops trader, and three owners of small factories manufacturing dresses, belts, and umbrellas.

Public attention focused on Maria again. Her case was a judicial sensation: a woman who had already been sentenced to death was being retried for the same offense. Many had a sadistic curiosity to see the woman, who had mobilized most of the nation in her defense, in the docks again. Others believed the result of her trial would finally clarify the state's position toward capital punishment.

From the very first day, the courtroom of the criminal branch of the Court of General Session was packed. A capacity crowd gaped at Maria. The rich and famous put in appearances. These included Cora's cousin, the popular actress Cora Urquhart; Mr. John Drexel of Philadelphia, an avid Brazzà lace collector; and the actress Mary Anderson De Navarro. Italians were in the majority, but, of course, the front-row seats were not reserved for the residents of Little Italy. First came the city's prominent citizens, intellectuals and socialites, then the law students and girls practicing stenography. There were also several students of psychiatry, due to the growing connection between that field and the law. Journalists were plentiful, and all the major immigrant papers had sent reporters: two Italians, two Jews, a German, and two Irishmen. Among the representatives of the five attending American papers was Charles Chapin from the *World*. The illustrators from the daily newspapers sat at their own reserved table.

Several lawyers were present and they were especially interested in the possibility that the defense might seek an acquittal on the grounds of insanity or epilepsy. If this line of defense succeeded, it would be a significant innovation in the American justice system. There was just one precedent in America, which had occurred a few months earlier at the trial of Michael McGowen. The young man had killed his fiancée in a particularly savage manner. His lawyers saved him from the death penalty by arguing that he was epileptic, and he was sentenced instead to life in prison.

In a recent statement, House had hinted at a hereditary illness in Maria's family. In any case, Paragraph 21 of the New York Penal Code ruled that "mental illness does not lift the individual from penal responsibilities except at the exhibition of evidence demonstrating that, at the moment of commission of the act, the person was not capable of understanding the nature and the quality of the act." Would the defense be able to prove that Maria was "not capable of understanding" at the moment of the murder?

No mention of epilepsy or mental illness had been made at the first trial. How would the new trial influence what had taken place sixteen months earlier? Both the defense and the prosecution had reasons not to dwell on the previous trial: the one because it had ended with a guilty verdict, and the other because of the prosecution's reprehensible conduct. The reputation and credibility of both sides were at stake.

Maria sat next to Mrs. Foster. She wore black from head to toe: a blouse with gigot sleeves, a pleated skirt, a hat with two feathers, and kid gloves. Her eyes were slightly reddened and her face perhaps too pale, but her expression was calm, almost detached. She stared at the east wall on the right, where the Fates were pictured: in the middle was the old hag spinning, with a skull at her feet and flanked by two comely maidens. Behind Judge Gildersleeve's desk was an allegory of Justice: a woman with stern black eyes holding the scales. Never once did the girl look at the jury, or the public, or her relatives sitting in the second row next to Father Ferretti. From time to time she whispered to Rebecca Foster, who would hand her a bottle of salts.

Those who had attended the first trial were surprised at Maria's new bearing. Many asked themselves how the girl could belong to a family which her lawyers had described as touched by insanity or illness; she seemed absolutely incapable of committing any reckless act, let alone violence. But the truth was that Maria was not well, physically or mentally. She had been sleeping badly, and, according to Matron Smith, she was prone to fits of amnesia. She was so weak that Dr. Ward, the prison physician who refused to comment on her alleged epilepsy, had supplied her with peptonoids so that she might recover strength without the labor of digestion.

On Friday, November 20, the prosecution opened the trial. Lauterbach listed all the details of the day of the crime. Agents Hay, O'Reilly, and O'Rourke repeated their story. The razor (Exhibit A) was shown to the judge; this time the prosecutors also showed the jury Maria's cotton calico dress (Exhibit B), caked with faded bloodstains. Maria stared at the sight of her dress. "Yes," she whispered when asked whether she recognized it.

There was an impromptu discussion on whether the defendant had been arrested on the street while washing her hands in Porzio's bucket, or in her rooms. House took this opportunity to point out that, where immigrants were concerned, police reports were rarely accurate. He also reminded the jury that the police had been the first to get Maria's last name wrong, an error which was perpetuated by journalists and lawyers.

Deputy Coroner Dr. John B. Huber described once more the gruesome sight of Domenico's throat at the time of the autopsy and stated that the man had lost every ounce of his blood.

Domenico's brother, Louis Cataldo, had been tracked down at the last minute, and the prosecution was hoping he would indulge in some animosity toward Maria. Not at all: He said he had ceased to associate with his brother two years prior to his death, that he did not care about the murder, and that he had nothing to say.

Bernardino Ciambelli of the newspaper *Il Progresso Italo-Americano* was called to the stand. He had interviewed Maria at the police station an hour after her arrest. He testified that two facts had emerged from her disconnected speech: prior to seducing her, Cataldo had offered Maria a mysterious drink. Later, she had gone to live with him because she was too ashamed to return home.

"How did she appear to you?" House insisted on asking him during the cross-examination.

"She seemed not to know what she was saying. She was talking in a disjointed way."

"Did she tell her story of her own free will?"

"No, I had to repeat my questions several times."

"Did she admit to ever having wanted to wound Domenico Cataldo?"

"She said that in the apartment that morning, when she was rejected again, she had had the impulse to attack him, but could not do it in her mother's presence."

"Are you sure of that?"

"One doesn't invent these things."

"Did she say if Domenico Cataldo beat her?"

Ciambelli could not remember that. House was able to make him admit that his recollection of that meeting had merged in his mind with a story he had written later. The quick notes he had taken of Maria's statements were not reliable.

Then came Vincenzo and Caterina Manguso, owners of the bar where the murder took place; the boy Michael Snyder, who had seen her wash her hands; Maria's employer Mary Tilley; Mrs. Deleva, Domenico's old neighbor; and, finally, John Gerders, owner of the Chrystie Street bar where Maria had a drink with Cataldo. Their accounts were more thorough. It became clear that Domenico had abused Maria's good faith, that the two had fought fiercely, and that he had taken her to the Chrystie Street bar.

At three that afternoon, House made his opening statement to the jury: he spoke clearly and simply, without affectation. He lingered on the Barbella family's extreme poverty:

"They were peasants from southern Italy," he said. "Poverty brought them to this country . . . Domenico Cataldo never had any intention of marrying Maria . . . One day he showed Mrs. Barbella a photograph of two women and said: 'These two are mother and daughter. Both have been mine. When the mother began to insist I marry the daughter, I left. Will I marry Maria? Look at this picture. As you can see I refused to marry a beautiful girl. No, I will never marry Maria!'

"We will present to you a witness who will testify to that under oath," House announced firmly. "We will also bring you a man who saw a knife in Cataldo's jacket just moments before Maria Barbella attacked him. We will bring to court a person who will swear to the fact that Cataldo boasted of having given the girl a drink that eliminated all her capacity for resistance. That witness will swear that he was called to the district attorney's office and that, having told his story, he was told he was not needed."

"Lawyer House!" blurted a red-faced McIntyre. "This is absolutely false! It is an infamous lie!"

"Well, and my witness will swear to it," answered House, resuming his narrative. He was a talented storyteller and possessed the novelist's gift for sequence, nuance, and understatement, deftly inserting his few surprises. The public was mesmerized and followed the familiar story as though they were hearing it for the first time. At the highest point of his narration, he revealed the defense's strategy:

". . . We must evaluate Domenico Cataldo's character only in so far as it allows us to understand the situation. The central reason for the tragedy is another one. The hand that wielded the razor that killed Domenico Cataldo was the hand of an epileptic."

There was a murmur of astonishment: the psychiatry students seemed disappointed, while the lawyers present in the public gallery opened their notebooks. House continued his narrative:

" 'Only pigs marry!' was the man's odious insult. At that moment, Maria's eyes flashed; everything around her darkened. She fell to the ground, senseless. Afterwards she stated she did not remember anything that had happened. Gentlemen of the jury, this is not a matter of an act of folly generated by a troubled mind. The hand that held the razor did not belong to a healthy woman. No. At that precise instant Maria Barbella suffered an epileptic seizure." House paused, then repeated loudly. "This may seem like a desperate plea. It has only been used four times in the history of criminal justice, twice in England, once in France, and only once in this country. But let it be clear that this line of defense is not a subterfuge but rather an absolute certainty. We have no choice: In any case you will hear Maria's family history and that will be enough to dissolve any doubts you may have. However, I warn you: the woman who killed Domenico Cataldo died immediately following her action. That woman today leads a different life. It is up to you to decide whether that life should be interrupted or not."

Maria sat, pale and absolutely still. Her hands were joined as though in prayer. She knew nothing about epilepsy and had never given much thought to her fainting spells. Even her sister Antonia sometimes had them. The Ferrandina doctor had diagnosed them as typical symptoms of puberty. "It means you are growing up," her mother had told her. And yet her mother, too, would faint, perhaps due to fatigue from overwork, perhaps due to the terrible winter gales or the violent summer heat. The doctor had recommended daily infusions of chamomile and sage. Once, after the death of an infant brother, the doctor had given her mother some white tablets. Two years in a row her mother had miscarried.

In America, it was Domenico who had made her sick: sick at heart, sick with fever, sick with nightmares. One night, for example, she had dreamed of a man with no eyes who sawed her body in half while Domenico held her arms. She had also dreamed of a scorching fire, and a crying horde of cats in heat. Maria called that world of terrifying images a "heavy dying sleep."

Leopoldo Porzio, the grocer with the shaggy black hair, was called to the stand. His eyes under the thick dark eyebrows were wary. He had been in America seventeen years and still spoke little English. His deposition was more explicit than the one he had given at the first trial. The two translators compensated for the absence of shocking revelations: Benedetto Morossi with his tendency to shout, and Paolo Vergara with his gesturing. It looked like a pantomime.

"What did she do then?" asked prosecution lawyer Lauterbach. Porzio mimed putting his hands in water, lifted them, and shook his fingers. The jury was embarrassed. "She immersed her hands in the water I'd been using to wash the windows," thundered Morossi. "She lifted her hands and said. . . ."

"Forget it," Lauterbach interrupted.

"Well, what did she say?" asked McIntyre.

"I don't remember . . ." answered Porzio.

Paolo Vergara shook his head.

"And what did you do?"

"I continued to clean the store."

The prosecution turned the witness over to the defense.

"Did you ever speak with Domenico Cataldo when he came to live near your store?" asked House.

"Yes, he used to come in to do his shopping."

"What did he say?"

"Two or three days before he died, he told me the girl had run away from home with him. 'She's not the first,' he said." Porzio looked heavenward and shrugged.

"Objection!" McIntyre burst out. "This has nothing to do with whether the woman was of sound mind when she killed Cataldo."

"We are not saying she was of unsound mind," Friend shouted from the table where he sat next to House.

"It does not seem to me," interjected Judge Gildersleeve, "that the defense is arguing the defendant was not of sound mind at the moment of the crime. I believe the defense has carefully avoided making such a statement."

"We propose that the defense make their statement now," retorted McIntyre. "We do not think their thesis of epilepsy is valid. Simple epilepsy does not make its victims lose recognition of what is happening around them. Alexander the Great was epileptic. As were Julius Caesar, Napoleon, and George Washington. Epilepsy does not justify a crime. . . ."

"Really?" Friend exclaimed. "The law supposes Maria Barbella was of sound mind."

House continued: "But the epileptic's mind is sound only when not in the grip of spasms from a seizure."

Here followed a long discussion about Domenico's words to Leopoldo Porzio. McIntyre insisted for more than an hour that they were pertinent only if Maria had killed in self-defense. This was a turning point, on the basis of which it would be decided whether to take Domenico's character into account or, as had happened at the previous trial, to ignore it completely.

"Surely," said House. "It is our duty to show how the man's behavior with women may have influenced Miss Barbella's state of mind when she attacked him! No testimony was admitted on this point at the first trial. The Court of Appeals, in its granting of a new trial, has stated that all testimony in favor of the defendant was improperly ignored."

But Judge Gildersleeve was not swayed. He ordered that Leopoldo Porzio's statements regarding Domenico be struck from the record.

"What did Maria look like?" House asked Leopoldo while turning triumphantly to the jury.

"She was . . . pale. Eyes like glass and foam at the mouth. She wiped her mouth with her hands and then put them in my bucket . . . She did not seem normal."

The prosecution attorneys jumped to their feet. After another argument they were able to have that statement struck as well. Leopoldo Porzio was not an expert and therefore could not judge Maria's state. But House and Friend were satisfied. The court stenographer could erase words from the record, but certainly not from the jurors' minds.

CHAPTER TWENTY·ONE

"*Simple* epilepsy will not save Maria from the electric chair," announced the *World*.

For all its cruelty, Charles Chapin's paper was probably right. And yet, saying that the girl had been in a seizure at the moment of the killing was more convincing than the "code of honor" explanation. House and Friend had carefully evaluated the various possibilities and had chosen the illness argument. An appeal based on Maria's cultural roots, or on her rights as an outraged woman, or even on momentary insanity, would have garnered support from some minorities, such as suffragettes and Italian-Americans, but not from national public opinion. The trial would have become an ideological battleground and the defense, no matter how courageous, could not hope to succeed.

Referring to his first months of research on the case, House told the *New York Journal:* "We were in the dark. However, when the Court of Appeals granted a retrial, the situation had already become clearer."

The vital information Cora had gathered in Ferrandina transferred the case from the political arena to the scientific one. Maria was no longer the victim of an indigent class or of an inferior condition due to her sex. She was no longer a woman forced to kill because of a barbarous southern Italian custom, nor a murderess for money. She was an epileptic.

It had not been easy to verify Cora's findings and to obtain the Barbella family's clinical history. As Edward Hymes, the newcomer to the defense team, explained: "Mental illness is taboo in every family. It is like a curse and inevitably causes shame. Maria and her parents were too frightened and superstitious to be of any help to us. We continuously told them it would all be to their daughter's advantage, but they behaved as though they did not know what we were talking about."

The lawyers pieced together a complete family history; in addition to Cora's findings, they had also found defects on the father's side.

The *Herald* managed to obtain a description of the history and published it on November 21 under the ruthless headline: "MARIA BARBERI'S HEREDITARY TAINT. FAMILY TREE OF A DEGENERATE."

Maria. Age 24. Began to speak later than her brothers and sisters; frontal headaches since childhood; vertigos with and without headaches; frequent epileptic convulsions in the first three years; epileptic attack with fall at ten produced scar; absence of all tickling sensations; constant tremor of eyelids on their closure; feeling of not being liked; insomnia; frequent bad dreams; would not learn dancing.

Maria's predecessors: two cases of alienation; three cases alcoholism; maternal grandfather, probably epileptic, died in old age in an asylum; maternal grandmother died of apoplexy; maternal uncle died after four years of convulsions; paternal uncle died of injury; mother epileptic; father excessive drinker when young; several others subject to fits of anger.

Brothers and sisters: one died of convulsions; one of
teething complications; two of typhoid; and one of marasmus;
of five living, all bear scars from falls; all slow in learning.

The trial quickly became a medical convention attended by
specialists in every field. Cheiro, the renowned palmist who
had consulted at the White House, visited Maria at the Tombs
and made plaster casts of her palms.

"Crossed lines mean unhappiness and suffering," he
explained to the *World* on November 21. "Miss Barberi's palms
are literally covered with these little crosses. She also has a
curved line, twisted and fragmented on both palms, crossing
the heart line and breaking it in two. This line shows a possible
disastrous love affair, and in her case, it crosses the life line at
about twenty years of age. The head lines are fragmented at
both extremities, indicating a confused and wavering mind."
Cheiro then came to an empirical conclusion about Maria's
destiny: it was to be difficult, brutal, and brief.

The astrologer Fred Backe visited the Barbellas in their new
home at 218 Bowery. Filomena confirmed the place and date
of her daughter's birth, on October 24 at Ferrandina. But she
could not remember the exact time of day nor, surprisingly, the
year. The father thought it might have been 1872, but he was
not sure either.

"So many children," he said softly. "And several died . . . I
think Maria was born at night."

"This might explain her introverted nature," said Backe. He
prepared her chart, admitting that, without the hour and the
year of birth, the results could not be accurate.

The sudden doubt about Maria's age surprised everyone,
including her lawyers. The girl could be younger than twenty-
four, but by how much? Could she possibly be a minor, which

would change everything? It was a purely academic question. Arriving at Ellis Island, Maria's father had declared 1872 as her year of birth. Only her Italian birth certificate could have contradicted this, and Cora had been unable to find it in Ferrandina.

On November 23, Maria's attitude did not change. Her eyes were still fixed on the great fresco of the Fates. If, by any chance, she had shifted her gaze to the public seated in the courtroom, most likely she would have seen a doctor. The defense had called four of them: Charles Dana, professor of mental illness at the Post Graduate Medical College; Dr. Frederick Peterson of the Vanderbilt Clinic School of Medicine; Washington Jacoby, an expert on epilepsy; and Alois Hardlika, professor of anthropology and criminology at the New York State Institute of Pathology.

For its part, the prosecution had gathered five specialists: Dr. John Fitch, chief of psychiatry at Bellevue Hospital, sat to the jury's left. On the opposite side were Robert Newton, a specialist in nervous illnesses, and Allen McLane Hamilton. Dr. Carter Gray was near the district attorneys, and Dr. Graeme Hammond sat next to Maria. Among the spectators were many other physicians who searchingly observed the girl's every move: they took great interest in the way Maria nervously twisted the handkerchief she held in her hands.

The defense called Eligio Lanzilotti, a 65-year-old tailor who lived at 233 West 29th Street. In the ten years since he had left Ferrandina, he had not learned a single word of English. Morossi was translating.

"Did you know Antonio Buonsanto, the defendant's maternal grandfather?" asked House.

"Yes, I did. We worked together for two years."

"Did he suffer any illness?"

"He used to have seizures, sometimes even in the street."

"How many times did you see him in that state?"

"Two or three."

"Do you remember when Mr. Buonsanto was taken to Aversa?"

"It happened in the Ferrandina market square. He attacked a group of young men and fought with them until they managed to wrestle him to the ground. That day they took him to the lunatic asylum."

Juror number 6, Max Freund, raised his hand. "How did you know that was where they took him?"

"Because they took him to Aversa."

"How did you know there was a psychiatric hospital there?"

"It's still there. Everyone knows that. In our region we always say, 'Watch out, or they'll take you to Aversa.' Even the children know what that means." Juror number 6 sat down.

"Did you ever see Mr. Buonsanto again?" asked House.

"No. I never saw him again. He died in the asylum." The witness paused, then added: "Poor Antonio. He was a good man."

"Did you think his behavior was rational or irrational?"

"Objection!" thundered McIntyre. After some arguing back and forth, the witness was allowed to answer.

"Irrational."

"What do you mean by 'irrational'?"

"A person who behaves like an animal," Lanzilotti explained.

"Objection! I ask that the answer be struck from the record," McIntyre shouted. Gildersleeve did not sustain his objection. House then asked Lanzilotti whether he remembered anything else about Maria's relatives.

"Her uncle, Giovanni Barbella, never wore a coat in winter. He was a drunkard. One day he went into a bar and bought everyone drinks, then suddenly ran out crying like a woman. No one could understand why. One day I saw him walking down the street half-naked, and they had to rush him home.

Another time he almost set the house on fire. Once he was trying to uncork a bottle, and he broke the neck with his teeth and chewed on the glass."

"Did you know Maria's grandmother, Maria Buonsanto?"

"Yes, I did. Maria was named after her grandmother. She drank, and she often burst into tears for no reason."

"What can you tell us about Giuseppe Barbella, Maria's grandfather?"

"He drank too."

The tailor recounted how he had been at the Barbellas' house one day when Maria's little brother, Giovanni, had a fit of convulsions. They feared the worst, but the boy survived.

In the courtroom, all eyes except Maria's turned to Giovanni. He had fallen asleep with his head leaning against his mother's shoulder, and she kept her face hidden in a black shawl.

House turned the witness over to the prosecution.

"In what way are you related to the defendant?" McIntyre asked right away.

"But . . . I am not related to her. . . ." the man answered with some perplexity. The assistant district attorney seemed satisfied and dismissed the witness.

Pasquale Pellettieri, another tailor from Little Italy, was next. A native of Laurenziana, in the Basilicata region, he had lived in Ferrandina for twenty-eight years before emigrating to America. After the Barbellas arrived in New York, three of their children had lived for six months in his house at 276 Elizabeth Street. According to his testimony, there were frequent arguments, and Antonia cried often. One day she fell to the ground and remained stretched out on the floor: she seemed dead, because she was chalk-white and her eyes were wide open. Then suddenly she regained consciousness. For several days after the incident she had been weak and unable to do any housework.

A long-time friend and contemporary of Maria's parents, Pellettieri looked sad. This may have been due to his heavy eyelids, downcast eyes, and heavy black whiskers. Several times he was asked to speak more loudly, and even Morossi could barely hear him.

He told how once, in Ferrandina, the procession following the Madonna of the Cross had left behind a wake of agitated women surrounding a human figure on the ground. Lying on the cobblestones was Filomena Barbella, felled by a hysterical seizure.

"Objection!" shouted Lauterbach. "The witness is not an expert and therefore cannot define the woman as 'hysterical.' "

"There are four or five different kinds of fits and only a doctor could distinguish between them," McIntyre intervened. The phrase was therefore changed from "hysterical attack" to "convulsions." It remained to be established whether poor Filomena had only had that one seizure or whether there had been others.

"I don't know," answered Pasquale. "That was the only one I witnessed. The women were shouting that she was possessed by the devil. Filomena was trembling and screaming: her eyes looked like glass, she was foaming at the mouth and her tongue was moving from side to side. So I ran to call the doctor, who gave her something, but she couldn't calm down. We managed to take her home but things did not improve. We didn't have a special priest for that kind of thing in Ferrandina, so we sent for Father Luigi from Matera. He gave her extreme unction on her forehead. Then he swung the censer over her head and around the bed three times, saying prayers in Latin to chase the devil away. After that, she slept deeply for about two days. When she woke up her breath smelled of lavender and she didn't remember anything." Pasquale stopped. Beard, the stenographer, raised his head, dipped his pen in the inkwell, and paused. The onlookers waited anxiously for the conclusion of the dramatic testimony. "Maria's mother is a good woman. Sometimes she gets angry," sighed Pasquale, "but her rages never last long."

Maria looked at him and it seemed to Mrs. Foster that there was a vague smile on her lips.

"And what can you tell us about the defendant's father?" asked House.

"All I can say is that sometimes, before Maria was born, we used to drink together."

"Nothing else?"

"Oh, we played in the village band together for a time, but Michele Barbella was always off-key. He couldn't even manage the cymbals." This caused scattered laughter and Judge Gildersleeve had to use his gavel to restore order. Mr. Barbella did not bat an eyelash. Maybe he hadn't understood.

Pasquale Pellettieri's deposition was over. But just as he was rising from his chair, House intervened.

"Is it true, Mr. Pellettieri, that you have lost a son?" he asked softly. Had Vergara been inattentive no one would have heard, but the translation came automatically.

"My only child died last night," the man answered as he left, leaving an ominous silence in his wake.

Fifty-year-old Rocco Recchia, of 50 Chrystie Street, was the next witness. He owned a barbershop at 61 Bowery. He had been the Barbellas' neighbor at Via de' Mille in Ferrandina and had emigrated with them. He confirmed the other depositions, adding that Filomena had had seizures for at least eight years, always after the death of one of her children.

"Sometimes I was a substitute doctor, so I know what I'm talking about," Recchia said firmly.

House asked him to explain.

"I was good at bloodletting when it was needed," he answered readily. "At least twice a year I applied a snow-filled bladder to the nape of Filomena's neck after a fit. That was what the doctor said we should do."

"What kind of bladder?"

"Any kind. I got it at the butcher's. In Ferrandina, we store the snow in deep cellars. When we had no snow, I used cold water."

He also told two stories about Maria's younger sister, Antonia. At Ferrandina, while washing laundry in the river one day, the girl had fainted and wounded her head as she fell. Just after the Barbellas were evicted from their first house on Elizabeth Street, Recchia, feeling sorry for them, had taken Antonia into his home. During one of her seizures, the girl had almost thrown herself out a window. He had been able to grab her just in time, and when Antonia revived she did not remember a thing. Recchia repeated that, although he did not know modern medicine and could barely read and write, he had acted as a doctor many times.

"Here also, when they fall ill, they send for me. . . ."

"We ask the witness to kindly keep to the facts," McIntyre interrupted impatiently.

"That is exactly what Mr. Recchia is doing," House pointed out. The judge did not react and the witness continued.

"I am not a doctor, as I was saying, but I am able to identify some illnesses and to cure them: not with pills, but with herbs and other methods. I learned everything I know from my father. Before the first physician arrived from the province, my father took care of the sick in Ferrandina. I sincerely believe that Filomena and Antonia's attacks have something to do with epilepsy."

McIntyre was visibly upset.

"And what can you tell us about the defendant?" asked House.

"Not much. I know for sure that she had several attacks when she was little. I wouldn't know what kind. In one of her falls she cut her forehead and her elbow and the doctor gave her some stitches. . . . I was present with the doctor. Almost everyone in that family had health problems, so it's difficult to remember. . . . But if we are talking about Filomena and Antonia I know what I'm saying."

McIntyre's cross-examination did not succeed in confusing or casting doubt on the witness. Recchia said he could provide the assistant district attorney with the names and addresses of people in Ferrandina who had witnessed many unpleasant episodes involving the Barbella family. As far as Maria was concerned, he repeated he had never personally seen her fainting as a child, but that he was present when the doctor had given her stitches.

Maria did have two small scars: a small one on her forehead, near the hairline, and a larger one on the right arm, just above the elbow. The Sing Sing official had only recorded the second one, perhaps because when she had arrived at the penitentiary, Maria had rolled up the sleeves of her dress. But was it possible to prove now that the scars had been caused by an epileptic fit? Maria herself did not remember anything about her injuries.

McIntyre was about to say something, when House asked that Maria be allowed to show her scars to the jury. The judge assented.

"Come, Miss Barbella. Please, show the jurors your scars," said House, helping the girl to her feet. Maria walked mechanically up to the jury, took off her hat, and stood motionless, staring at the floor. House lifted her hair, revealing a scar near the right temple. One by one the twelve men leaned forward and looked at it. Then she put her hat back on, took off her jacket and rolled up the right sleeve of her blouse. Again the men leaned forward and scrutinized her scar, which was about four inches long. Finally Maria pulled her sleeve back down, put her jacket on, and returned to her seat.

McIntyre turned to his colleague Lauterbach and rolled his eyes skyward as if to say: "All right, so what?"

CHAPTER TWENTY-TWO

$\mathcal{N}$o one could miss the presence in the courtroom of Moishe Ha-Levi Ish Hurwitz, the well-known Yiddish playwright, who had attended Maria's first trial. The "Professor" made his entrances with a following of acolytes and always appeared at a crucial moment in the proceedings, as though he knew in advance what was going to happen. On Monday, November 23, Hurwitz sat at a good vantage point against the wall near the entrance. He did not want to miss a single word of the Barbella family's testimony. All except Maria had been called to testify: the parents; her thirty-year-old brother Giuseppe; twenty-two-year-old Antonia; twenty-one-year-old Carlo; Giovanni, thirteen; and Carmela, twelve.

When Walsh, the clerk, called Filomena Barbella's name, the small woman with sunken, deeply-ringed eyes approached, dragging her feet. She was shrouded in her black shawl, through which shone two large gold hoop earrings. Now and then Maria looked at her mother, who was perched on the seat, her feet dangling above the floor.

Swaying her body back and forth in the regular rhythm that had rocked to sleep many ill-fated children, Filomena told the story of her life. She was married at fifteen. After two miscarriages, she had given birth to eleven children. Four died before reaching the age of two, one shortly thereafter. Now she was fifty. Yes, her father died in the asylum. At fifty-nine, her mother was paralyzed by an apoplectic fit. Unable to move and not allowed to drink alcohol, she died a year later screaming for wine. Her brother Francesco? He died of convulsions at the age of four. Uncle Giuseppe? He was known as "Beppe Matto," since he always acted crazy. The interpreter explained that "Beppe" was the Italian diminutive of Giuseppe, and "Matto" simply meant crazy. When Aunt Loretta, the beauty of the family, suffered from her terrible tantrums, she would bang her head against the wall and scratch at her own face with her chewed-up nails.

As she spoke, Filomena concentrated on Vergara's translation. With some reticence, and with a subdued expression, she described her family's secret shame. Attorney Hymes had rightly called it a "curse." Filomena had resigned herself to family instability, and made of this resignation her only strength.

Carlo and Giuseppe were relatively healthy, like their father. Giovanni had had convulsions until the age of seven; Antonia had not had any since her marriage; Maria, on the other hand, had miraculously survived more than one violent seizure.

"Maria is like me," said Filomena. "The Madonna protects her!" To everyone's surprise, she had no idea what epilepsy, or "pepsy" as she called it, was. Her explanation for the illness was simpler: all those fits and falls were God's will. He gave each his own cross to bear.

House called Giovanni, who approached the jury with a determined step. His hair was cut short, revealing the strange shape of his head: small in front, bigger in the back, with the left side bulging. Filomena pointed out the hairless white patches on the right side of her son's head.

"How did he get these scars?" asked the lawyer.

Maria Barbella
come appare ora al nuovo processo

Maria Barberi's Mother.

Father of the Italian Girl.

Maria Barbella and her parents.

"During a convulsive attack. He fell on the stove."

"Giovanni, when did lawyer Friend have you cut your hair?" McIntyre asked sarcastically.

"Saturday night, sir," the boy answered.

"No!" cried Friend. "I had nothing to do with it!"

Muffled laughter was heard among the public.

"Giovanni, show the jury your tongue," said House. The boy grinned and complied, and the jurors saw that the right side of his tongue was torn.

"He cut it falling from a bridge," Filomena explained. "They brought him home bleeding and foaming at the mouth."

Filomena's answer was accompanied by an inexplicable burst of laughter: turning to see the reason for it, House saw that Giovanni still stood with his tongue out. Smiling slightly, the lawyer told the boy he could return to his seat.

"Did Maria learn to speak before or after the others?" he then asked Filomena.

"Much later. We knew she wasn't dumb, because during her fits her screams sounded like words. Then she was dazed for days and so weak she couldn't walk like the others." Filomena's dialect was certainly crude, but her tone was engaging, her gestures expressive, and her language picturesque. "A dark cloud crossed my eyes. . . ." was how she described one of her attacks. Her invocation to Domenico was recalled as: "In the name of Our Lady, I entreat you to marry her!" She showed how she used to hold the unconscious child Maria by pressing her arms to her chest saying: "I held her close to my heart."

"Describe to us her sleep."

"It was troubled. Often she cried out: 'Fire! Fire!' and I would wake her up: 'Maria, what is it?' But she never remembered anything."

"Has Maria ever tried to commit suicide?"

The lawyer had to repeat the question twice.

"Yes . . ." said Filomena reluctantly. "It was just before we left Ferrandina. We were sitting outside. Maria and Antonia started to quarrel. The next thing I saw was Maria running into the house with her father right behind her. Minutes later, he came back with Maria in his arms. She had tried to throw herself from the roof, but couldn't remember anything."

Gildersleeve then gave Filomena the opportunity, which Judge Goff had denied her, to recount her meetings with Domenico in minute detail. The exclusion of this testimony had been one of the main reasons the new trial had been granted.

Filomena said that, two weeks before Domenico's death, she had even gone to his stall at Canal Street to beg the man to marry her daughter. One day, she went to her daughter's place. Maria was crying and Domenico pushed her violently into the next room, slamming the door. "It's only a stupid quarrel," he said by way of explanation. But from that moment on, Filomena feared for Maria's life.

McIntyre vehemently attacked the picture that was being painted by her testimony. Pointing to Edward Hymes, the lawyer with a psychiatric specialty assisting House, he thundered:

"This gentleman states that there are predetermining causes to the epileptic attack in whose grip, it is supposed, the defendant was at the time of the crime. As far as I know, an epileptic fit arrives like a bolt of lightning out of the sky and is not due to a sequence of events. All of this has nothing to do with the murder or with whether Maria Barbella is insane or not." McIntyre gave the word "insane" an insinuating tone.

"Insanity! Maria is not insane, Mr. McIntyre," said Hymes. "She's an epileptic!"

"Objection, Your Honor!"

Vergara did not translate, but the squabbling voices had frightened Filomena, who began to rock from side to side, covering her ears with her hands. Many had the impression she was about to give a demonstration of the family illness, and the medical experts on both sides observed her with avid curiosity. Minutes passed, but she slowly regained her composure. Gildersleeve's voice was heard sustaining McIntyre's objection.

"We ask the witness to keep to the facts of the morning of the murder."

Vergara communicated to Filomena that, if she was not too tired, she should now try to remember the moment of the killing. With a strangely detached voice, Filomena began:

". . . Signora Manguso was telling me to leave, otherwise the quarrel would not stop. . . . Suddenly there was a scream. Maria collapsed to the ground. Domenico fell on top of her, and then he wasn't there any more. I ran into the street screaming: 'He killed her! She's dead! She's dead!' Then I don't know. I heard the police had taken her away alive, but they only let me see her the next morning."

House motioned Filomena to stop, and Vergara helped her back to her seat. Her testimony had lasted more than two hours.

Then 58-year-old Michele Barbella took the stand. His gray mustache and rumpled hair made him look more like a fearless sailor than a peasant turned tailor. McIntyre asked him a series of questions designed to incite him, which he handled quite well.

"Were you ever addicted to alcohol?"

"When I had the money, yes, I used to drink. But I quit the day I turned thirty."

"Is your memory good?"

"I don't know."

"Where was your daughter exactly, when you saved her, that time on the roof?"

"She was at the edge of the roof."

"And you grasped her with one hand and pulled her back?"

"With both hands."

"I imagine she was foaming at the mouth. . . ."

"I don't remember that."

"Did you ever ask your daughter to leave Domenico Cataldo and come back home?"

"No."

"Why not?"

"I went once to see him, not her."

"And you did not try to bring her home?"

"No."

"Did you ever use violence against Domenico Cataldo?"

"No."

"Did Giuseppe and Carlo use violence?"

"No. We did not tell our sons where Maria was."

"Did any member of the family attempt to bring her home?"

"No."

Giuseppe Barbella, the eldest son, was then asked whether he had seen Maria after Domenico's death.

"At the Tombs and at Sing Sing," he answered.

"What did she say?"

"I asked her how she was and she said she was afraid to sleep, and so she stayed awake."

"What did she mean by that?"

"The dreams would kill her, that's what she said."

"Did she ever mention Domenico?"

"No."

"And you didn't talk to her about the murder?"

"No."

However, under House's questioning, Giuseppe admitted he had asked Maria about the crime, adding that she had thrown her arms around his neck, crying. "My brother, I don't remember what I did!" had been her words.

Antonia Barbella Mattei looked a lot like Maria, but had lighter hair. Defense attorney Edward Hymes questioned her. Her convulsions had stopped after the birth of her first child, but she still suffered terrible migraines. Sometimes she had a pain in her right leg, so acute that she couldn't walk. She took off her hat and showed the scar on the back of her head, a result of her fall on the riverbank. Hymes' second question surprised everyone in the courtroom:

"Describe your dreams to us, please."

McIntyre objected contemptuously and Judge Gildersleeve observed that everyone dreams.

"Yes, but there are dreams and dreams," Hymes specified. "We know dreams derive from cerebral action, and the argument is pertinent to this case."

"If a girl dreams of being devoured by a lion, that is of no help to us," House interjected, "but if she dreams regularly of falling from a cliff or something of the kind, it becomes important. We want this on the record."

McIntyre turned to House sarcastically: "I suppose that having discovered the origin of these nightmares, you will send someone to Sixth Avenue to buy a book on the subject. Of course, it may be true that every dream has an explanation. It can even be admitted that this witness has the same dream every night, in which she falls from a cliff that is higher and higher each time. We are ready to concede that every member of the family has an identical dream. . . ."

"I only want that which I can prove," Hymes replied.

"The defense wouldn't be surprised if even Mr. McIntyre had some bad dreams," quipped House.

The rap of the judge's gavel put an end to the discussion, and Antonia was given permission to describe her dreams, all rather terrifying.

Prosecutor Lauterbach cross-examined her. Antonia hesitated even at the ritual questions. Where had she lived in the city? She could not say exactly. Lauterbach became aggressive.

"Why is it that you and all the members of your family do not remember a thing about what we ask you, but you remember everything when House asks the questions?"

"I have moved several times and I don't remember the street names and numbers."

"Has anyone suggested you answer 'I don't recall' when we are questioning you?"

"No, sir."

"Are any of your children mentally retarded?" McIntyre asked abruptly.

"I don't know. . . . They behave like all children, except maybe they cry a bit too much."

"Are any mentally retarded?" he insisted.

"They are too young, I wouldn't know. . . ." The defense objected and McIntyre explained: "Every authority on the subject of epilepsy holds that, after two generations of epileptics, the third has mentally retarded members. . . ."

"What authorities do you refer to?" asked House.

"To those working in New York."

Drs. Newton and McLane began to confer in whispers. So did Drs. Hardlika and Jacoby, while Dr. Charles Dana scribbled something down. McIntyre asked to see the children.

"Could you bring your eldest to court tomorrow?"

"Yes, if he doesn't cry."

"Well, crying or no, I order you to bring him here tomorrow."

"If his father consents," Antonia dared to retort, but the judge informed her she had no choice.

Carlo Barbella was short, and also prone to fainting. He had recently lost consciousness on the street, scarring himself above the left eye.

"Ah! Another scar!" McIntyre said sarcastically. "The Barbella family coat of arms!"

Someone in the public burst out laughing and the judge's gavel was heard. Carlo could not remember having had a single pleasant dream since he was born.

"Speak louder, please," Hymes told him.

"This is my voice, I can't speak any louder."

"Why didn't you learn English?"

"I can't."

"Why not?"

No answer.

Carmela Barbella was by far the prettiest of the family. She was slender, with shiny black hair and regular features. In good English she said she hated school because she always had a headache and it was difficult to concentrate.

"It's aching now," she specified. She, too, stated that her dreams were never pleasant and she often dreamed of falling.

McIntyre suggested her nightmares were due to indigestion. "What do you usually eat for dinner?" he asked.

"Bread and milk."

"Don't you often eat macaroni?"

"No, we only have macaroni on Sundays. . . ." she muttered, and burst into tears. Diet was a sensitive point of prestige in Little Italy.

"Why didn't you mention your headaches and your dreams at the other trial?"

House protested that McIntyre was trying to cast doubt on the credibility of the witness.

"Not only that," was the immediate reply. "I will cast doubt on the statements of every single witness we have heard so far. I have formed a certain idea of these proceedings. . . ."

Giovanni Barbella, dressed up in his sailor suit with a big blue collar, was last to be called. He confessed he had once seen Domenico and Maria together near Thirteenth Street. She had disappeared from the house and her parents were looking for her, so he told them. When he was asked what school he went to, he said, "The public one on Marion Street." Unlike his sister, he did not hate school. But his teacher often sent him home.

"Why?" asked House.

"I fall asleep. . . ."

"Why?" repeated the lawyer.

Giovanni didn't know exactly, maybe it was because of his headaches or the buzzing he often heard in his ears. At this point, House lingered on the boy's irregularly-shaped head, suggesting that Giovanni's problems were somehow related to it.

"The shape of this head has nothing to do with the case," McIntyre reacted. "If irregularly shaped heads indicate mental deficiency, I can produce right here and now a person whose irregular head has brought him fame and honor."

Everyone wondered whom that could be. Julia Sage, who sat in the first row, concluded that it might be Judge Gildersleeve himself. He was the only prominent person in the room whose head seemed out of proportion with the rest of his body.

CHAPTER TWENTY THREE

"*M*aria Barbella's decisive hour. Today She Will Play Her Part on the Witness Stand in a Fight for Life," the *New York Journal* announced on the morning of November 25. By 10 A.M., a large crowd had gathered at the barred entrance of the criminal courts building. Their shouts reached into the courtroom: "Ma-ri-a! Ma-ri-a!" Banners and signs were not lacking, although some said: "CHAIR FOR THE MURDERESS." The street was blocked to traffic, but still the police had their hands full. The "Professor" waded through the crowd at the head of his retinue. His stage drama was soon to be completed, and as far as he was concerned, every demonstrator was a ticket sold.

Another author was present: the writer Julian Hawthorne, son of Nathaniel. His recent novel, *A Fool of Nature*, published under a pseudonym, had just won a ten-thousand-dollar prize. Julian was attending the trial as a reporter for the *New York Journal*. Responding to the public furor, he wrote:

> Every day, on our planet, thousands die who are no different than the little seamstress Maria Barberi and the shoeshine Domenico Cataldo and no one takes any notice. And yet,

because the two were lovers, and the woman killed the man, thousands today follow the trial with interest.

On the witness stand, Maria sat stiffly with her hands in her lap, as usual. When she began to speak, the onlookers, who expected to hear the crude accent of the downtown tenements, were surprised by her graceful English. Her voice was barely audible, but Julian Hawthorne noticed that she exerted a spell, holding the audience as only great tragic stage actresses do. "One had to strain one's imagination to discern the situations she described," he wrote.

> It was like peering through a murky fog, so confused at times were the characters and their impulses. Yet, it was impossible to look away, to hold the ear from listening. In her story were the elements of the great tragedies of this mortal life. That small Italian peasant felt the same passion and despair that move the heroines of history and poetry. She was the sister of them all. That creature had aroused the desire of a man, had loved him, and had become his slave. He had jeered at her, betrayed her, and she had killed him. Looking at her, I could not comprehend how she could have done it in a state remotely approaching a normal one. It was not in her to do it. A foreign force must have possessed her. No, she could not have possibly done it on her own . . .

As she spoke, Maria remained absolutely erect and did not gesticulate. Why did she stop at Domenico Cataldo's stall? Because he called her by her name. He knew her name before she knew his. Her lawyers questioned her as though she were a child. "Were you a good girl before you met Domenico Cataldo?"

"Yes, sir."

"Honest?"

"I was honest."

Then they asked her some questions about her family. She said that her grandmother was the first drunken woman she had ever seen, and also the first person she had seen dead: she had died screaming and her mouth was all crooked. Uncle Giovanni once tried to set the furniture on fire, and another time he took off all his clothes and ran out naked in the streets. Asked whether she had ever been to school, Maria said yes, but she had had to stop because of an eye problem.

"My eyes burned like flames, and I always had a headache. Luckily, by the time I left school I already knew the alphabet and I could count to a hundred. . . ."

"Do you still suffer headaches?"

"Sometimes . . . I feel as if two hot coals are stuck inside like lumps in my head, and I hear a rumbling like a train going on and on, and then I can't stay on my feet. . . ."

She spoke clearly but softly, and often repeated her answers for Beard, the stenographer.

"Once I was at home by myself and I heard this rumbling in my head. I saw a flash of light and then everything went dark. Mama said she found me on the floor. . . ."

"Do you sleep well?"

"Yes and no," was the answer.

"What do you mean?"

"Sometimes I feel a great heat, like in summer, and an animal on fire leaps out and burns me," she explained. "It's not a dog, not a donkey. . . . It's something like a monkey, but it's not exactly a monkey. . . . He used to say I look like a monkey. . . ." She lowered her eyes. "Maybe he was right. . . ." she said in a whisper that was heard only by Dr. Hammond and Mrs. Foster, who sat next to her.

"Do you ever dream of cats?"

"Yes. . . . They jump out of walls. . . . My bed thumps like a heart, it is rising and falling, then I don't know. When I wake up, my bedclothes are on the floor."

"Do you remember when you tried to throw yourself from the roof?"

"I only know what my parents told me."

The experts, with the exception of Cheiro the palmist and Backe the astrologer, had all gathered within a few feet of her and studied her with an almost morbid fascination: Her physical aspect, her gestures, her voice, the least tremor of the lips and the eyelids, everything was being classified and recorded as normal or abnormal. Maria did not seem intimidated by the gentlemen's scrutiny.

"When was it that Domenico Cataldo asked you to marry him?"

"The day he called me by name. He said he was ready for marriage and that I was just right for him. He spoke as if he already knew me."

Despite a barrage of objections from McIntyre, House was able to have Maria state that she had gone to live with Domenico because she trusted him to marry her right away.

"What other choice did she have, after all?" shouted a woman's voice. The gavel rapped. "Silence! Silence is ordered!"

When McIntyre objected that betrayal did not justify murder, the juror Seliger cut him off, complaining that the witness was being interrupted too often; and, on behalf of the entire jury, he asked that all testimony about Maria and Domenico Cataldo's relationship be admitted. Gildersleeve reassured him: everything that was pertinent would be admitted. The prosecution did not look pleased.

One day, before she went to live with him, Domenico persuaded her to go for a walk. Suddenly he was thirsty and wanted a drink. "I was ashamed," said Maria. "I had never gone inside a barroom with a man before. He gave me a soda and mixed something red in it." She was trembling, but she continued. "I got dizzy, then everything went dark. . . ."

The prosecution objected.

"I don't understand," asked McIntyre, "whether what is being argued is the thesis of temporary insanity . . . excuse me, of epilepsy, as the defense likes to define it, or of seduction? This fact is not relevant!"

Gildersleeve did not sustain the objection and Maria continued.

"Sometimes, when I begged him to marry me, he hit me."

"And what did you do?"

"I cried. . . . And then we made up."

Three days before the murder, he had snatched a photograph of himself from her hands and thrown it into the stove.

"Why did you want a photograph of Domenico?"

"So I could look at it."

"Why?"

"So I could look at it, that's all."

"What for?" House said again.

". . . So I could see his face. . . ."

"But why did you want to see his face?"

"I love him. . . ." Maria used the present tense.

"What did Domenico Cataldo say to you on the morning of April 26?"

"That he was going back to Chiaromonte, and then he ran down the stairs." She opened her bottle of salts and inhaled. She had followed him, but when she got to the street she changed her mind and returned home.

"Why?"

"I thought I would put on a pretty dress in case he was going to marry me before leaving. So I opened the chest to take something and I saw the razor."

"Why did you take it? Were you thinking of hurting him?"

"I don't know, I don't remember . . . I thought only: how can I get married? How do I make him marry me? That's all I thought . . . I didn't want to live anymore . . . I took it for myself. . . ." She broke down, bent her head forward, and pressed her hands against her face. Was a seizure coming on? Mrs. Foster grabbed her arm, Maria brightened, but the Tombs Angel suddenly blanched. Her face lost all color, her shoulders slumped, and her head fell to her chest. The legal physician O'Hanlon ran up to her. Moments passed. Mrs. Foster then raised her head slightly, opened her eyes, and whispered:

"It's nothing . . . I'm alright. I just need some fresh air."

The doctor assisted her outside.

A guard opened a window and a pleasant breeze drifted through the courtroom. The judge was about to announce a brief recess when, from behind the hands that covered her face, Maria's voice was heard. The gavel stopped in mid-air.

" 'Only pigs marry!' " she sobbed. "Only pigs . . . And there was that rumbling in my head. . . ."

"What is the first thing you remember?" asked House.

"The blood on my hands. I thought I was cut . . . and that taste in my mouth. . . ."

"Do you remember having struck Domenico Cataldo with a razor?"

"No."

"Your witness, lawyer McIntyre," said House, turning to the district attorney. "I'm finished."

"Your Honor," said the prosecutor, "this woman has been on the witness stand for five hours and must surely be tired. As my cross-examination will be rather in-depth, I request an adjournment."

The judge asked Maria whether she was too tired to continue. She said, yes, she was, but she would try to go on. Gildersleeve granted the adjournment.

As McIntyre passed Maria on the way to the exit, she suddenly took his hand, bent forward, and kissed it. This gesture, a typical southern Italian expression of respect, surprised those present.

"Don't be angry with me," she pleaded. "I'll go on, if you like, I'll answer some more . . . Don't be hard with Maria. . . ." Visibly embarrassed, the assistant prosecutor hurried to the door. "It is not always easy to be a district attorney," Julian Hawthorne remarked in his *New York Journal* piece.

The following day was Thanksgiving, and the courts were closed. The *World* wrote on November 27:

> Maria Barberi passed a comfortable Thanksgiving in spite of the miserable night. She awoke with a scream in the early morning, and did not sleep again. . . .
>
> . . . She appeared contented, no doubt because of the letter she has received from Countess di Brazzà. The countess is in Italy and is expected here on December 8th.

Chapin had asked Maria for an account of the circumstances which she thought had made her so famous. The girl refused at first, but Julia Sage, who visited her at least once a week, advised her to accept. So she did:

> To the Editor of the *World:*
>   You have asked me to write a letter and I will try.
>   It's not easy when one is in great trouble and one cannot sleep or eat. I've learnt English, reading and writing in the last months, but at the moment even speaking is difficult.

I've been asked if my second trial is as hard for me as the first one. In some ways it's not as hard. When I was first brought into the courtroom, I didn't know the language and the customs of your country. No matter what they said, I thought it was against me. Now when my lawyers speak, I know they're trying to help me, and I understand at last what I've done. I did not understand then.

Since the trouble began, I've met many good American women. They are different from me. No woman can know what she would do until she has tried, and many women are good because they haven't had temptations.

I cannot write of my own case, except to say that I don't know how I did it. If a man is in fever and throws himself out of the window, people don't say it's a crime. They say: "He didn't know what he was doing." It was so with me. I was in fever. I didn't know what I was doing.

Cataldo was good to me at first. I was working in a sweatshop and I was lonely. I cannot write about our life together. He did not marry me. They say I've killed him and, of course, it must be true or I wouldn't be here.

After my first trial, I was sent to Sing Sing. I shall never forget how good Mrs. Sage was to me. She taught me everything I know today, even embroidery.

In the courtroom, only Mrs. Foster's presence holds me together. I'm glad when evening comes and I can go back to my cell, even if I'm always afraid of dreaming.

Mrs. Foster, Mrs. Sage, and the Countess di Brazzà have made me love America.

My religion has also helped me, and so I leave my future in the hands of God. He put me in this world, and He will decide whether or not I can stay here. If it's no, He'll give me the strength to bear whatever comes.

MARIA BARBELLA, the Tombs, November 24, 1896.

The trial resumed on Friday, November 27, with McIntyre's cross-examination, which had a single objective: to prove Maria killed Cataldo in revenge. He wanted to show that she had associated with him without a hope of marriage and that she stayed with him despite the abuse and the deceptions. In the end she killed him to pay him back for the many insults she received, especially the final one.

The assistant prosecutor began to ask Maria about her testimony at the first trial. Maria was terrified: Mrs. Foster was not allowed to sit next to her this time. The courtroom was again packed and there were many young women among the spectators. During the whole long cross-examination, no one left the room. Bodies strained forward and all eyes stared at the small woman fighting for her life. Only her voice was heard as she recounted her story: the one that suddenly had begun in a bare room on Chrystie Street, when, for the first time, she had found herself alone with a man . . . the first time.

Judge Gildersleeve asked how she had felt at the first trial.

"I was sick," she answered.

"And how do you feel now?"

"Much better," said Maria.

McIntyre began by addressing her as "Miss Barbella," but he soon abandoned every formality. As he delivered his questions, it was difficult to tell whether he was reading from the transcript of the first trial or asking new questions. Maria could not always identify or recognize her previous answers when he referred to them.

McIntyre seemed irritated by her memory lapses.

"I don't remember. It all happened in an instant. I don't know, it's like a dream, I don't remember," was her refrain. The assistant prosecutor was able to finish without losing his patience.

"It was a triangular duel," wrote Julian Hawthorne. "A duel between Maria Barberi, McIntyre the prosecutor, and McIntyre the gentleman."

House, Friend, and Hymes kept up a steady stream of objections to the fact that McIntyre read from the first trial transcript, which the Appeals Court had ruled to be unreliable.

"How can I prevent the prosecution from asking the witness what she stated in the past? The year and the month may differ, but the crime was committed by the same person," the judge pointed out.

"If this is Your Honor's opinion, then what the Court of Appeals has defined as unreliable becomes valid in this setting," House retorted.

McIntyre summarized his facts. "The witness armed herself with a razor, put it in her pocket, and went to the bar where her lover was," he said, all in one breath. "Is this not evidence of intent and premeditation? If I am prevented from proving this is so, I am prevented from carrying out my duty, and I may as well resign."

Gildersleeve allowed him to continue his cross-examination.

"You knew the razor was in the chest, didn't you, Maria?"

"My mind is blank. . . . I don't remember. . . ."

"Did Domenico Cataldo shave that morning?"

"I don't know."

"How is it that you don't remember anything of what you stated at the first trial?"

"I don't know. I was ill and I said anything that came to mind. . . . I didn't tell the truth and I didn't lie. . . . I didn't know what I was saying. . . ."

"Miss Barbella, perhaps you were truly ill, and yet you described in great detail your first meeting with Domenico Cataldo, what you liked about him, and so on. It's all written down, Miss Barbella, and it all makes sense. Your memory was vivid and . . . anyway, you really did not look ill to me," he ended.

"I was not well. . . . I don't remember anything," Maria insisted, looking him in the eye.

The public stirred and murmured. House jumped to his feet, red-faced with anger, and shouted: "Objection!" However Gildersleeve, having rapped his gavel sharply to restore order, motioned to McIntyre to proceed.

"When you returned home after what happened on Chrystie Street, did you feel any remorse?"

"No, sir," Maria said calmly. "I loved him and he loved me, and so I had no regrets."

"Did you ever think of harming him?"

"Once or twice," she admitted. "But I loved him anyway . . . I loved him every minute, even when he said that thing to me about pigs. It's just that I don't remember what happened afterwards. . . ."

"Why did you take the razor if you wanted to throw yourself in the river?"

"Because I didn't want to die slowly. I thought I would do something with the razor after jumping in." She always had her answer ready.

"I could not believe that a person playing a part, or following the direction of others, could speak in the way she did," Hawthorne wrote. "She truly gave the impression of having been blinded and bewildered by her emotions, so that she saw and yet did not see, heard and yet did not hear. . . ."

The sore question remained: Was she truly an epileptic? She described her recurrent visual flashes as bolts of lightning followed by clouds of fog. Could these be divine manifestations?

Mystical visions? She said she felt no guilt for having yielded to Cataldo or for his death, Hawthorne recounted. How was that possible? Since, like many southern Italians, she feared the wrath of God and was superstitious. . . .

"Maria didn't know anything about the psychological intrigues of Shakespeare and Balzac," Hawthorne continued. "but knew only what she had felt, and was able to distinguish between remorse and shame."

Given the testimony of this second trial, it seemed that she had never really blamed Cataldo and naively still dreamed of marriage. Hawthorne suggested a reason: ". . . Maybe Maria did suffer from epilepsy after all. Not the clinical disease the experts had come to observe, but rather the illness that afflicts the great victims of poetic illusion . . ."

"Maria, you say you did not repent of your act," McIntyre said reprovingly. "So why did you want to throw yourself in the river?"

"Because Domenico Cataldo did not want to marry me and I couldn't live with that shame."

"What did you say when your mother begged him to marry you?"

"I said: 'Don't cry, mother, don't believe it, he will marry me. . . .' "

"And so you truly thought he would do so?" McIntyre emphasized the paradox.

"Yes . . . I did and I didn't. I was like in a cloud."

"Do you remember telling me at the first trial, that you cut Cataldo in a fit of rage?"

"No, I don't remember that."

"Did you not say: 'Die! Die! You have ruined me!' "

"I don't remember."

"A police officer has stated that you told him you killed Domenico Cataldo because he ruined you. . . ."

"I don't know what I told the police," Maria shouted suddenly, bursting into tears. "I don't remember anything. . . ."

"Enough!" shouted House.

McIntyre refused to be branded a bully: "I am only seeking the truth. If all the eminent alienists present in the court will have reason to believe Miss Barbella acted during a seizure, or if they will doubt her responsibility, I will relinquish the case and ask the jury to dismiss it. But first I want to ascertain the facts."

"Proceed," declared the judge.

"Did you not say at the first trial that Domenico Cataldo had eight hundred dollars in the bank?"

"I don't know what I said."

"Do you remember saying that he was thinking of giving you half the money and that then he did not?"

"I have never wanted his money."

Darkness had fallen in the courtroom. The electric lights were turned on, a procedure that always aroused a certain surprise among the public. McIntyre left his place at the table and approached the small woman in the chair. The judge leaned forward. The stenographer bent his head to listen, while his hand ran quickly over the sheet of paper. Vergara, the interpreter, became more attentive. Maria seemed on the verge of fainting again and shielded her eyes from the blinding lights with her hand. Her voice wavered between a resounding forcefulness and a weak whisper. McIntyre put the question to her:

"Did you know Domenico Cataldo had other women?"

House sprang to his feet, ready to object, but Maria's answer was immediate.

"Yes, I was jealous."

"And you never got angry with him? You don't mean to tell me you weren't jealous?"

"Yes, I was."

"You were jealous, but you were not angry. . . ." The assistant prosecutor was about to spring his last trap.

"It's hard to explain. . . . I loved him very much," Maria answered desolately.

"You loved him enough to kill him. . . ."

"They say I did it, but I don't remember . . . I don't remember," she repeated as though she were in a trance. The assistant prosecutor did not insist. The cross-examination was over.

Mrs. Foster took Maria by the arm and led her to the Bridge of Sighs. The public, affected, did not move. For six and a half hours, the little immigrant had resisted the onslaught of one of the most illustrious minds of the American legal profession.

At that exact moment, the vessel S.S. *Fulda* of the Lloyd, Bremen Steamship Co. was leaving the Bay of Naples en route for Gibraltar, with New York as its final destination. Among the 310 passengers were Detalmo and Cora. Their daughter Idanna was among the 56 children on board.

CHAPTER TWENTY-FOUR

On Monday, November 30, a problem arose in House's defense strategy. The problem was Nando Tavolacci, the man who was playing cards with Domenico the day Maria came into the bar with a razor hidden in her pocket or sleeve. Having talked privately with House about Cataldo's stiletto during the summer, Nando promised the lawyers he would testify; actually he was preparing to go into hiding. An entire weekend spent questioning his neighbors, who were rather tight-lipped, yielded no information that could lead to him.

"We haven't seen much of him lately. His new barbershop on Long Island must be doing well. No, we don't know where he is. . . ."

Caterina Manguso refused to help them again: she had managed to find him once before, and the lawyers had let him get away.

House exploited the witness' absence as well as he could:

. . . The absence of the man who saw a knife in Domenico's waistcoat pocket is more significant than his presence. Surely he was afraid of ending up like Domenico Cataldo, even though we cannot imagine how. Domenico's private life remains a mystery: He did not seem to have any friends, nor any relatives aside from his brother Louis, the street sweeper. But one can never say. Nando Tavolacci may belong to that significant group of Italians for whom testifying at a trial automatically means trouble. . . .

Captain Smith from the East Fifth Street station confirmed that one of the personal effects found on Cataldo's body was in fact a knife. McIntyre objected: "It is well known that Italians are in the habit of carrying a knife. The fact is only pertinent to the case if the defense attorneys intend now to suggest that their client could have acted in self-defense, which would change things drastically, of course. . . ."

House approached the judge. "Your Honor," he began with a firm voice. "If a man goes around with a knife, it means he is also capable of using it. . . . But this is not the point. Nando Tavolacci, in effect, saw a simple blade. We do not know whether Domenico had tried to use the weapon against the defendant. However, we know for certain that Maria Barbella fell to the ground and that to this day she is unable to remember a thing about the murder: this is the crux of the tragedy. Your Honor, let us not forget that a life is at stake here. We certainly cannot deny the jury an exact picture of the moment in which the crime was committed. . . ."

Sitting as usual next to Rebecca Foster, Maria seemed completely indifferent to the proceedings. The previous night, her screams had kept everyone awake. Matron Smith had had to give her a sedative. The girl knew she might have to testify again and this frightened her badly. She would not be able to withstand another third degree. But Judge Gildersleeve suddenly called McIntyre and House to the bench. After a brief consultation,

House approached Maria and told her that her interrogation was over. For the first time, the onlookers saw her smile.

Julia Sage was called.

"Maria is not the type of woman who can devise and carry out a plan to take a human being's life," she stated. "I think she still loves Domenico Cataldo. During the nine months spent at Sing Sing, I saw her every day and she never, not even once, showed resentment toward him. 'The worse thing is that my Domenico is dead!' she told me one day. I have read the transcript from her first testimony, and I see no contradiction with what she has always told me. She had taken the razor to kill herself. Why doubt that? Suicides are common enough. During the first trial, someone testified that she grasped Domenico by the hair and cut his throat. 'What does that mean?' she asked me once. 'I never took Domenico by the hair.' I firmly believe Miss Barbella is innocent."

"Very well, Mrs. Sage, but what can you tell us about her alleged epilepsy?" McIntyre asked her.

"That subject I leave to the doctors."

"Do you mean to say that, in the nine months she spent at Sing Sing, Maria Barbella never had a seizure?"

"Her health was a source of constant worry to me. That is all I can say. I am not a physician, but simply the wife of the warden of a state penitentiary," she replied firmly.

Rebecca Salomé Foster took her place at the witness stand. She was visibly nervous and restless. While she wanted to protect Maria, she was not at all certain that the girl suffered from epilepsy. Of course, Maria was weak: her blood pressure was low and she lacked appetite. However these were not symptoms of epilepsy, but rather common complaints among female prisoners. Of course, Maria was psychologically frail and very sensitive; yet she had never fainted in prison, and while everyone at the Tombs had heard her screaming at night from terrible nightmares, was this enough to define her as an epileptic? No, Mrs. Foster did not really agree with the defense strategy. Like Cora Di Brazzà and Julia Sage, she attributed the murder to a momentary loss of reason. She therefore feared the experts' questions.

"I met Maria Barbella on May 11 of last year," the Tombs Angel began. "After that I visited her every day until July 18, when she was transferred to Sing Sing. For a whole week from our first meeting, the girl did not speak at all; then, little by little, I convinced her to tell me something about her family, her country, and her work at the sweatshop. However, she never spoke of the crime: at the least hint of it she would fall into a gloomy silence. I will never understand how she survived that first trial . . . She was constantly on the verge of a nervous breakdown."

"Which did not occur, however," was McIntyre's ready remark.

"That is not exact," Mrs. Foster answered coldly. "When a person shuts herself off as Maria did, something is wrong. In my fourteen years' experience at the Tombs, I remember nothing more disconcerting than my meeting with this simple peasant girl. At first she did not understand me. Now she does. Despite her emotional frailty, she has come a long way. And this is due, in my opinion, to her great sensitivity towards others. . . ."

McIntyre called Emanuel Friend. The lawyer jokingly refused to state his age, as there were too many pretty ladies present. In the moment of levity that followed this statement, Maria looked around at the crowd for the first time. Friend told of when he had escorted the prisoner during her transfer to the Tombs from Sing Sing. When the Fourth Avenue street-car passed through Thirteenth Street, Friend asked Maria whether that street reminded her of Domenico's death. "No," she had answered serenely. "I used to live here, that's all I remember."

Frank S. Beard, official stenographer of the Second Circuit of the criminal court, was the next witness. Beard swore to the accuracy of his original transcript, and repeated the most important parts of Maria's testimony at the first trial, while McIntyre read the answers she gave the second time.

To the question of why Maria had taken Domenico's razor from the chest, the original answer had been: "Out of exasperation." Now the girl stated that she wanted to kill herself. When she had been asked where she was when she opened the razor, she had answered: "Right behind him." Now she said she could not remember. In her first testimony she had repeatedly stated she struck her lover in a moment of rage. Now all she remembered were the famous words "Only pigs marry!" The rest had disappeared.

These comparisons were crucial. A buzz rose from the court-room, and Gildersleeve's impatient request for silence only increased the turmoil. The jurors were attentive. Beard read from the transcript loudly, while Maria held Mrs. Foster's hand tightly and House shouted his objections.

"Your Honor, this is inadmissible! That testimony was struck by the Court of Appeals! What I ask, Your Honor, is why the Court of Appeals granted a new trial if the preceding testimony contains all the accurate answers."

Gildersleeve did not respond, nor did he sustain the objection.

"It's scandalous!" House exclaimed in a voice loud enough for all to hear.

The next witness was Benedetto Morossi, the interpreter whose tedious translation had put Maria at a disadvantage during the first trial. His English had improved a little, but not by much. Having emigrated from Venice seventeen years previously, Morossi had passed two public exams to be able to work as an interpreter. His testimony was briefer than his oath.

"I correctly translated all the questions put to Miss Barbella before Judge Goff, as well as her answers."

District Attorney Lauterbach then called Dr. John Ervine, the Sing Sing physician. Ervine had visited Maria every day, as her cell was in the infirmary. At first the girl tried to avoid those visits: when he came into the cell she would hide in a corner in terror, certain he had come to electrocute her. It was a few weeks before Julia Sage and the matrons were able to convince her the man was just a doctor.

McIntyre interrupted him and asked him about epilepsy. But Dr. Ervine was cautious:

"I am a general practitioner, sir," he answered. "It would not be fitting for me to talk about epilepsy in front of the eminent experts present in this courtroom. However, I must admit that I have rarely seen such an irrational fear in a person. Although it was July, she trembled constantly. You can think what you like but, as far as I'm concerned, her nerves had given in. Bringing her back to relative normality was not easy. It was not just a matter of prescribing sedatives: it was a real psychological challenge."

Anthony Comstock, president of the Society for the Suppression of Crime, said that he heard Maria's first statement at the Essex Market prison: "What she said made no sense. Maria was completely beside herself."

House and Friend were worried about their witness Francesco Cianelli, a plumber from Newark, New Jersey. Would he disappear like Nando Tavolacci? But the man showed up, and was even on time. Maria's lawyers had great hopes for his testimony. He spoke of Cataldo as a "heartbreaker" who boasted about his conquests to his friends. Three weeks before his death, Domenico had spent an evening with Francesco in a bar. After several beers, he admitted that some of his women had been unwilling, but, with a glass or two, everything was resolved. "Italian women are not used to strong liquors," Cataldo had said, laughing.

The jury never heard Cianelli's testimony, because Gildersleeve ruled it out after the first sentence. House jumped to his feet and a bitter discussion began between the defense, the judge, and the two assistant district attorneys. But the judge did not change his position and the plumber was dismissed without any explanation. Cianelli returned home, wondering why he had ever taken the trouble to go all the way to Manhattan.

Caterina and Vincenzo Manguso, who were managing the bar on the morning of April 26, were called one after the other. When Domenico had come to live in the neighborhood, he had told them Maria was his wife and they had believed him. The couple's testimony was not all that conclusive. Everything had happened at once. A scream was heard. Maria fell. Domenico tripped on her and then staggered out.

"How much time passed between the moment Domenico ran out and Maria's exit from the bar?" asked House through Vergara.

"I don't know," Caterina Manguso answered. "I had turned around to put on my shawl and take the keys to the bar and she was no longer there. When I saw the blood on the floor, I didn't know who had been hurt."

"How much time went by between the moment Maria entered the bar and the moment she cut his throat?"

"If I told you thirty seconds, or a minute, I would be lying. I was too confused. . . ."

Caterina Manguso admitted having said, before the first trial, that she didn't remember anything, and that therefore her presence in the courtroom would be useless.

Francesca Porzio, wife of Leopoldo the grocer, was from Viggiano, near Ferrandina. She had gone up to Domenico's apartment once, soon after the couple moved in. She had found him sitting at the table eating, while Maria was crying from behind a door, refusing to share the food with him. " 'Don't take any notice of that ugly monkey,' the man had said. 'She complains and torments me, she does nothing else.' I felt sorry for her. She used to come into the store and buy things, but always moved furtively and left in a hurry. The mother would sometimes stop in for a chat, but she never mentioned her daughter's troubles." The Porzios had found out that Maria was not Domenico's wife only a few days before the murder, when the man had announced he was about to return to Italy to his legitimate wife and children.

Morossi was the one who translated Angelo Piscopo's critical testimony. Angelo had been Maria's next door neighbor. Early one morning, about ten days before the tragedy, he was having breakfast with his wife when he heard someone crying in the entrance hall: it was Maria. They asked what had happened and she answered: "Nothing . . ." They had just returned to the kitchen when a scream brought them hurrying back to the entrance, where they found Maria in the grip of convulsions. So they took her to their bed, and Mrs. Piscopo sprinkled her face with cold water and rubbed her forehead until the girl regained consciousness.

McIntyre demanded to know what kind of scream it was, and the witness described it as well as he could. McIntyre asked if, by any chance, he could imitate it. It was a big mistake.

"Yes, sir," Angelo answered excitedly. The tall thin man stood up and gave the awful, gasping cry of the epileptic. It was an unmistakable scream. Angelo threw his head back and lifted his arms, rotating his hands upwards and then stopping them in midair. He stayed there, rigid, and yet trembling from head to foot.

"Sit down!" thundered McIntyre, but the damage was done. The jury had seen what the prosecution was seeking to deny. Angelo Piscopo was about to repeat his performance, but Lauterbach stopped him by reminding him that what counted when testifying were words, not gestures.

"How can I remember the words, since nothing whatsoever was said?" asked the witness impatiently. "Maria was unconscious for about ten minutes."

"Not more than ten minutes?" asked McIntyre.

"Who knows? I didn't look at the clock."

"Why are you rolling your eyes, Mr. Piscopo? Is it to show what Miss Barbella was doing?" asked McIntyre.

"No, sir. When I'm nervous, I always do that. It's a tic. I showed what Maria did when I was standing up."

"Was Domenico at home that morning?"

"No, he wasn't there. But whenever he was, we used to hear a lot of shouting and crying. . . ."

"Did you see Maria after the murder?"

"Yes. I saw her sitting at the kitchen window, all dressed up to go out, but I don't think she saw me. . . ."

By then it was past nine in the evening, and the first phase of the trial had come to an end.

CHAPTER TWENTY-FIVE

The battle of the experts began at ten on the morning of Tuesday, December 1, and ended nine days later. To the perplexity of the lay audience, the courtroom echoed with polysyllables relating to epilepsy, degeneracy, the early stages of alcoholism and the last stages of paresis, cranial dimensions, bregmatic irregularities, and so on. Maria, of course, did not understand a word of those scientific arguments and became more and more pale as the hours wore on. Mrs. Foster wondered how such a simple, if cruel, thing as a desperate act born of betrayed love could give rise to such complexities. Each scientist provided his own seemingly vital contribution. One addressed the whole range of human evolution, and even the first hominids were evoked on behalf of the little peasant from Basilicata.

Erudition overflowed and Latin quotes were countless. Did Maria forge her own destiny, or was she a passive tool in the hands of fate? Mrs. Foster was astounded. She had never heard anything like it at a trial. Such a collection of doctors and scientists had never been seen before in a courtroom. The onlookers followed the display with curiosity mixed with amazement.

Invoking the privilege of ignorance, the "Professor" and his entourage were absent from almost the entire medical debate.

Obviously the playwright and director had failed to see in it the potential for satire. Not so the reporter from the *New York Journal,* Julian Hawthorne, whose piece on December 3rd did not really amuse the medical community:

> Are your ears of different size?
>
>   Is your hard palate extremely high?
>
>   Are you less ticklish than others?
>
>   If affirmative answers to these questions describe your peculiarities, it is worthwhile noting it down. It will become important if you ever happen to kill a man and have to stand trial for murder.
>
>   Not only are your physical departures from the modern human being important but, if your father or brother has hair on his chest, do not forget that . . .

Dr. Alois F. Hardlika, a specialist in the combined sciences of criminology and anthropology, was the first to testify for the defense. He was slim, of medium height, with thick, untidy black hair falling over his forehead. He had studied in Italy with Professor Lombroso, with Professor Bourdel in Paris, with the criminologist Behr in Germany, and in America with Dr. Altman, the famous alienist. As a resident physician at the Middletown insane asylum, he had seen an average of forty epileptics a day for the past two years.

Hardlika had measured, weighed, and analyzed each member of the Barbella family.

"Are you aware," McIntyre began, "that Professor Langer in Vienna has found an error of .3 inches, defective, in Benedict's instruments?"

"No," answered Hardlika.

"You made your measurements with Benedict's instruments, did you not?"

"No, I used Glissière's calibers, Anthelme's cephalometer, and Broca's bregmatic indicator."

"Oh!" McIntyre exclaimed weakly, as Hardlika went on to expound his results.

"The defendant's father has large tufts of hair on the shoulders, and the neck and chest are extraordinarily hairy." The scientist spoke in the proud tones of a parent describing his newborn. "The bottom part of the chest juts out in an abnormal manner."

The spectators looked at the serene Italian in the second row with renewed interest.

"What do you have to tell us of Giuseppe, Maria's brother?" asked Hymes.

"His ears are of differing dimensions: the left one is 2.20 inches long and 1.35 wide, while the right is 2.26 inches long and only 1.18 wide."

The crowd reacted like a group of tourists turning to look at a monument, but Giuseppe's ears were hidden by his hair.

"In some parts of the body," added Dr. Hardlika, "I found that his reflexes were exaggerated or, on the contrary, beneath the norm. I also found several scars."

"And Mrs. Barbella? And Carlo? Antonia? Carmela? Giovanni?" One by one, Hardlika listed their anomalies. Giovanni's great asymmetrical head had interested him especially.

"And now let's talk about Maria," said Hymes. "Have you examined her?"

"Of course, three times."

"And what did you find?"

What Dr. Hardlika had found filled a forty-page report, a copy of which was given to each juror. He restrained himself from reading the whole thing out loud, and limited himself to listing the most important results, all in one breath. They were laid out in a chart as follows:

Height: 4 feet 10 inches;

Blood circulation: good;

Skin: healthy;

Eye color: hazel tending toward gray;

Hair color: black, thick;

Temperature: 100 degrees F (tongue);

Pulse: 90;

Breathing: 28 (short);

Form of head: subrachycephamic, Broca index, 81.9;

Circumference of the cranium: 20.50 inches;

Length of the face: 4.68 inches;

Height of the forehead: 1.88 inches;

Nose length: 1.98 inches; nose width: 1.20 inches;

Thickness of the lips: 0.66 inches;

Teeth: good;

Eyes myopic with normal pupils;

Often hears buzzing in the ears;

Smell and taste: normal;

The tongue shows a marked deviation toward the right;

When smiling the right corner of the lips is not as far away as left from the median line. . . .

Dreams: dreams mostly of fires; sees cats mostly black.

Vertigoes occur at night.

Finally Hardlika drew his conclusions: Despite the fact that Maria did not display any measurable perversions, she was nevertheless a smaller-than-average Italian, slightly ill-formed, with various symptoms of a low I.Q.

McIntyre treated Hardlika with open derision.

"Doctor, have you ever seen the museum freak, Jo-Jo, the man with a dog's face?" the prosecutor asked him solemnly.

The scientist thought it over for a minute. "No," he answered at last. Gildersleeve had the question struck from the record.

Hymes spoke next, reading a statement which covered more than fifteen pages, listing all the moral misdeeds of Maria's ancestors, her infantile convulsions, the fits and falls of her brothers and sisters, repeating all the measurements and deductions the witness had just provided. He told the story of the murder and described Maria's appearance and behavior during the first trial, as well as during the times spent at the Tombs and Sing Sing.

After an hour and twenty minutes he finally reached the end of the question:

"Now, Dr. Hardlika, supposing all these statements to be true, do you think that on April 26, 1895, the defendant was in a state of mind capable of distinguishing right from wrong and of evaluating the consequences of her act?"

"Do not answer!" shouted McIntyre, jumping to his feet and leaping toward the witness. McIntyre wanted the question struck. First off, he attacked the phrase: "The maternal grandmother was of substandard intelligence." The assistant prosecutor was certain the record did not confirm this, which brought about a tedious examination of the transcript and a three-hour discussion. Then McIntyre criticized every page of Hymes's statement. Many of his objections were upheld.

Soon after, the prosecutor began a ruthless cross-examination of Dr. Hardlika, pointing out that he was only twenty-eight years old.

"Weren't you a cigar maker at one point?" McIntyre asked, smiling.

"Yes, out of necessity. I made cigars to pay for my studies."

Gildersleeve remarked that there was absolutely nothing wrong with cigar making, and House pointed out that one of the greatest American magistrates, Judge Daniels, had paid his way through university by shining shoes.

McIntyre then produced from under the table some great sheets of heavy paper, which he spread out. He showed one sheet to Dr. Hardlika, who looked at it curiously. The paper had been pierced with a needle and the holes formed an ellipse.

"It's the outline of a man's head," the assistant prosecutor said. "Do you see anything strange?"

The scientist examined it from every angle. "Well, no," he answered after a while. "It's just that it is abnormally. . . ."

"Abnormally long?"

"Exactly," confirmed Hardlika.

"The head is so long," remarked McIntyre, "that the New York Central Railroad is flourishing; so very long that Consuelo is now the Duchess of Marlborough. Doctor, this is the outline of William Vanderbilt's head."

Hardlika looked embarrassed. The crowd stirred, while McIntyre handed the specialist another drawing.

"What do you think of this head?" he asked him.

Hardlika studied the shape. "Well, it's not quite normal," he answered cautiously.

"Is it the head of a degenerate?" McIntyre pressed him.

"No, I wouldn't say that. . . ." muttered the scientist. He had barely saved himself, as the outline was of Senator David B. Hill's head.

The test continued. The judge, who was restless, leaned forward as Hardlika studied another piece of paper.

"The shape and the dimensions of this head appear to be normal," the doctor asserted confidently, "maybe it's a little too big."

"Are there any signs of degeneration?"

"No, none."

This was a prudent answer, as the subject was Judge Gildersleeve himself.

The assistant prosecutor was about to hand Hardlika another sheet when House stood up, shouting that McIntyre was tormenting the doctor. "It's an old trick and I'm surprised that Mr. McIntyre would stoop to such methods to demonstrate his thesis. . . ." House declared.

"Sir!" roared the assistant district attorney. "Sir! I have never
been attacked in the courtroom before. . . ."

The judge rapped his gavel energetically, and Hardlika was
excused from classifying other distinguished American citizens
as idiots, lunatics, or criminals.

"Do you agree with the fact that various grades of responsibility exist?" McIntyre then asked.

"No," was Dr. Hardlika's answer. "If a person is irresponsible, how can he be more or less so? There can be no degrees."

"Now, what do you mean by normal and abnormal?"

"There is no man who can answer this question," stated
Hardlika. "It is something that varies with race, the social conditions, the customs and habits, the latitude. . . ."

While this duel went on to the public's great delight, Maria
and her family seemed indifferent to everything.

Hardlika cited the case of an Italian soldier who had shot an
officer during an epileptic seizure, without remembering what
had happened.

"Of course," said McIntyre, "but that was a case of madness. . . . There was no motive, right?"

"Yes, that's right . . . apparently not."

"Yet the man was tried, found guilty, and shot. Was he not?"

"He was."

"Doctor, do you think all epileptics are mentally ill?"

Hardlika answered evasively: leaders such as Alexander the
Great and George Washington had epilepsy, as well as poets
such as Coleridge, without detriment to their military or literary exploits.

At this point Edward Hymes of the defense asked the court
whether Dr. Hardlika could answer the famous question: "On
April 26, 1895, was Maria Barbella in a state of mind that

would permit her to distinguish good from evil and to evaluate the consequences of her act?"

Gildersleeve motioned him to continue.

"She was in a state of mental aberration, caused by a slight epileptic seizure."

"When did the aberration take place, before or after the seizure?"

"It was a part of the seizure."

"Does this mean she was in a state similar to that of a sleepwalker?"

McIntyre objected to the comparison, and the doctor was not allowed to give a clinical description of sleepwalking.

"What is your definition of mental insanity?" asked McIntyre.

"As Spitzka points out in his great work on the subject, it is almost impossible to give a definition of mental illness. . . ." Hardlika waffled.

The professor of mental illness Dr. Charles Dana was called to the stand next, and Hymes was asked to repeat his question. The doctor, however, wanted first to give a brief introduction on epilepsy.

"Latent epilepsy," he explained, "better known as psychic epilepsy, often manifests itself with a violent impetus toward a person or thing that is within reach. The state of *stupor* which derives from it, that is of confusion and disorientation, is common to all epileptics. Sometimes, after this phase, the subject has vague memories of what happened, but usually there is a total loss of memory."

"Is it true that during their fits, epileptics use more force than necessary?" asked Hymes, remembering that Maria, in severing those vocal cords that had so often lied to her, had almost decapitated her lover.

"That's true," Dr. Dana confirmed.

McIntyre came forward. "Let us suppose that the defendant has stated that, had the mother not been present, she would have struck Domenico an hour earlier. Would such a statement by any chance change your opinion regarding her responsibility?"

"Not at all," answered the doctor.

"Let us suppose there were no evidence the girl is an epileptic, what then would your opinion be?"

"I cannot suppose that there is no evidence, because there is," asserted the doctor.

"Suppose then that the subject pulled the razor from the sleeve where she had hidden it, pulled back the victim's head to expose the throat and make the cut a decisive one, and, having struck the blow, had thrown the razor away, then telling the officer who arrested her that she did all this in an excess of rage because her lover did not want to marry her. . . . Would this not prove the presence of a memory which is incompatible with the theory of irresponsibility due to epilepsy?"

"Someone may have told her what she did," Dr. Dana hazarded.

"And if the murderess remembered exactly the victim's last words, could she maintain that she lost her memory?"

"She could not."

"Now, doctor, I ask you to suppose that the defendant did make all these statements."

"In that case there would be no doubt: The woman has retained a memory of what took place."

"Well then: if she had had a convulsive seizure without loss of memory, how would you define what she had?"

"Epileptoid automatism," Dana stated.

"But, doctor, how is it possible that a person in such a state should take a razor from her own sleeve, open it, cut a man's throat, withdraw and throw the razor away?"

"All I can say is that in my opinion Maria Barbella did not know who she was, where she was, and what she was doing. . . ."

"And yet she knew very well who Cataldo was and why!"

"Epileptics often display homicidal tendencies toward those they love. . . ."

The exchange continued for several hours. Mrs. Foster was in the grip of an anxiety she had never felt before. McIntyre dragged Dr. Dana along twisted hypothetical routes, but the doctor firmly defended his initial opinion: Maria was epileptic.

Dr. Frederick Peterson was president of the board of directors of the Craig Epileptic Colony and a professor at the Vanderbilt Clinic School of Medicine and Surgery. He stated that in his examination of Maria he had found a paralysis of the right side of the face. Her general condition was abnormal. He agreed with his colleagues that, at the terrible moment of Domenico Cataldo's murder, Maria was, to all intents and purposes, in a sleepwalking state and therefore was not aware of what she was doing.

McIntyre attacked him. Dr. Peterson, a shy man by nature, lost confidence. On his way to the witness stand he had seen on the assistant prosecutor's table copies of his most important scientific papers and, with great surprise, even the latest edition of his collection of poems, which was titled *In the Shade of Ygdrasil*. McIntyre opened the book and read aloud the passages which had struck him in relation to Maria's case. From a poem, entitled "The Idiot," he recited this stanza:

> *The horrid vacant visage leers*
> *And shows its heritage woe:*
> *Its scars—the sins of ancient years.*
> *Could any love or hate it? No!*
> *Pity may give her tears. . . .*

While everyone was left wondering what these lines really meant and why the attorney had introduced them at all, Dr. Peterson was visibly embarrassed. Fortunately for him, the prosecutor then closed the book and focused on the doctor's scientific literature, which addressed the "stigmata of degeneration."

Among these, Peterson listed premature graying of the hair and a sparse beard (alopaecia and phocomelacia.) For a living example, Dr. Peterson shyly pointed to Dr. Graeme Hammond's mane of hair and Dr. Safford Newton's beard. Both were witnesses for the prosecution. Being a dwarf or a giant also were signs of degeneration. Attorney Friend, who was short, was of that category.

"Doctor, have you ever examined your ears?" asked McIntyre.

"I have," answered Peterson, smiling, "and I think they're not so bad."

The rest of the courtroom escaped his scrutiny. In the end, Dr. Peterson explained that simply having one or two obvious physical defects did not at all constitute a sign of degeneration.

Dr. George Jacoby, an epilepsy specialist, stated that in some cases the subjects retained a vague memory of their seizure, but that it often faded. "An epileptic, for example, could set a house on fire and watch it burn," he explained. "He may at first remember enough of the flames to describe them, but may soon afterwards deny ever even having witnessed the fire . . . Maria Barberi lost consciousness at the precise moment in which the man uttered those fateful words. Had Domenico kept his mouth shut, he might still be alive today," he concluded.

Richard M. Wattenberg, juror number 12, stood up. "Does a person always lose their mind when they are in a state of trance?" he asked, giving rise to an erudite digression. Jacoby explained that, among the Indians of the western plains, and the Balinese in the Dutch East Indies, "trance" did not mean loss of mind but rather a higher state of consciousness. "In the epileptic trance," he explained finally, "the subject has no idea of what they are doing."

Dr. Allen McLane Hamilton was the first expert witness for the prosecution. According to him, Maria was fully in possession of her faculties at the moment of the murder. Had she been in the grip of an epileptic seizure, she would have attacked any person present in the bar and not necessarily the man who betrayed her. At Hymes' question: "What does being of sound mind mean to you?" Hamilton answered:

"I don't know, how about you? There is no standard of mental health, but a man is generally considered to be of sound mind when he does not display substantial differences from his fellows."

Dr. Allen Fitch had a fastidious sense of humor which the defense attorneys found particularly grating. About him, Hawthorne wrote:

> Dr. Fitch came, moreover, recommended by an army of thirty thousand insane persons, and more epileptics than he cared to specify. But all that to no avail. Mr. Hymes discovered in his testimony symptoms of mental fog that would have done credit to London in November, and even precipitated an explosion that seemed likely to endanger more lives than Maria's.

"Let us suppose that a person sees a flash of light and then complete darkness," said Hymes, "and then finds herself in a different place; that she is foaming at the mouth, and then remembers absolutely nothing of what has happened from the moment in which she saw the flash and the one in which she wakes up . . . What would you say her state of mind was?"

"Well, something along those lines could happen at the Turkish baths. . . ." Fitch answered calmly.

"This is a joke, doctor, not an answer," shouted House, leaping forward. "We are here debating on a woman's life, and you, a respected expert, sit on the witness stand making such comments!"

McIntyre accused House of being offensive. But the lawyer would not be silenced: "Your Honor, we want Dr. Fitch's answer to go on the record. We will make good use of it!"

But the expert had answered in absolute good faith. He tried to explain, but could not make himself heard above the lawyers' din.

"Mr. House, there has been a misunderstanding. I meant exactly what I said. However I did not at all mean to say that Miss Barbella was in a Turkish bath. I believe the young lady knew perfectly well that the sharp blade could wreak irreversible damage. . . ."

Dr. Safford Newton had visited Maria in the Tombs several times. He had found her to be of sound mind and body, and attributed her hysteria to her solitude.

"In any case doubts are arising among alienists as to heredity as an explanation for epilepsy," he specified. "The percentage of cases in which heredity determines predisposition ranges from 11 to 31 percent. The most common cause is linked to trauma of the brain during birth or shortly after."

"What are the things that can bring on an epileptic fit?" Hymes asked him.

"In some cases indigestion, excesses, lack of sleep. . . ."

"And what do you say of emotional traumas?"

"Yes, sometimes. Any kind of emotional shock can unleash an epileptic seizure."

Dr. Newton's final statement was also the last the jury heard:

"Every single one of Maria Barbella's actions the morning of the murder show that she was in full possession of her mental faculties. Taking the razor from the chest and hiding it were, in my opinion, voluntary and fully conscious acts."

"EPILEPSY OR BARBARISM?" ran Chapin's headline:

... It is not that Maria Barberi was ever insane or that she is now irresponsible, or that emotion deprived her of reason, but that, owing to heredity from 'degenerates,' she had an epileptic seizure during which she cut her lover's throat in a sort of somnambulistic trance without knowing it.

The truth is that indignant shame and the rage of a woman betrayed and scorned explain the murder fully, epilepsy or no epilepsy. The girl is simply a barbarian and did as a barbarian would naturally have done under the circumstances.

Perhaps there is no one in New York who wishes to see her suffer the extreme penalty of the law, but most people are unlikely to forget that laws are made to restrain barbarism. ...

Friday, December 10, was the day the verdict was to be delivered. In front of the courthouse, Franklin Street was packed with people, although the biggest crowd was under the Bridge of Sighs: Maria would cross it at 9:55 that morning.

Special permits were needed to enter. All the jurors' wives had made use of their privileges, and two of them, Mrs. Marcus Seliger and Mrs. David Allen, had not missed a single day of the trial. While Julian Hawthorne, thanks to his press pass, made a smooth entry, Professor Hurwitz had to make use of all his eloquence in order to set foot inside the courtroom.

Maria crossed the bridge swiftly, provoking a strange furor in the crowd beneath, as happens in a bicycle race when the leader passes a crowded bend.

In the courtroom, while House's energetic closing statement rang out, Rebecca Foster studied the jurors. Their calm, almost impassive expressions concealed doubts and certainties which would affect Maria's fate. The Tombs Angel could not find comfort in the fragmented, ambiguous testimony of the past three weeks. What had that immense flood of words demonstrated? In her opinion, the army of experts had not affected the controversy. The defense had declared Maria not responsible while, according to the prosecution, Maria was herself at the moment of the crime. The doctors had confirmed both points of view. When opposing sides both sponsor expert opinion, the result is usually balanced, and the average jury member finds himself in the position of a medieval prince surrounded by astrologers. To whom, Mrs. Foster asked herself, would the royal favor go? In medieval disputes, the astrologers themselves risked their heads if they lost. In this case, Maria was the only one risking anything. The gravest threat came from McIntyre's comparison between her two depositions, from the first and the current trial.

"This girl's destiny was set from the very day she was born," Frederick House said with pathos, "because her family was marked by a terrible disease that is transmitted by heredity. Against this destiny Maria could not, and cannot, do a thing. The prosecution states that the mother's and the sister's seizures were not epileptic convulsions, but rather hysterical attacks. However, if this family's clinical history is accurate, we are forced to concede Maria Barbella at least the benefit of the doubt. . . .

"If Maria was of sound mind at the moment in which she struck Domenico, then she is responsible for the death of a man. But the law in its clemency states that, as soon as the question of responsibility arises, the burden of evidence falls on the prosecution. And because the seed of doubt has been sown, it is now up to the prosecution to prove that when she killed Domenico Cataldo, the girl was legally and morally responsible for her action. The only truth here is that Maria Barbella suffers from epilepsy. Distressed at Domenico's insults and unaware of her own illness, she killed a man whom, at any rate, the city certainly will not miss. . . ."

This last comment was greeted by an ovation. The women, who were on the verge of rushing to show House their approval, were blocked by the doormen and returned to their seats.

"This is not a public square!" shouted Gildersleeve.

The crowd in the courtroom took Maria's side almost to a man. When McIntyre stood to speak, the applause turned to silence. Once more he felt forced into the role of the devil's advocate, which, although unpleasant, had become familiar to him. Calm and detached, McIntyre summarized his thesis with compelling logic:

"As we have established beyond any reasonable doubt," he began, "the crime was deliberate. Maria Barbella's ability to distinguish good from evil was questioned only by experts called by the defense. Had all the esteemed physicians agreed on her lack of responsibility, I would have closed the case, despite my and Mr. Lauterbach's personal convictions.

"Maria Barbella is not only responsible for her lover's murder; she is first of all responsible for allowing Domenico Cataldo to seduce her. There is no man capable of forcing a woman to do something she does not consent to," he stated loudly. "There is no man capable of forcing a woman to drink unless she is thirsty," he added, among growing murmurs. "Cataldo drank more than half of the same drink as Maria and yet he did not lose consciousness of his own actions. His refusal to marry her does not justify a homicide." He was no longer addressing the jury, but rather the turbulent crowd. "It does not justify that!" he shouted. "The defendant last year provided a version of the facts, and this time not even that. I have nothing more to add. . . ."

Judge Gildersleeve then gave his charge to the jury. He repeated the main points of the testimony, lingering over the evidence presented by the prosecution's specialists. He explained how to distinguish among different degrees of murder, ending with:

"The jury must judge the defendant guilty, unless it considers her of unsound mind."

It was five in the afternoon. While the jurors filed out, Maria was led to an adjacent room.

"Voices were heard and there was a certain to-do," wrote Julian Hawthorne.

Someone said the jury needed legal counsel on a controversial point; in any case, forty minutes later word was sent that a verdict had been reached. The men solemnly returned to their seats. "It will doubtless be murder in the first degree . . ." someone muttered. Gildersleeve's brief charge had tipped the balance in that sense.

The clerk took the roll. Three or four voices betrayed strong emotion. The first juror asked: "What is your verdict? Guilty or not guilty?"

"Not guilty," announced Melchior Ullmer, juror number eight, with a smile.

"May God be praised!" a woman's voice shouted. It was the voice of the Tombs Angel.

The steamer S.S. *Fulda* had reached New York at four that same afternoon. Cora called the offices of House, Friend &

Grossman as soon as the carriage dropped them off at the apartment she and Detalmo had rented.

Frederick House himself answered: he had just come back from the court.

"I'm delighted to hear from you, madam," he said. "Stay on the line, there is a person here who wants to speak to you. . . ."

The lawyer handed the phone to Maria, who jumped to her feet, beaming with happiness. She had never spoken on a telephone before, and House had to show her how to hold the receiver.

"Hello! Hello!" shouted Maria. "I love you, they have let me out of prison. I'm free!"

"I can't wait to see you!" Cora was overjoyed. "I have just arrived and we are at 254 Madison Avenue. We will expect you with your family tomorrow morning. . . . I can't wait to see you," she said again.

"It's the first time I speak on the telephone, madam, I have so many things to tell you. God bless you. Yes, oh . . ." Maria thought of something to say: "Have you been to the prince's wedding in Rome?"

"Yes, and I also went to visit the Pope," answered Cora. "He gave me something for you. You'll get it tomorrow morning. . . ."

The December 13th *Herald* described the meeting between Cora and Maria:

. . . Maria and her family, father, mother, and little Giovanni, whose head caused such a sensation during the trial, drove from their home at 218 Bowery in the carriage sent by the Countess di Brazzà to pick them up. Maria was dressed in an elegant black gown.

The countess received them in her apartment. The family bowed low before their benefactress and thanked her for all her kindness. She denied herself to all who sent up their cards and sent down word that she was not in. The countess, who aside from being a philanthropist is also a talented writer, was making preparations for a trip to Boston for the publication of her new novel *An American Idyll.*

The Barberis sat upon the tufted, upholstered chairs and told the countess that nobody had been as good a friend to them as she had.

It was a strange group to behold. Little Giovanni, with his hands on his knees and his eyes bulging from his head, sat on the edge of a chair, mesmerized by a clock. The mother with her black shawl over her chest, and her thin fingers interlaced, fixed her eyes only on the countess. The father nervously twisted his dingy, slouch hat.

Maria was entirely at ease. She sat primly in the chair and talked in a low voice. She has many of the ways of a well-bred woman now.

The countess congratulated her in English and expressed surprise to see how much she had changed. She asked if the canary was still alive.

"Of course, Cicillo is still alive!" the girl exclaimed, laughing. Later she would go to the Tombs and fetch it. She hadn't taken it home with her the night before, only because the Tombs Angel thought it might catch cold.

The countess spoke in Italian to Maria's parents, and even patted little Giovanni's head. Then she gave Maria an amber rosary from Italy which had been blessed by the Pope himself. Attached to it was a small gold medallion with a portrait in relief of Leo XIII.

Meanwhile the count, who is an inventor, was ready with his photographic equipment. He asked the Barberis to pose for a portrait. Various shots were taken, first of Maria sitting with her relatives, then of the countess herself standing next to her protégée in the middle of the group.

The last portrait was of Maria with the eight-year-old beautiful Countess Idanna smiling on her lap. . . .

The next day Maria traveled alone for the first time in her life. She took the train to Sing Sing, where she spent Christmas with Warden Sage and his wife, Julia.

On December 14, the *Abend-Blait* newspaper announced the opening of *Maria Barberi: A Soul on Fire,* a tragedy in four acts by Moishe Ha-Levi Ish Hurwitz. The Yiddish-language performances began the following Saturday at the Thalia Theater on the Lower East Side. It played every night until the end of January 1897, with two performances at Christmas and New Year's. The *World* hailed it as a "sensational success," and *Il Progresso Italo-Americano* wrote that the theater was always crowded with Italians who did not understand a word.

On December 31, the front page of the *New York Journal* carried this headline: "MARIA BARBERI A HEROINE! Risked Her Life to Rescue Woman From Flames."

Mrs. Dolly Hogan, the wife of a printer who lives in the same house as the Barberi family, accidentally set fire to herself yesterday. Her apron, saturated with kerosene from a broken lamp, was set on fire by contact with the stove while she prepared her husband's dinner. It was 5 P.M., and with her sweet soprano voice, known in the tenement, she was singing "My Pearl is a Bowery Girl."

Miss Barberi was knitting near the window that looks out onto Mrs. Hogan's balcony. But suddenly a scream caused her to look up. Mrs. Hogan was in flames on the balcony. Maria grabbed a blanket and ran up the stairs, bursting into the flat and out onto the balcony. The skirt, ablaze all over, sent the flames swirling above Mrs. Hogan's head. At the risk of setting fire to herself, Maria beat out the flames with her own hands, and tore off the blazing garment from her neighbor. Then she wrapped the blanket around the burned woman.

Mrs. Hogan, who was rushed to Gouverneur Hospital by the firemen, is in serious condition and might not survive.

Everyone agrees that if Maria Barberi had not appeared at the critical moment, Mrs. Hogan would have died on the balcony. . . .

EPILOGUE

*T*he first woman to die by electrocution was Martha M. Place of Brooklyn, who was executed at Sing Sing on March 20, 1899, two years and three months after Maria Barbella's acquittal.

In the Tombs, Warden John J. Fallon's reign of malice ended the year Maria was freed. On January 6, 1896, twenty of his own staff charged him formally with cruelty. The resulting investigation led to his removal, but the Tombs retained an infamous reputation.

At Sing Sing, Warden Omar V. Sage remained in charge until his retirement in 1901. On January 9, 1917, he died of heart failure at the age of 82.

Judge John W. Goff had sentenced Maria to death at her first trial and, eventually, she passed a sentence on him. Her mistrial precipitated a debate which led to the abolishment of a vestige of colonial rule that allowed political and judicial functions to overlap.

Goff favored the strict mandate of the death penalty, but he was lax when it came to respecting the separation of powers. In 1895, he received a total salary of $16,000, partly for his position as a judge and partly as a member of both the Sinking Fund Commission and the Board for the Revision of Taxes and Assessments. He was also allowed $2,000 a year to rent an office outside the courthouse. He was forever hurrying out of the courtroom to attend political meetings.

Maria's trial sowed doubts which put an end to Goff's judicial career. It was eventually decided that he was not, in fact, a judge. Under modern statutes, he was merely a municipal officer. John W. Goff died of pneumonia on November 9, 1924, at the age of 76. Judge Otto Rosalsky had this to say to the *New York Times* reporter who interviewed him for the obituary:

"He felt that the world must be taught that the commission of crime carried with it punishment. He also believed that if we carried leniency too far or yielded to sentimentality, the result would be the degeneration of society."

John F. McIntyre's twenty-year career as assistant district attorney was distinguished. He prosecuted 614 murder cases and lost only 34. In 1897, shortly after Maria's acquittal, McIntyre resigned and set up private practice. He was approached by Irish-American societies to undertake the defense in England of Edward Ivory, an Irish Fenian charged with plotting to kill the Queen. McIntyre was the first American lawyer to defend a client in a British court. In 1916, he became a judge in New York. At the age of 72, on January 19, 1927, Judge McIntyre died of pneumonia at his home at 163 West 77th Street.

Lawyer Emanuel Friend pursued a brilliant career in criminal law. On the morning of November 1, 1904, he went to his office in the Pulitzer Building as usual. In the course of business, he wrote a check for an overdue life insurance premium and asked the clerk to deliver it. The clerk objected that it could just as well be mailed, whereupon Mr. Friend joked, "No, you'd better take it now, as I might drop dead this afternoon."

That day he left the office early, and later collapsed of heart failure in his home at 28 Hamilton Terrace. He was 51 years old.

Edward Hymes, the pioneer of psychiatric evidence in criminal trials, became an American chess champion, representing the United States in the cable matches against England from 1897 to 1903. He died of pneumonia in May 1938 at age 67. Although he was not remembered primarily as a ground-breaking lawyer, his field of psychiatric defense has evolved over the years into a powerful tool, often used to manipulate the truth.

On January 24, 1907, lawyer Frederick House accepted an appointment to the Board of City Magistrates, and in July of the same year was elected its president.

"The system is flawed. . . . Sometimes I think I've chosen the wrong line," he once had told Cora. Perhaps for this reason, in 1917, at the dawn of the automobile age, House accepted the assignment to serve as judge in New York's Traffic Court. And it was to this trifling domain that his remarkable sense of fairness was confined. He served for eighteen years through the administrations of five mayors, and died of pneumonia in

1925 at the age of 68. It is doubtful whether any of the 300,000 cases he tried as a traffic judge brought him the same gratification as Maria's acquittal.

On January 17, 1919, Charles E. Chapin, the city editor of the *World* who had blackmailed and harassed Cora, entered Sing Sing as a confessed murderer. He had killed his wife.

". . . Of Charles Chapin it can be truthfully said that he came willingly, even eagerly, to prison," writes Warden Lewis Lawes in his memoirs, *20,000 Years in Sing Sing.*

Chapin became the editor of *The Bulletin,* the prison paper. Nine years before his parole review, he died of pneumonia on December 30, 1930.

Joseph Petrosino, Cora's bodyguard, began a crusade against the Mafia which led him to an early grave. He had pursued his assignment overseas, investigating Italian connections to American organized crime. He was shot to death in Palermo, in a deserted corner of the Piazza Marina, late on the evening of March 12, 1909.

Attracted by the gunshots, a sailor from the warship *Halabria* found Petrosino hanging by one hand from the grating of a nearby window, blinded by blood from a head wound, but still struggling to lift his revolver. He was 48 years old. On his person were found notes on Mafia membership in the United States and in Sicily, as well as several postcards addressed to his bride of eighteen months: "Adelina Petrosino, 233 Lafayette Street, New York."

The Neapolitan Camorra denied responsibility for the murder, blaming the Sicilian Mafia. Not since the assassination of King Umberto I of Italy, eight years before, had the Italian colony in New York experienced an equal commotion. Cries of despair filled densely-populated Mulberry Bend, where Petrosino was so well known.

"*E morto! Il povero Petrosino!*"

A month later, on April 12, Petrosino's funeral procession drew a crowd of 200,000 along the route from the old Church of St. Patrick on Mott Street to Calvary Cemetery in Queens. One thousand policemen accompanied the police band, which played Verdi's "Requiem March."

Cora's bodyguard, the first Italian-American hero of law enforcement, was described at his burial as "a man with the seal of nobility, not on parchment, but in his heart."

On the morning of Saturday, February 22, 1902, a fire which spread from the Seventy-First Regiment Armory to the adjoining Park Avenue Hotel claimed eighteen lives. Rebecca Salomé Foster, the Tombs Angel, was among the victims.

"She was caught by the back draught and successive waves of flames," reported the *New York Times.*

Her February 26th funeral at the Calvary Episcopal Church on 21st Street, by Gramercy Park, was the scene of a remarkable gathering. In the same pews with judges and lawyers sat reformed prostitutes and thieves. Philanthropists and clergymen mingled with prison guards, court clerks, and children from the slums. Hundreds stood in the rear of the church and in the side aisles.

A small woman dressed in black approached the casket with a bouquet of violets and knelt beside it throughout the service. Her name was Maria Barbella.

In April 1904, a monument to Mrs. Foster was installed in the Criminal Courts Building. Sculpted by Karl Bitter, it included an ". . . allegorical tablet portraying the Tombs Angel comforting a young man. The inscription read: 'On Her Lips Was the Law of Kindness.' "

President Theodore Roosevelt, one of the first contributors to the monument's fund, wrote: "It is a pleasure to testify even in so small a way to the work of Mrs. John W. Foster. . . ."

When the Criminal Courts Building was demolished in 1938, the Foster memorial was relegated to the basement of the new building at 100 Centre Street. There it remained, virtually forgotten, until 1983, when art historian Michele Cohen of the New York City Art Commission discovered it in an inventory. Mrs. Foster's memorial is currently under restoration at the Metropolitan Museum, and will eventually be reinstalled in the hall of the Criminal Courts Building.

In an interview with the *New York Times* on April 1, 1900, Mrs. Foster confided that the most disturbing memory of her life was the night she had spent with Maria Barbella in the death cell at Sing Sing.

"I resolved," she said, "that if I could alleviate the suffering of just that one woman, my life would have been well lived."

A few days after Maria Barbella's acquittal, Cora Slocomb di Brazzà's novel, *An American Idyll*, was published in Boston, with 70 of her original illustrations. The *North American Review* of January 1897 wrote:

> . . . The Countess di Brazzà comes for the first time before the American public in a strictly artistic capacity. It must be admitted that she has produced a unique story. Its hero is a handsome, blue-eyed European of wealth and position, devoted to scientific pursuits.

In his scientific thirst for new worlds to explore, he pays a long visit to the chief settlement of the Piman Baja Indians of the Sierra Madre, about whom little is known.

The heroine, a young Piman girl, Ampharita, "the silent one," becomes his guide on specimen-gathering expeditions. . . .

Civilization and Savagery meet in two choice representatives, and the credit does not exactly lie with Civilization in the sequel. . . .

In its scientific accuracy, the story has the value of a treatise on the Piman Indians. The truthfulness of her insight reminds the reader of the tenderness of Helen Hunt Jackson. . . .

Cora's public life ended in 1906, at the age of 44.

"It happened suddenly," writes Detalmo in his memoirs. "She had a breakdown and, after that day, she was never the same again."

Was it the pressure of a benign tumor? Was it a consequence of the typhoid which had almost killed her in her early twenties? Or was it simply mental exhaustion? We will never know. She became ill, without warning, on a hot May afternoon. She was passing through Bologna on her way back to Brazzà from the earthquake-devastated region of Calabria, where she had organized relief. While trying on a new outfit at her dressmaker's, she suddenly became frantic and began to tear at the fabric. By the time Detalmo arrived, she had been hospitalized and did not recognize him.

On June 8, her new life began in Imola, near Bologna, under the close care of the remarkable Dr. Cesare Ferrari. His revolutionary ideas anticipated the work of the well-known British psychologist, Dr. Ronald Laing.

The park surrounding her building reminded Detalmo of Brazzà. Cora occupied a private apartment on the ground floor.

She never left her rooms. Ten years after her protégée Maria had left prison, Cora entered hers. Detalmo could not live away from his wife, even though the chances of seeing her were rare. For fourteen years, until his death, he divided his time between Brazzà and Imola, where he sojourned for long periods as a guest of Dr. Ferrari. On each visit, he brought with him Cora's favorite flowers, the wild violets of Brazzà, wrapped carefully in moist cotton so they would not lose their scent.

Cora had always feared fire, and now was obsessed about it. New Orleans had had more fires than any other city in the world, and her father had served as a volunteer fireman. Her monologues were confusing. Had she seen a great fire as a child? Or had it been a dream in which she had watched her father stride into the flames?

She was spared the news of the fire which destroyed Brazzà and of her own mother's death a few days earlier. The First World War passed unnoticed. When Detalmo's visits stopped in 1922, she did not understand that he had died. She missed her only daughter's wedding to my grandfather, a dashing cavalry officer, as well as the births of her three grandchildren. My grandmother, Idanna, died in January, 1940. But this, too, escaped her.

Cora, who had been a driving force in so many lives and the catalyst of so many events, took her leave from life silently, almost unnoticed, while her adopted country was being ravaged by yet another terrible world war. She passed away in Rome on August 24, 1944. She was eighty-two years old. Only her large and luminous aquamarine eyes had not changed.

Less than a year after her release from the Tombs, Maria Barbella married a man from her village.

"MARIA BARBERI WEDS," trumpeted the *New York Herald* headline on Thursday, November 4, 1897. *After a Courtship of Less Than Twenty-four Hours She Becomes Mrs. Francesco Paolo Bruno.*

. . . At half-past six yesterday afternoon, three carriages rumbled up to the [Tammany Hall] club house, and the braves, who were celebrating the Tammany sweep, swarmed out on the stoop, expecting to greet Mr. Van Wyck, Mr. Sheehan, or some other big guns of the wigwam. Instead they were confronted by a bridal party headed by Lawyers Frederick House and Emanuel Friend and Civil Justice Lynn. The situation was explained and the front room was cleared for action.

Unfortunately the groom had neglected to provide a ring, but an Italian relative relieved his embarrassment by loaning her own ring which was returned after the ceremony.

The braves did the right thing by opening a keg of beer and drinking to the health of the happy couple. . . .

The *World* picture of the wedding showed Maria still dressed in mourning. Her only festive adornment was a bouquet of fresh violets. Her new thick-lensed spectacles aged her. Her husband, a twenty-five year old barber and son of former neighbors of the Barbellas, had just arrived in New York from Ferrandina.

"I never saw him until Tuesday," Maria told the *New York Times.* "I didn't want to marry him. I wanted to wait a year, but my parents wouldn't let me."

Other than the report of her attendance at the funeral of the Tombs Angel, there are few traces of Maria after her wedding,

and I am unable to find a Mr. and Mrs. Francesco Paolo Bruno
in the 1900 Brooklyn census at their last-known place of residence, 227 Central Avenue. I journey back to Italy to continue
my search. Had they returned to their native village of Ferrandina? I am curious to find out whether Maria had any children.
When and where did she die?

Like Cora, I reach Ferrandina in the fall. Cora had traveled
there by carriage, I go by car, because there is still no train station. Cora had been a guest of the mayor, but I rent a room
from the keeper of a "Sali e Tabacchi," a typical Italian store sell-
ing cigarettes, Nivea cream, salt, and lottery tickets. Ferrandina
still lacks a hotel. It has one gas station and no movie theater.
The village carpenter doubles as an undertaker. Three main
churches serve 9,000 inhabitants. The postman still brings news
from relatives in North America. The married women hurry
about in black shawls. The ninety-eight-year-old niece of Rocco
Recchia, the barber-doctor who testified at Maria's second trial,
is still alive. Like other old women, she adheres to the traditional black bodice, the embroidered white blouse, and full
black skirt. A framed five dollar bill hangs next to her husband's
photograph on a whitewashed wall, alongside a Madonna. Her
one-room house is sandwiched between similar houses, and its
front door is also the only window. Mrs. Recchia has the smile
and the voice of a young girl. She speaks to me in her dialect.
We sit outside in straw chairs, and her gnarled hands seem to
crochet by themselves. The smell of fresh bread fills the air. She
suddenly asks me to help her rise. She wants to take me somewhere, and we end up four doors down at the baker's shop,
where a small inquisitive crowd surrounds us while she offers
me a fresh warm loaf of bread; then we part.

Young men still sit at the cafe in the piazza, playing games of
Neapolitan Briscola, sipping anisette, and forever discussing

emigration, no longer across the Atlantic but to the industrial cities of the north.

The palaces of the two rich families who once owned all the land are still standing. A recent tremor has cracked their walls. The earthquake's scars can be seen seen everywhere. People speak about the repairs they are planning with the promised government emergency funds that, two years later, have not yet arrived. Their hopeful tones betray impotence and fatalism. I finally understand why even "Christ stopped at Eboli," some miles away, without venturing any further.

A chemical plant, temporarily shut down, dominates the valley. From the distance it looks like a ghostly Camelot resting on the left bank of the Basento River.

At the dead end of Via de' Mille, I find number 8. The two-story house is abandoned but still standing. Electric wires dangle from the same roof where Maria's father once prevented her from leaping to her death. I call out the name "Barbella" to a neighbor staring at me from a window, but the woman shakes her head. "Never heard of it." It is the same with other villagers. When Michele Barbella emigrated with his wife and children in 1892, he left nothing behind, not even the family name.

Don Vincenzo Comble of the Chiesa del Purgatorio, a large, jolly man in his late forties, takes my search to heart. The most popular priest in Ferrandina, he becomes my guide. Don Vincenzo has traveled to Ferrandina's immigrant communities in Canada and Brooklyn, celebrating Mass among them. His brother is the postman. Don Vincenzo introduces me to the old parson of the Chiesa Maria Santissima della Croce on the piazza in the heart of town. Unlike Don Vincenzo, this priest is lean, grumpy, and old. He leads me into the sacristy and points to a dark Baroque armoire with carvings of cherubim.

"The records are in there," he mutters.

"Is it locked?" I ask.

"Yes, and I have the key. Come back tomorrow," he says with a grin, to torture me.

"I'm here only for a few days. I've come very far and I'd be grateful if you would allow me to look at the books today. . . ."

"Impossible," he replies. "Anyway, it's a waste of time, you'll never find the name of the woman you're looking for. Besides, I'm sure that her family didn't belong to this parish. . . ."

"I can try," I insist. "Please, I'll give a donation to Saint Rocco, he will help. . . ." I had already noticed in a corner of the church a silver, life-size statue of Ferrandina's patron saint, heaped with votive offerings.

The priest's expression changes slightly, not that he smiles. He looks like someone who doesn't particularly like human beings, someone for whom God simply means a small franchise, a secure roof over the head, and two meals a day. His shabby habit and his black wide-brimmed hat endow him with unearned respect, which he knows how to exploit. In Basilicata, priests and bandits are equally respected.

Sighing, he finally unlocks the armoire with a heavy, baroque key. Inside are six shelves laden with volumes bound in burgundy leather. The dates, engraved in gold leaf on the spines, range from 1650 to 1940. The most recent books are bound in cardboard. Quickly I turn the yellowed pages, aware of the priest's impatience. I scan the christening records. But, among the baptisms registered in 1872, I cannot find Maria's name. I continue on into the following four years, and still cannot see it. Perhaps the priest is right after all, and the family did not belong to this parish. It had never crossed my mind that Maria might have been born earlier. Just to make sure, I check in the opposite direction, turning to the years 1871, 1870, 1869, still nothing. As I nervously turn the pages, the priest is motioning me to leave. Then my eyes fall on her name: "Maria Barbella, born at 6 A.M. on October 24, 1868: father, Michele; mother, Buonsanto Filomena. . . ."

Maria was not 22 years old when she killed Domenico Cataldo, but a good five years older! When Cataldo rejected her, she may well have lost hope of ever getting married. In her mind, it may have been her last chance. In 1895, an unmarried woman in her late twenties was already doomed to a life as a spinster. Had Cora's eyes seen these very pages? These records, after all, have been preserved in the sacristy, in the same armoire, since the seventeenth century. Did these thoughts also cross her mind? Did Cora purposely conceal Maria's true age in order not to highlight her vulnerable position at the time of the killing? These are crucial questions, which can't be answered.

Later that day, I tell Don Vincenzo that Maria had eventually married a man from Ferrandina by the name of Bruno. As we walk through the village, I show him her New York marriage certificate and the newspaper reports about her wedding. "There are many Brunos in Ferrandina," he remarks, stopping suddenly in front of a shop where a man is filing the hind shoe of a sleepy mule. "Here is one: the blacksmith Giuseppe Bruno." Giuseppe says that his great-grand-uncle was called Francesco Paolo Bruno, and that, yes, he had married a woman by the name of Maria. As far as he knows they are both buried in America. He can't understand why I am so interested in his family. Don Vincenzo mentions Maria's story. Giuseppe Bruno's eyes open wide: he has never heard of it. He tells me that his great-grand-uncle had the reputation of being a black sheep, a real troublemaker. I thank him for all his help and move on.

Refusing to give up, I go to the small City Hall building, hoping to discover more about Maria's husband in the municipal archives. It is surprisingly easy. The clerk opens a huge volume. I immediately spot Francesco Bruno's "Situazione di famiglia," his official "family situation":

> Bruno, Francesco Paolo of Giovanni, born in Ferrandina on July 13th, 1872, barber; married on January 20th, 1900, to Fabbrizio Maria, of Pasquale, born in Ferrandina on June 15th, 1878, peasant. Emigrated to the United States of America. . . .

The blacksmith Giuseppe is right: the name of Francesco Paolo's wife had indeed been Maria, but the woman on record was not the "Maria" of my search. He must have married Maria Barbella in 1896 only to get his American papers. Perhaps he had made a deal with her parents, and they had married her off, to bury the past. One day he must have simply deserted her, left New York, and returned to Ferrandina to fetch the sweetheart he had left behind. He brought the second "Maria" to America posing as his lawful wife.

In 1902, two years after Francesco Bruno's Italian marriage to Maria Fabrizzio in Ferrandina, Maria Barbella was living with her parents once again, this time in a tenement at 116 Chrystie Street, four doors down from the room where Cataldo had seduced her with a drink and the promise of marriage.

In October 1899, she had given birth to a son whom she named Frederick, probably after Lawyer Frederick House, who had saved her from execution. In that same year, Martha M. Place of Brooklyn received the distinction of being the first woman to die in the electric chair.

The death penalty has fared variably since then. In 1995, the year marking the centennial of Maria's death sentence, New York State resumed capital punishment after a moratorium of thirty years. It joined another thirty-eight states, of which thirteen continue to use the horrific method of the electric chair:

Alabama, Louisiana, South Carolina, Georgia, Florida, Kentucky, Virginia, Tennessee, South Carolina, Indiana, Ohio, Nebraska, Pennsylvania, and Connecticut. New York will impose the death penalty by lethal injection.

Italians are no longer an underclass in the United States. African-Americans have now taken their place on death row. African-Americans accused of killing whites are far more likely than any other category of offenders to receive the death sentence.

The rate of execution has dropped since 1895, when two hundred persons were executed in a single year, while in 1994 only thirty-one condemned inmates were killed. Nevertheless, it is estimated that an average of two hundred fifty new death sentences are passed each year. At the end of 1984, there were 1,405 persons on death row. Now, a decade later, the number has swelled to 3,009.

While the issue of the death penalty tears at the moral fiber of American society, the cost of capital punishment is staggering. According to *The Economist* (March 11, 1995), the expense of a single execution in the United States ". . . amounts to between $2 and $3 million. That is roughly the same cost as incarcerating three prisoners in a maximum-security prison for 40 years. . . . California spends close to $100 million each year on capital punishment and all its paraphernalia." Yet, over the past eighteen years only two people have been put to death in the Golden State. Society's love affair with the death penalty has become extremely costly for taxpayers.

As of November 1995, there were fifty women on death row out of a total of 3,000 inmates awaiting execution. The executions of women constitute less than 3 percent of the total of approximately 18,500 executions recorded since 1632. The last woman executed in the United States was Velma Barfield, in North Carolina on November 2, 1984.

In their study of women who commit murder, Dr. John Kirkpatrick of the University of New Hampshire and John A. Humphrey, professor of sociology at the University of North Carolina, observe that:

> . . . Among men, a lot of homicides occur over the most trivial things—leaning on a car, say, or not paying 50 cents owed. It's as if these men are on the edge of violence and anything can precipitate it. But in order for women to kill, it has to be perceived by them as a life-threatening situation affecting their physical or emotional being. . . .

I have been haunted by the possibility that somewhere in this dense ocean of beings that is New York City may reside a direct descendant of Maria Barbella. Perhaps I have sat next to him on a bus, spoken to her in a shop, or watched a film in the same movie theater. The chances of her son Frederick having survived into his nineties are slim. But did he have children? Maria's sister Antonia had two. And what about the youngest sister, Carmela? Giovanni, the younger brother with the asymmetrical head, died of tuberculosis on February 25, 1914, at the age of 27. He had become a film projectionist in the developing business of "moving pictures." Carlo, who had followed in his father's footsteps as a tailor, died of a heart attack at 36. And what happened to Giuseppe, Maria's older brother?

I begin with the phone directory. In Manhattan, there are three listings under Barbella; one of them lives on East 13th Street, just a block away from where Maria killed Cataldo. Twelve Barbellas are listed in Brooklyn, three in Queens, the Bronx, and Staten Island. Skeptically, I look up Barberi and find two in Manhattan; six in Brooklyn; five in Queens; and only one each in Staten Island and the Bronx. I decide not to call but to write to each and every Barbella and Barberi.

Weeks pass without a single reply.

When did Maria's parents die? Of all the newspapers, only the *New York Times*'s obituary index goes back to the turn of the century. Looking under Barbella, I am surprised to learn that it is Rocky Graziano's real family name: The obituary I come across is his father's.

There is no listing for Michele or Filomena Barbella. On February 20, 1992, searching blindly in the Municipal Archives, against all odds, my eyes fall on Maria's father's death certificate: Michele Barbella, the tailor from Ferrandina, died of cerebral apoplexy on April 30, 1905, at the age of 67. He passed away in his home at 165 Mulberry Street and was buried at Calvary Cemetery, Woodside, New York.

I cross the 59th Street Bridge and drive to the two-hundred-acre City of the Dead I have often seen in the distance, the largest Catholic Cemetery in the United States, with a quiet population of 6,000,000. I walk through stark rows of graves and more graves. I pause for a moment at the tomb of Cora's heroic bodyguard, Joe Petrosino, and then continue on to section 28, range 2, Plot F, Number 8. Under a small gray tombstone, engraved with the name "BARBELLA," is the family plot. Here rests my only link to Maria's progeny.

In the Calvary Cemetery records, this communal plot was reserved by Maria's sister Carmela on May 10, 1905. The burial of Maria's aunt, Filomena Gianpiccolo, who had once entered the Tombs concealing a stiletto, was later registered, on October 10, 1917, by a woman named Maria Greco. Could this Maria Greco have been Maria Barbella? Did she marry a second time?

The office of Calvary Cemetery informs me that, unfortunately, they are not allowed to disclose the names and addresses

of the relatives who have been paying the yearly maintenance
fees of the Barbella plot. But letters can be forwarded, and so I
write to Maria's relations, in care of the Calvary Cemetery. On
April 5, 1992, the Calvary Cemetery returns my letters. The
postman's stamp on the envelopes reads: "Addressee unknown."

It is now a hundred years after Cora and Maria's epic battle for
justice. I long to find a great-grandchild of Maria's so that we
may celebrate together the sparing of a life.

ACKNOWLEDGMENTS

$\mathcal{E}$leven years have passed since I first became acquainted with the life of Cora Slocomb di Brazzà and the story of Maria Barbella. I cannot possibly mention all the names of those who helped me throughout my research. But among the friends and colleagues who gave me reason to persevere, I must thank Gabriel Morgan, who worked with me on the second draft of the manuscript; Sharon Kitagawa, who created a computerized version of that text when I was still using a manual typewriter; Hugues de Montalembert and Luc Bouchage for revisiting with me places of the past; and Susan Bergholz for her valuable support.

In New Orleans, the native city of Cora Slocomb, my gratitude goes to: Edith Haupt, the only surviving relative of Cora's family; Jimmy and Minnie Coleman; and Rose Lambert of the Louisiana State Museum.

In Ferrandina, the native village of Maria Barbella, I will always remember the jovial kindness of Don Vincenzo Comble of the Church of Purgatory; Francesco Serafino, municipal archivist; and Pierino Pierro, who was my guide and advisor.

In New York, I am grateful to Henry Schwarzschild of the National Coalition to Abolish the Death Penalty, and to

Linda Thurston of Amnesty International for their profound interest.

I have written this book in different phases of my life, and I must thank all those who offered me the seculsion to write: Carole Wyman in Boulder; Lisa Green in Fort Lauderdale; Carlo and Daniela Frua and Olivia Motch in Long Island; Basil Charles in Mustique; and in Chile, both Michael Westcott in Algarrobo and my aunt Eugenia Pirzio Biroli in Puerto Cisnes, Patagonia.

For their resourceful help, I also thank Laure de Gramont, Claudio Cutry, Mariangela Topazzini Tondello, and Alvise and Carla Alvera.

For their faith in me, I thank: my mother, Marina Piccolomini, and my uncles Detalmo and Giacomo Pirzio Biroli, who helped me to unveil the life of their grandmother Cora; my father, Puccio Pucci, and my brother Giannozzo.

I owe an enormous debt to Maria Campbell for her treasured guidance.

Lastly, I must mention Terence Ward, whose presence beside me turns every task into a poetic experience.

Idanna Pucci